Michelle Hollingsworth is a trusted, kind, and compassionate voice for all moms, all seasons. She has been that person to me, and I'm so grateful she has taken the time to share her wisdom in this beautiful book. Get copies of *WorkHearter* for all your people and allow it to infuse courage and stubborn love into the hearts of moms as work at what matters most.

—Kimberly Stuart, author of *Star for Jesus*
*(And Other Jobs I Quit)*

Michelle is a relatable mom who has experienced the different seasons of parenting and learned how to catch the butterfly moments of wisdom in each one. She is a trusted friend who leaks out the love of Christ with her life hacks for moms.

—Bob Goff
Chief Balloon Inflator
Nonprofit www.lovedoes.org
Speaking www.bobgoff.com
Workshops www.dreambigframework.com
Coaching www.coachingwithbobgoff.com
Retreat Center www.oakscenter.com
Author of four NYT Bestsellers: Love Does, Everybody Always, Dream Big and Undistracted

# WorkHearter:

## Meditations for Moms, Season by Season

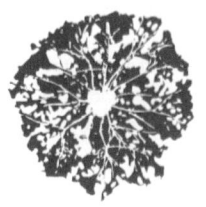

Michelle Hollingsworth, EdD

*WorkHearter: Meditations for Moms, Season by Season*

© 2023 by Michelle Hollingsworth.
Print Edition

All rights reserved. No portion of this book may be reproduced, stored in a retrieval system, or transmitted in any form or by any means—electronic, mechanical, photocopy, recording, scanning, or other—except for brief quotations in critical reviews or articles, without the prior written permission of the author.

Published in Nashville, Tennessee, by WorkHearter Press.

Other credits:
Book Cover Design: ebooklaunch.com
Author photo: Raechel Curtis of
Photography by Rae in Nashville, TN
Typesetting: BB eBooks Co., Ltd.
Sketch art: Rachel Marie Prince and Rebekah Lamberth

Scripture quotations marked BSB are taken from the Holy Bible, Berean Study Bible, BSB. Copyright © 2016, 2018 by Bible Hub. Used by permission. All rights reserved worldwide.

Scripture quotations marked CEV are taken from the Contemporary English Version. Copyright © 1991, 1992, 1995 by American Bible Society. Used by permission.

Scripture quotations marked CSB are taken from the Christian Standard Bible®. Copyright © 2017 by Holman Bible Publishers. Used by permission. Christian Standard Bible® and CSB® are federally registered trademarks of Holman Bible Publishers.

Scripture quotations marked ESV are taken from the ESV® Bible (The Holy Bible, English Standard Version®). Copyright © 2001 by Crossway, a publishing ministry of Good News Publishers. Used by permission. All rights reserved.

Scripture quotations marked HCSB are taken from the Holman Christian Standard Bible®. Copyright © 1999, 2000, 2002, 2003, 2009 by Holman Bible Publishers. Used by permission. HCSB® is a federally registered trademark of Holman Bible Publishers.

Scripture quotations marked KJV are taken from the King James Version. Public domain.

Scripture quotations marked LSB are taken from the Legacy Standard Bible, Copyright © 2021 by The Lockman Foundation. All rights reserved.

Scripture quotations marked MSG are taken from THE MESSAGE. Copyright © 1993, 2002, 2018 by Eugene H. Peterson. Used by permission of NavPress. All rights reserved. Represented by Tyndale House Publishers, a Division of Tyndale House Ministries.

Scripture quotations marked NASB are taken from New American Standard Bible®, Copyright © 1960, 1971, 1977, 1995, 2020 by The Lockman Foundation. All rights reserved.

Scripture quotations marked NASB1995 are taken from New American Standard Bible®, Copyright © 1960, 1971, 1977, 1995 by The Lockman Foundation. All rights reserved.

Scripture quotations marked NIV are taken from the Holy Bible, New International Version®, NIV®. Copyright © 1973, 1978, 1984, 2011 by Biblica, Inc.® Used by permission of Zondervan. All rights reserved worldwide. www.zondervan.com. The "NIV" and "New International Version" are trademarks registered in the United States Patent and Trademark Office by Biblica, Inc.®

Scripture quotations marked NKJV are taken from the New King James Version®. Copyright © 1982 by Thomas Nelson. Used by permission. All rights reserved.

Scripture quotations marked NLT are taken from the Holy Bible, New Living Translation. Copyright © 1996, 2004, 2015 by Tyndale House Foundation. Used by permission of Tyndale House Ministries, Carol Stream, Illinois 60188. All rights reserved.

ISBN 979-8-9893089-0-3 (eBook)
ISBN 979-8-9893089-1-0 (HC)
*Printed in the United States of America*

For my wonderful children: Blake, Skyler, Bekah, and Ella Gray. I hope you never question your worth or God's love for you and always know how thankful I am that He chose me to be your mom.

*Many are the plans in a person's heart, but it is the Lord's purpose that prevails.*

*Proverbs 19:21 NIV*

*Hey mama*
Hey mama of babies, you are doing great
You are thriving even if only surviving
I see your tired eyes, screaming inside those late-night cries
If you need to cry, cry out to Jesus, it's never too late
Take all the rest you can get
Long lost dreams you'll soon forget
Mama, Look at you
You're brand new too
Cut yourself some slack
Stop wishing you had your old body back
Your old body couldn't do what you can now
This too shall pass even if you don't know how
You are creating the future
With your sacrifice and nurture
Don't be mad, don't be sad
Even wearing those industrial-size pads
If ever there is a time to be had
This is the time to be glad
Long nights now without sleep
One day soon change will come bittersweet
Breathe in, breathe out
This is what life is all about
Hey mama of littles, you are doing fine
Even when your kids whine
Keep wearing all the hats like a magician
Nothing can take away your intuition

Mistakes will be made
Many prayers will be prayed
These are the days you'd never trade
No matter how much it paid
Oh mama, take their little hand
You will never be more in demand
No other prize could be so grand
You are the center of their universe
And their favorite nurse
Welcome to the best job perks
This is the most rewarding work
Hey mama of teens, you are doing well
Teenage years can feel like hell
You're so busy giving
They're doing all the living
You can't win
But you develop tough skin
All you want back are those baby snuggles
These years bring more juggles, more struggles
They are fighting for independence
All they need is acceptance
Hold your tongue on that sentence
Raising them up right
Seems like such a fight
Calling you lazy
Making you crazy
Mama don't get angry
Even when they push you away
They really want you to stay
Pray, pray, pray
It passes by quickly

This time can seem so tricky
Hey mama of bigs, look how far you've come
All grown up on their own from the seeds you've sown
Blessed these days if you get to see them some
Don't worry mama, there's no place like home
Well, I'll be
What do you know?
What do you see?
Mama, look at you, you grew up too
Now you're a pro
Time to let go
Take His hand
He knows the plan
Breathe in, breathe out
This is what your purpose was all about

## Table of Contents

*Introduction: WorkHearter* — xv

Part 1: Spring Showers — 1

Part 2: The Sweetness and Sweatiness of Summer — 105

Part 3: The Finality of Fall — 211

Part 4: The Weary Days of Winter — 305

*Acknowledgments* — 409

*Scripture Reference* — 413

*About the Author* — 417

## Introduction: WorkHearter

> Whatever you do, work at it with all your heart, as working for the Lord, not for human masters, since you know that you will receive an inheritance from the Lord as a reward. It is the Lord Christ you are serving.
>
> Colossians 3:23–24 NIV

Our greatest calling is guiding others to know more about Christ and His gift of salvation. We sometimes think only theology experts can do this, but God calls all of us to help others, using our unique gifts. The blessing of motherhood is one such gift. Sounds like a great idea in theory, right? But as moms, no doubt we work hard but also we work wholeheartedly: we are WorkHearters. And as *WorkHearters*—there are so many things that get in our way.

While we are busy caring for the daily life of another human being, we also carry the burden of training up our children in God's Word. This weight can feel heavy, like an assignment we can't possibly pull off between making mac and cheese, tending to bruises, combing out pigtails, and the spinning plates of work, family, and community.

As adults, we go through changes as we age and grow in wisdom and experience. Likewise, our children go through seasons of change as they grow and learn. In the midst of our busyness, there are moments that define the course of our lives.

These moments aren't all big life-changing moments. Some are small experiences but have a large impact on us. We stop, look around, take a breath, realize we have learned something profound in that instant. Many of these moments change us for the better. Big or small, they are all meaningful.

There is good news in the midst of the busyness: we have what we need. The best instruction book we have for parenthood is from God Himself. Every day is different, every child is unique. We juggle constant change—but Jesus never changes. Hebrews 13:8 tells us Jesus Christ is the same yesterday, today, and forever.

As mothers, we can take solace in the fact that we can weather any season with Jesus as our helper since He will not change. It is encouraging to know we are never alone—not in the hot humid days of summer, the rapidly changing days that come with fall, the forced rest of the bitter cold days of winter, or the blooming rainy days of spring. The Father sees us where we are. He is with us, helps us, walks with us and strengthens us.

This book is a collection of stories that may resonate with a story or two you also share. We are all connected by our God the Father. I know that there is nothing new under the sun and my story belongs to His story. Whether you read this now or years from now, Isaiah 55:11 lets me know God's Word will never return void. No matter our similarities or differences on this journey, Jesus endures. I am an imperfect person sharing what I have learned along my imperfect journey of motherhood so this book will not be perfect either. Some life decisions I made were out of survival mode, but when I chose to seek God's will for my life, I not only survived but thrived. God's infallible word should be the ultimate resource for us to stay in line with His good, pleasing and perfect will.

As moms, we work so hard inside and outside the home to provide for our families and often lose ourselves in the process of wading through our own struggles. We know our children are gifts from above, and they add immeasurable value to our lives, vastly more than any dream they take. They are the greatest work we will ever do. Some say being a mother is the hardest job they ever had but a job is what you get paid to do. Work/Purpose is what you were born to do. Motherhood is our purpose. We work at what matters most with a heart filled with God's love.

"Nothing in the world is worth having or worth doing unless it means effort, pain, difficulty... I have never in my life envied a human being who led an easy life. I have envied a great many people who led difficult lives and led them well," Theodore Roosevelt said. Different seasons will bring different challenges and require different comforts. As you work with your whole heart every waking moment and even the sleepless ones, remember He is never far. Even when you don't see or hear or feel His presence, He is close.

So take heart, mom. Here is a year's worth-give or take-of reflections on faith, reasons for hope, ideas to contemplate, and stories for meditation, spread out at a pace a WorkHearter can manage. This book is my perspective of the work God has done in my life and helped me realize I have no need to fear. I hope it blesses your life in some way. May God bless you and keep you.

# PART 1

# *Spring Showers*

Rainy days and blooming buds bring newness and fresh air to our weary-from-winter bones. God's Word showers us with renewal every day—it's as easy as opening it up and being open to it. New relationships and new seasons of parenting are all about growth and learning what works and how to prune what doesn't—all apt descriptions of the spring renewal.

Motherhood in the spring is close to gardening and planting seeds for a future harvest. What works for one of our children may not prove fruitful for another. Learning new ideas and unlearning old habits are like spring cleaning—sometimes starting over and decluttering. Use this time to observe, learn, and perhaps try something new!

Trees don't need to be told to bloom in spring. They just do. God wants you to bloom renewed after a season of rest. Remember, no one tells the trees to rest in winter either, they just do. They wouldn't bloom otherwise. What looked like a dried up dead tree, blooms new again.

Stormy seasons can happen during spring too. If thunderstorms or tornados strike, strong communities are quick to help each other rebuild. Storms or setbacks in life produce a resilience that gives you the ability to recover quickly. When raindrops fall after you have been through a stormy season, it won't matter because you know you are stronger.

## Meditations of a Mama's Heart

> May these words of my mouth and this meditation of my heart
> be pleasing in your sight,
> LORD, my Rock and my Redeemer.
>
> Psalm 19:14 NIV

I'm guilty of inwardly calling myself negative names. Especially when I mess up, so it happens often. I heard my own mother call herself names when she made a mistake. My own daughter has called herself a failure when her newborn baby didn't sleep. As if we are supposed to be perfect as moms. Our words to ourselves as mothers can positively affect our outlook and attitude. Instead, we need whispers of encouraging words to ourselves to be uplifted. If the opposite is true, we are discouraged. What we speak to our children yields the same power. I have often regretted words I've spoken out of frustration or anger almost immediately.

David knew that God was worthy to search our words and our hearts. God is the only one powerful enough to help us keep our spoken words and our unspoken thoughts away from an earthly perspective. We can ask Him to keep our words and thoughts directed toward God's perspective.

The good news is that no matter how long our hearts have been unpleasant or what words we have negatively spoken,

He is the redeemer. He is our Rock to lean on when troubles cause our hearts to worry and our language is affected. Fear of failure can cause negative self talk to be louder than self love talk, but God is love and there is no fear in love (1 John 4:16-18). Remember, all new moms are on a level playing field with no advantage given for education, age or experience. Our education, experience, status and background don't matter to our babies.

## WorkHearter Wisdom

None of our effectiveness as mothers is dependent on our own work, skill, or experience. It is all dependent upon our Lord. We are never out of His reach. His mercy and forgiveness is abundantly ours. Join me today saying this simple prayer seeking to please the Lord with our words and our thoughts in our daily life, in our relationships, and in our distractions.

## Living Interrupted

Rest in God alone, my soul,
for my hope comes from Him.
He alone is my rock and my salvation,
my stronghold; I will not be shaken.

Psalm 62:5–6 HCSB

How we grow up affects us as adults and as parents. I was the oldest child in the home and I was fighting for a chance to be heard among my younger siblings. I learned a character trait of interrupting out of survival. I was afraid I would forget or not be able to participate in any conversation with my parents if I didn't interrupt to have my needs heard. Those who don't know me see me as rude when I interrupt, but it is a bad habit I am working on. It is the trait I dislike about myself the most. I never learned how to *hold my horses*. I am impatient. Although I try not to, I am still a work in progress.

    Being a mom, I am interrupted more than I'm not. I live in a constant state of interruption. My thoughts are interrupted with intrusive fears, doubts and worries. Life has not been the same since I became a mother. Babies are the champions of interruption. They interrupt our sleep, daily routine and plans with their needs, but they are the sweetest blessings. When I was thinking of what could go wrong as a new mom, my baby would smile or coo and, in that moment, I became joyful instead of fearful. As soon as children grow and even before they can speak, they interrupt us when they have a need. They are not the interruption, the need is. Even if it's as simple as boredom, it's a need to them. Sometimes they need a connection in that moment. The questions, the pleas, and the rambles from those I am raising seem nonstop. Interruptions can be exhausting, and living interrupted can shake our steadiness and focus. But, our children need to rely on us to be unshaken and love them uninterrupted so we can point them to rely on our heavenly Father.

## WorkHearter Wisdom

Our children need a place to be heard uninterrupted. More importantly, they need to know they are not an interruption. How can we learn to see these interruptions as blessings? Sometimes, heavenly things will interrupt our worldly things. Isn't it glorious to know Jesus will listen to us without interrupting our prayers, pleas, and rambles? He never tires of us. Our needs are not an interruption to Him. When you feel unheard, overlooked and exhausted, go to Him and find rest. He will not only listen to you uninterrupted, His love will never be interrupted in your life.

# *PRAYER IN ANY SEASON*

*This, then, is how you should pray:*
*" 'Our Father in heaven, hallowed be your name, your kingdom come, your will be done, on earth as it is in heaven. Give us today our daily bread. And forgive us our debts, as we also have forgiven our debtors. And lead us not into temptation, but deliver us from the evil one.' Matthew 6:9-13 NIV*

As one tired mama to another, I know we don't have to do this alone. We can pray like Jesus and use scripture to fight our battles. The Word of God is a sword used as the most powerful tool against temptation.

Even when we don't have any words to pray due to exhaustion, grief, interruptions or the feeling of defeat, the Holy Spirit will intercede and pray for us. When we are weak, He is strong for us.

I know you are strong. Look at what you can do in one day with no sleep. I'm cheering for you to *Stay strong, mama.*

*In the same way, the Spirit helps us in our weakness. We do not know what we ought to pray for, but the Spirit himself intercedes for us through wordless groans.*
*Romans 8:26 NIV*

## Crows and Songbirds

And even the very hairs of your head are all numbered. So don't be afraid; you are worth more than many sparrows.

Matthew 10:30-31 NIV

Let your conversation be always full of grace, seasoned with salt, so that you may know how to answer everyone.

Colossians 4:6 NIV

I can't carry a tune. I am more like a crow than a songbird. Every time I'm at church afraid to sing above a whisper because I know I'm off-key, I notice a songbird will be near me. I was attending a beach church service, and the acoustic worship leader's guitar battery went out, leaving only his voice. I wanted to be louder to join in with the worship, but I know my singing can make some cringe. When—what do you know?—a songbird came stood right beside me singing louder than I ever could. His song carried me.

There are 33 different species of sparrows across our country, but all sparrows are considered songbirds. Songbirds are not affected by the crows. They sing their song regardless of who's around. It's who we choose to listen to and focus on. I focused on the songbird's voice instead of my own.

Sometimes criticism is like listening to crows. It's loud and obnoxious. It feels harsh. Our tone can be harsh even in truth. But the encouraging words of a songbird can lift the spirit and drown out the crows, even if their songs are softer. Crows and songbirds coexist in all environments. Crows are extremely intelligent but harsh. Crows don't forget a face and will teach other crows how to identify a mean human being. Songbirds will sing the same song over and over to mark their territory. Their songs are useful to everyone around them, no matter how repetitive the tune.

## WorkHearter Wisdom

Our testimony is the repetitive song of our life story. The tune can sound like a crow or a songbird, but it is our song to sing. The harsh notes that sound like a crow can serve as a warning seasoned with salt, and the sweet, soft melodic notes point toward the repeated grace and redemption we've been given. Our children are the songs in our life that carry us through and drown out the harshness of this world. Let them sing to you today. Their voices are the most beautiful instrument created. Speak back to them with grace, and remember how worthy you are to our heavenly Father-worth more than many sparrows. Don't be afraid to sing like you are worthy. Sing it like you mean it sister!

# Water the Plants

> For he will be like a tree planted by the water,
> That extends its roots by a stream
> And will not fear when the heat comes;
> But its leaves will be green,
> And it will not be anxious in a year of drought
> Nor cease to yield fruit.
>
> Jeremiah 17:8 NASB 1995

One of the biggest issues of contention in my marriage is taking out the trash (second only to the toilet time situation). My husband feels like he carries the burden of trash management for the whole house with no assistance in taking it out. I compare it to my doing all the dishes or laundry, but somehow trash is worse than those household tasks, in his opinion. Trash stinks, it gets heavy, and once the trash container is full, he has nowhere to put the overflow. Also, he has to push it down to the road no matter the weather. So, his task is visible but not perpetual like mine. But, neither task is permanent.

In our home, we have assumed roles over necessary tasks —some that we do individually and some we partner in completing. As mentioned, my husband takes out the trash. That is a task he has always done, whether I have to remind/nag him to do it or not. I do the laundry even when it stinks, whether I get it put away quickly or not. Those tasks are individual in our house. Those must be done by one of us.

We both must intentionally water the plants. When we see the leaves start to brown or look sad, one of us will just water them because they need it—not because we are asked or expected to do it. That's a partner task we have. We both have the responsibility to recognize a plant that needs watering.

Our children need lots of watering to grow spiritually, mentally, emotionally, and physically. They need nourishment in all these areas. Parents work hard to meet the physical needs by providing clothing, shelter, food and water. We even strive to meet the emotional needs by showing love and affection. Mental needs can be nurtured by words of encouragement.

But spiritual needs may the most overlooked area our children have in today's culture. As parents, we must intentionally do a better job of helping our children grow spiritually, and not leave this task to Sunday school teachers, Bible study leaders, and youth ministers. This is a partner task we need to take the responsibility for that is perpetual, visible and permanent:give the water needed to grow and bear fruit. Otherwise, we are tending to a garden without water. Knowing that we need to keep an eye on physical, mental, emotional and spiritual burnout or drought, we also need to take out the trash and keep it out of our relationships. As we reflect on who we hang around, eventually we can see areas that are starting to stink.

## WorkHearter Wisdom

Our family relationships need to be watered to grow: firmly planted and rooted in God's Word in order to thrive. If we don't help our children grow spiritually, who will? Who is making the intentional effort to water the plants/relationships/spiritual growth in your home?

## Spring Forward: Standard Time

Behold, I am making all things new.

Revelation 21:5 ESV

He cuts off every branch in me that bears no fruit, while every branch that does bear fruit he prunes so that it will be even more fruitful.

John 15:2 NIV

See how the farmer waits for the land to yield its valuable crop, patiently waiting for the autumn and spring rains.

James 5:7 NIV

In spring, we "spring forward" one hour. I miss that hour for at least a week which is 168 hours!

Time is a funny thing. The one minute before a class or meeting is over, an airline check-in time is available, or a concert sale begins is the longest sixty seconds to tick by … but the last moments we spend with loved ones speed by.

That same hour we spring forward seems longer than sixty minutes when it's gone. I feel tired both after spring forward *and* fall back of daylight savings time changes. Gaining or losing an hour drains me physically. I drag around in a daze wondering why it's so bright at five o'clock in the morning and still daylight at seven p.m. I know I need to spring into action due to the sunlight outside, but I'm still in rest mode from a winter season. I struggle the same but in a different way when winter starts. I want to be productive and struggle to rest at the start of winter season. Seasons change us slowly.

As parents, our spring season with active children activities might include sports, school, church, and new clothes and shoe shopping for their growing bodies. This season also needs to have room and time for watering the seeds of faith that are planted. After a long season of rest, we can spring into action by guiding our children with instructions in light and love for a full harvest later.

Pruning is also a standard part of spring. Pruning by a parent could mean removing unhelpful/unfruitful parts of our life or our children's lives. It may be removing something considered fun. Pruning may be removing something that is good but not great to have room for great. Too much good can overcrowd the great. Good could be something we are doing that's right but we do it for the wrong reasons. Pruning may be painful, but we don't have the luxury to pause pain. The rainy showers of painful early spring seasons bring flowers after the rain passes. We can't see the buds or blooms the pruning will show when they are getting water during restful seasons. They are there below the surface soaking in the rain needed now to grow later. With His help, we can do this mamas.

## WorkHearter Wisdom

What do you think of when you read that God is making all things new? Reflect on a season of pruning that you experienced that was uncomfortable. Did you become comfortable with the discomfort? How can we patiently wait for those fruitful seasons?

# Stray Hair

What do you think? If a man owns a hundred sheep, and one of them wanders away, will he not leave the ninety-nine on the hills and go to look for the one that wandered off? And if he finds it, truly I tell you, he is happier about that one sheep than about the ninety-nine that did not wander off. In the same way your Father in heaven is not willing that any of these little ones should perish.

Matthew 18:12–14 NIV

"So I say to you: Ask and it will be given to you; seek and you will find; knock and the door will be opened to you."

Luke 11:9 NIV

I have always had long hair. Ever since my mom cut my hair into a bowl cut in third grade and all the boys told me it was ugly, I vowed to have long hair the rest of my days. I like being able to pull it up in a ponytail and a hat when I want to. Sometimes, though, long hair can be irritating. Stray hairs will hide on the back of my shirt or run down my arm when they fall out (thank you, hormones). It happens so often, I shouldn't be alarmed. But there are times it feels like a bug is on my arm and I must find the stray hair and get it off my body immediately. To witness this in person is quite comical. These irritating stray hairs become the bane of my existence. It becomes my only focus and priority in those moments. Never mind the thousands of hairs intact on my head, finding the stray one is all that matters in that moment.

Jesus spoke about having a flock of one hundred sheep and one wandering off from the ninety-nine. He spoke of the joy of finding the one. It was the focus and priority to find the one.

I want my children to know how lucky they are that Jesus seeks us out and rejoices over every single one saved. He doesn't use majority rule. He seeks out the minority who are lost, alone, afraid, and hurt. He gives the us the same focus to help protect little ones. He put the mama bear instinct in our hearts to strive to protect because He gave His life to protect each one of us. Our priority and focus is to protect our children in every generation. It should concern us as much as a stray hair to find the one missing or hurting.

### WorkHearter Wisdom

How can we help the next generation uphold the sanctity of life? How can we teach them their worth and value? If you don't know where to start, ask Him to show you. For me, a good place to start is putting away the many distractions. Let's vow to put down the cell phones more and distance the distractions to focus on the child that needs us more. Hold your children tightly today. Look our gifts in the eye and show them they are the priority and focus they deserve to be by reflecting joy and lighting up when you look at them.

Part 1: Spring Showers

## Spray or Stream

On the last and greatest day of the feast, Jesus stood up and called out in a loud voice, "If anyone is thirsty, let him come to Me and drink. Whoever believes in Me, as the scripture has said: 'Streams of living water will flow from within him.'"

John 7:37-38 BSB

When we built our house, my husband ordered a huge sink faucet that was too large to use on a small coffee-bar sink. (He tends to mismeasure when he's making a hurried decision.) So we moved it to our laundry room, where it was more size appropriate. Like our kitchen sink faucet, it has two settings—spray or steady stream, depending on preference. Preference is a tricky concept. When I wash the dishes or hand-wash laundry in the sink, I prefer the stream setting. I know the direction and area the water will go, and it does a better job by directing the stream, in my opinion. My husband prefers the spray. I know this because every time I go to the sink after he's used it, the setting has been changed to spray.

The spray goes everywhere and more gets outside of what I'm trying to rinse than inside. My husband and I differ on this preference but I do more of the dishwashing chore, so I notice. I see the spray as wasteful, with water going outside and splashing. Even though it gets on my nerves, I don't get upset having to change the setting. I just click the button and quietly smile. It's an unspoken inside joke between the two of us. The dishes and laundry still get washed. No harm, no foul for a change in preference.

His personality in parenting is similar. He wants to do it all and give it all. His style of parenting is carefree and spontaneous. I want a steady routine with structure. Our conflicting parenting styles cause some disagreements. These disagreements cause conflict. My husband's way drains me, my way drains him. Our daughter recognizes this when we are worn down and uses it at times to her benefit. Even though she needs the routine and time management sometimes, other times she enjoys the spontaneity. Neither way is wrong or wasteful with her.

## WorkHearter Wisdom

When reading scripture, I need a steady stream of time to study the word. I need quiet to focus. My husband and daughter prefer music in the background during Bible study; like a spray hose, they prefer the overstimulation experience that I need an escape from.

Neither way is wasteful if we learn. Our children could be different than us in what their spiritual needs are. They may need a steady stream or a spray hose, and their needs can differ in different seasons of life. We just need to let them drink in that living water when they are thirsty.

# Quiet Moments of Contemplation: Romans 8:28 NIV

And we know that in all things God works for the good of those who love him, who have been called according to his purpose.

I never thought God would work everything that happened in my life to good. How can anyone take a divorced mom and work it to good? How can anyone take a messed-up credit score and work it to good? How can anyone take a college dropout and work it to good? Well, He did. He gave me a new marriage and more beautiful children. He gave me a way to own my own home and start a business. He helped me finish college. Best of all, He gave me the gift of salvation.

I also have been called to live a life of purpose. My ultimate purpose is being a mom. I will never have any greater purpose or calling than pouring all my efforts into my children. I am far from perfect, but the verse doesn't say He will work all things for those who love Him and are perfect. He knows we are not, and He knows there will be times that things will not be good. We will experience bad. We will even cause the bad. I know because I have caused the bad. But His Word says He will work those things for good. And I love Him even more for that.

## In the Thick of It

The kingdom of heaven is like a man who sowed good seed in his field. But while everyone was sleeping, his enemy came and sowed weeds among the wheat, and went away. …

"An enemy did this," he replied.

The servants asked him, "Do you want us to go and pull them up?"

"No, he answered, "because while you are pulling the weeds, you may uproot the wheat with them. Let them both grow together until the harvest. At that time, the harvesters: First collect the weeds and tie them in bundles to be burned; then gather the wheat and bring it into my barn."

Matthew 13:24–25, 28–30 NIV

As a parent, I live in the weeds. I feel like the weeds are stronger and thick enough to withstand any expert parenting tricks I have in my toolbelt. Weed seasons for me are specifically associated with parenting during teen and toddler years. Thick weeds during the teen years may look like changing hormones, mood swings, and defiance. Nothing we do during this season will be right. Even the best moms will feel like failures. Teens will be mad at their mama because they have so much emotion. It's impossible for them to hold it in, and they can only let it go in a safe place. You, mama, are their safe haven, their home—their sanctuary. Historically, those fleeing from the law were immune from arrest in religious sanctuaries. A sanctuary is a place of comfort or protection for all.

Similarly, toddler weeds may resemble tantrums, autonomy, and defiance, as well trying to seek independence. Both seasons have proven to include shame and self-doubt for our children.

The thick weight of burden and responsibility that comes with being a parent brings even more challenges. Evil is tangled up in our society, social media, schools, and everyday life. Weeds needs to be cleared carefully. Don't pull up the plant you want to save when you pull or spray the weeds—and don't uproot your child's sense of self when you discipline them. Blooms happen when weeds are pulled but sometimes they have to be allowed to coexist for the sake of the plant. Just as a plant can compartmentalize an injury, it doesn't mean it can overcome it and thrive. We can't challenge our children every minute or prevent their mistakes during these seasons. We have to let them release their fears and emotions safely, then sit with their decisions and subsequent consequences while we love them through it. Love and discipline can coexist.

### WorkHearter Wisdom

Jesus used a parable comparing the similarities of heaven and weeds. Just when we are in the thick of weeds and the enemy seems to uproot every good seed we've planted as parents, the harvest comes. He tells us later in the chapter that the weeds are evil and everything that causes sin but one day they will be thrown into the blazing furnace. When that day comes, "the righteous will shine like the sun in the kingdom of their Father" (v. 43). We know that evil exists, and it spreads sin. We only need to raise our children to be lights in a dark world, so they may shine bright among the weeds and will stand out. God will sort the evil out. It's not up to us to pull out all the evil in this world or constantly prune, it's up to Him. He will harvest what we plant because it's all His dirt and fields anyway. When we are in the thick of parenting, our primary purpose is to cultivate the wheat in our children for the harvest, not to constantly spend all our time pruning or pulling the weeds which can cause wounds and stress. And, pray for rain.

PART 1: SPRING SHOWERS

## **Lost All Senses**

Because of the LORD's great love we are not consumed,
>for his compassions never fail.
They are new every morning;
>great is your faithfulness.

Lamentations 3:22–23 NIV

Opponents must be gently instructed, in the hope that God will grant them repentance leading them to a knowledge of the truth, and that they will come to their senses and escape from the trap of the devil, who has taken them captive to do his will.

2 Timothy 2:25–26 NIV

When we get angry, we lose all common sense and act out in hurtful ways. The sense that would normally stop us from being mean disappears as we have a temper tantrum. We know how to push the buttons of those we love most. Because hurt causes hurt, parents and children alike can cause compassion to turn cold.

Every winter, I get the feeling of losing all my senses—not in an angry way, but in a cold bitter way. I get cold and bitter when I am in a winter season and forget how warm the sun feels on my winter-numbed face in early spring. I lose track of how fragrant the flowers smell every spring when I am in the midst of winter. I miss the songs of birds. As we age, we lose tiny bits of our senses of sight, hearing, taste, smell. Our eyesight eventually gets poor, our hearing weakens. My eyes get bored from the dreary days of winter and crave the sight of green grass and budding blooms. Our sense of taste grows dull. We lose our ability to smell and our fingers can have numbness so we can't feel. Seasons of spring bring us new senses. Spring brings new blooms to see and smell, new songs from birds to hear, and new warm sunshine to feel.

We forget that His compassions are new every day in every season, and they will never fail. When you lose all sense or all your senses, and all you can do is cry Jesus, He will give you a renewed sense.

### WorkHearter Wisdom

Loss can feel like we will be consumed and numb from winter, but spring is in our grasp and ever present with every new day. Jesus's grace, compassion, and mercy are new every morning. Every morning we have the chance to regain our senses and enter a spring season. Children are the best representation of forgiveness we will ever see this side of heaven. They wake up every morning to spring in their hearts with fresh mercy, forgiveness, hope, and unconditional love for their parents. Mamas don't always deserve this bright, shiny, new-every-morning love, but we need it in every season.

## Worrying in the Weeds

Who of you by worrying can add a single hour to your life?
                                    Luke 12:25 NIV

The seed that fell among thorns stands for those who hear, but as they go on their way they are choked by life's worries, riches and pleasures, and they do not mature.
                                    Luke 8:14 NIV

My husband is meticulous about his landscape. He is constantly trying to get rid of the weeds. At times, we get busy or distracted and weeds start to take root in the plant beds. I try to be a good wife and nip them in the bud early in the morning before it gets too warm. I grab the weeds and toss them in the yard. Some of them are prickly and I need gloves to get down to the root without getting my hands nicked or scratched. The root system on some weeds is deep, not superficial. That's why we don't have to properly water a weed or put any fertilizer for them to thrive. Other roots are shallow and easily pulled up with minimal effort.

I worry during troubling times but I also find myself worrying in peaceful times. I worry the peace will end. When days are good, I worry about what can ruin them. I do this because I have seen the weeds take route in my life—both shallow and deep. I do this for myself and for my children. If my daughter has a friend that is negative influence, I worry she will be persuaded to make a bad decision. Even if it's not happened, I worry it will. I let the worry become a weed itself during a time of transition. I don't rejoice with the sprouted plants. I forget to see the grain produced. I worry because I've seen the bad sprout up with the good. I forget about the rest of the story. I forget about the harvest. Instead of focusing on the weeds and thistles, I need to focus on the harvest. A small seed of faith can produce the tallest of trees. Weeds/thorns can try to choke out the seed, but faith spreads faster and lasts longer than a weed can ever grow.

### WorkHearter Wisdom

Do you tend to forget about the coming harvest? What do you do to self-correct? Consider seeking inspiration in God's Word. Remind yourself the seeds you plant now will grow strong in a tender heart in spite of the weeds. Let's plant our seeds of faith so they grow tall and keep our hearts tender to the hearts of others.

# Catching Butterflies

Therefore, if anyone is in Christ, the new creation has come: The old has gone, the new is here!

2 Corinthians 5:17 NIV

Butterflies are everywhere, but we tend to only notice them in the ugly spots since they stick out in contrast. At construction sites in the spring and summer, you will likely see a contrast in the muck and the mud. Butterflies often fly around the ugly. When we were building in our backyard, they were a welcome sight after looking at piles of dirt all the dreary winter long. For me, the butterflies meant new growth and green grass would be coming along soon with warmer weather. They land on the muck, mud, and fresh poured concrete.

I always thought they only flew in pretty flower fields until I saw they frequently visit the stinky areas—and I got my camera out to catch an image of the contrast with a butterfly landing on mud puddles. Researching this behavior online revealed they are looking for salts. The salt helps them reproduce. Butterflies don't see the dirty mess. They see what they need in the mess.

Contrasts in life like this are easier to see. When someone is sick, the beauty in their eyes or smile is more noticeable than when they are well. Maybe because it is a welcome sight. When our eyes have only seen dreary days, a fluttering butterfly symbolizes a new day-complete metarmorphosis-is coming soon.

## WorkHearter Wisdom

When my kids have a bad day, they need to catch glimpses of butterflies. They are looking for the salt in us. They need encouraging words during seasons of gloom. So look for butterflies in the dark ugly seasons. In the muck and mud, they are easier to spot and you can likely catch a glimpse of brighter days to come soon. Be the beauty in someone else's eyes when they are stuck in the muck and mud of an ugly season of life.

PART 1: SPRING SHOWERS

## You Recognize It in the Eyes First

When he saw the strength of the wind, he was afraid. And beginning to sink he cried out, "Lord, save me!"

Matthew 14:30 HCSB

For where your treasure is, there your heart will be also. The eye is the lamp of the body.

Matthew 6:21–22 NIV

My sophomore year of high school, our English teacher had a well-known saying to get attention in every class. He'd say "Eyes here" while he motioned at his head if we were not looking at him or paying attention while he was teaching. It may have been his best way to keep us from going to sleep. It is memorable to this day. It wasn't until I was a high school teacher myself that I began to think he did it because he could tell by our eyes if we understood the lesson he was trying to teach us.

We all can tell a great deal by someone's eyes reflected in our own experiences. We can recognize sadness or loss if we have experienced deep loss. We can recognize illness in our children if their eyes are weak. We can see kindness in a crowd if someone's eyes are welcoming to us. We can see anger and even addiction in someone's eyes if we have witnessed it before in a loved one's eyes. You can often see many emotions and ailments in the eyes first—before any other signals or body language. It's hard to disguise our eyes. Jesus emphasized the importance of our eyes with "the eye is the lamp of the body." If we see clearly with our eyes, we will have wisdom.

In scripture, Peter could walk on water when his eyes were focused on Jesus. Jesus was in the forefront of Peter's vision because he wanted to be sure it was Him. But as a fisherman, Peter understood the power of wind. When Peter saw the strength of the wind and waves, his fear took over the forefront of his thoughts and he began to sink. Jesus said as He caught Peter, "You of little faith, why did you doubt?" (Matthew 14:31 NIV).

Seasons of doubt can come during any season. We don't have to be in a stormy season with waves rising and wind gusts to have doubts. In seasons of doubt, we eagerly wait for the season to change so we can feel less stuck. I've seen the strength of wind take down power lines and tall trees. In Tennessee, we get straight line winds and spin up tornados that can cause massive destruction. There are many things I love about spring like flower blooms and warmer weather, but I also dread those spring storms. In seasons of doubt, it's easy to forget that God is more powerful than any wind or storm. He gave us four seasons but only one spring, and those rain showers of one season bring forth the flowers of life.

## WorkHearter Wisdom

We need big faith to keep our lights bright as parents. What we focus on is what will carry us through our day and our children's day. If we put our fears or worries of the day in the forefront of our vision, we may not recognize a child who might be hurting. We may not see a kind smile extended to us while we are struggling to give a speech or presentation to a group. We can miss seeing a friend who is grieving a loss due to our clouded vision. We need clear eyes to receive and show the light of Christ to others. Focus our eyes on you Lord. Help us to see You clearly even during a storm.

## Peace Like a River

> Humble yourselves, therefore, under the mighty hand of God so that at the proper time he may exalt you, casting all your anxieties on him, because he cares for you.
>
> 1 Peter 5:6–7 ESV

A fisherman will tell you that there is not a more peaceful place on earth than a river or a lake. When I was young, I went fishing with my dad, made the mistake of not listening, and I got hooked in the head and eye by a lure when he was casting his line. I wanted to sit in the captain's chair elevated above the boat, so I did what I wanted not what I was told. I was humbled by what happened next. My dad cast his line perfectly, but instead of hooking a fish, his line caught me. I'm certain it was an accident, even if he had justified thoughts of cracking my skull as a rebellious teenager. My mom made him sell his fishing boat after that. I felt bad. It wasn't his fault, it was mine.

The same summer, I also had another humbling accident by riding our four-wheeler into a tree—breaking my wrist—because I wasn't paying attention. My dad bought that four-wheeler because he is a man who loves to buy toys no matter how old he gets. He sold it after that, but that's another story of my mom trying to protect us from what she deemed dangerous to us kids.

Since he didn't go fishing much after giving up his boat, he found peace again in the garden. He'd plant tomatoes, squash, cucumbers. A garden can be like fishing on a river. It's quiet and you have to wait. My dad had the same patience with gardening that he had with fishing.

I never understood that patience. You wait more than you actually fish or garden. I've learned, though, it's not about the wait, it's about what you learn through the cast or planting. Casting our love and planting seeds are the easiest actions we can take as parents of children to grow a great harvest.

### WorkHearter Wisdom

If you cast your line right, you will find the fish you've been waiting for. If you plant your vegetables right, you will harvest a crop. If you humbly cast your anxiety upon the Father, you will catch peace. If you plant seeds of faith, you will grow peace.

When we do the opposite and try to control or fear or worry about a situation we deem dangerous, we break the lifeline of peace we have with our Father. Sometimes being in the way when God casts his line of peace is simply not listening or paying attention. His peace flows freely like a river. Lord, help us be patient with what we plant today, pay attention and listen to your instructions and get out of the way.

## My Witness

But you will receive power when the Holy Spirit comes on you; and you will be my witnesses in Jerusalem, and in all Judea and Samaria, and to the ends of the earth.

Acts 1:8 NIV

My husband happened upon a head-on collision car accident shortly after it happened. He didn't see the events leading up to the crash, but he saw the aftermath firsthand. He was near a victim of the crash when he took his final breath. The experience occupied his thoughts for days. He told everyone he knew or even didn't know about the events of that day. He couldn't shake what had happened moments before he arrived at the scene. How quickly life can change. He also couldn't wash his hands of what he witnessed after. He needed to let people know. He may not have been able to prevent it from happening, but he had to let people know. It was on the forefront of his mind.

We are called to be witnesses to everyone we meet. It can be intimidating when we don't feel knowledgeable enough. Our children are anxious to learn from us. They are eyewitnesses to our everyday lives. When children are young, they believe their parents know everything. They watch us even when we don't notice them watching. We have the honor and opportunity to give them an eyewitness account of the difference Jesus has made in our life. They need to hear it. They need to see it. Our children should know our testimony of God's redemptive power in our life.

## WorkHearter Wisdom

We may not feel smart or theologically trained enough to confidently talk about Jesus to others, but we can talk about what we know. We can tell everyone about what He has done for our lives, how He has redeemed our story. How quickly our life changed once Jesus was invited into it. How can you share your account of what happened to you before and after meeting Jesus?

# One Last Request

Do not be anxious about anything, but in everything by prayer and supplication with thanksgiving let your requests be made known to God. And the peace of God, which surpasses all understanding, will guard your hearts and your minds in Christ Jesus.

Philippians 4:6–7 ESV

When I was younger, I would pray for things and say, "If you can grant me this, I'll never ask for anything again." I always did ask again. It was silly, but I was young. I thought what I was asking for would be all I ever needed. It didn't bring me peace; it didn't bring me joy. In some cases, it only brought me a few moments of wonder. And by wonder, I mean I wondered if my prayer was answered or if I would have had the same outcome whether I'd prayed or not. I naively thought each prayer would be my last request.

When I was a newlywed at age nineteen, I asked God to be married forever. I prayed this request every night. I had no intention to ever get divorced. I thought all I needed to do to stay married was to put in that last request. I wanted the peace that I didn't have to worry about my marriage, but I was not willing to take action to change my stubborn ways.

I argued. I was defiant. I worried. I was jealous. I was young. I was needy. I never imagined that our relationship would crumble so quickly. When my marriage began to deteriorate, I stopped praying. I originally asked God to stayed married forever, but when it got tough, I never brought my petition back to him with thanksgiving. I was unthankful in my request. Now with more years and wisdom, I pray for the peace to surpass my every thought and understanding and to guard my heart and my mind. I know what's it like to live without peace and to live with it. I choose peace as my continual request.

## WorkHearter Wisdom

God knew we would be anxious. He knew we needed the reminder to be thankful. He knew we needed peace to get past our own understanding of current situations in life. He knew we needed our hearts and minds guarded. He knew that our prayers would be many. He also knew that everything could be requested with no limits. We do not have to make last requests. We can make as many requests as we need or care to. Most the time, all we need is peace. He will grant us the peace we need ... if we only ask for it.

# Quiet Moments of Contemplation: Proverbs 3:5-6 ESV

Trust in the LORD with all your heart,
and do not lean on your own understanding.
In all your ways acknowledge him,
and he will make straight your paths.

You know this one, of course. But have you learned, yet, to release that stranglehold you have on *your own understanding*? Sure sister, we know how to acknowledge Him. I too have "Give Me Jesus" attire and list it in my own social media bio. But I need to work on my absolute trust and letting go of what I think I know. Absolute trust is having no idea or control of what is going to happen next and trusting God is taking care of the path you are on no matter the twists, turns and uphill battles. The classic hymns say it best: "Trust and obey, for there's no other way," and "'Tis so sweet to trust in Jesus."

## Perfect Storm/Perfect Timing

His way is perfect;
the word of the LORD is pure.
He is a shield to all who take refuge in him.

2 Samuel 22:31 CSB

There have been multiple times in my life when I thought a perfect storm brewing was a cruel joke. In hindsight, I see it as God's perfect timing.

My husband and I tried for years to have a baby. I sought alternative medicine/holistic providers, fertility specialists. We tried it all—until we decided to let it go and be content. I joined a doctorate degree program, he was given deployment orders ... and guess what? Of course, that's when I got pregnant.

I was extremely sick, a high-risk, geriatric pregnancy (the term *geriatric* alone will make anyone pregnant moody) and my oldest daughter was turning sixteen. We had planned a sweet sixteen party for her with several friends, which involved a limo, hibachi dinner, and a sleepover at a hotel. It was a perfect storm. My oldest daughter is my *rainbow baby* born after suffering a miscarriage, so I wanted to celebrate her for the ray of sunshine in my life that she is, no matter how bad I felt physically.

My husband was out of town on military duty so my

mom stepped up to assist. The girl squeals in their room got piercingly loud; we tried to sleep, but it was no use. At midnight, a knock on the door I assumed to be my daughter turned out to be my husband—he'd flown home to surprise me for a weekend visit. My mom put her pants on over her pajamas and hightailed it out of that room as fast as she could. She said, "I'm too old for this." I thought, "Touché, mama." I was almost 40 at the time expecting my 4th child, also feeling "too old for this."

My husband's arrival was perfect timing. In fact, the entire timing of this pregnancy was perfect. My oldest daughter, my rainbow baby, turned sixteen and able to drive herself one week before I was put on bed rest, and my husband arrived home from ending his deployment duty just one day before our baby girl was born.

## WorkHearter Wisdom

What I saw as a perfect storm of circumstances truly was God's perfect timing. Perfect meaning not one day or moment early, not one day or moment late. In all my planning and attempts to control life, I could not have orchestrated the timing of this major life event any more perfectly. All I needed was to humble myself and lean into his timing. I lived through the storm which was a temporary situation, and I came out of it clearly seeing the rainbow.

When have you experienced perfect timing? How has that helped you trust His plan more than your own?

## For Better or For Worse

> For whoever is not against us is for us.
>
> Mark 9:40 NIV

When you or your spouse stop fighting for the marriage, it ends and you grieve the unexpressed love when it's over. You grieve it because the love doesn't stop when a relationship dies, but your expression of it does. We want to belong to something that has ended, and it is tough to move forward without that sense of belonging to a spouse.

Our children also want to belong to something, particularly as they enter adolescence and teen years. Even if they are in a family that loves them, they will seek out friend groups to belong to. It is part of the transition into adulthood. It's easy to get caught up in wanting to belong so badly that you end up belonging to the wrong group—one without the same values or character that they have. A group whose actions are not helpful for them but potentially against them instead. This is the type of community that is not holding them accountable or challenging them for better but for worse.

I had a bad experience like that. The church had hurt me, and I wanted no part of it at the time. My love for the church died. Yet I grieved not belonging to a church body for years. I didn't have the biblical community I needed for support, accountability, and challenge. It was a battle in my life that I didn't anticipate. Jesus had to raise that death of love for the church inside of me to get me to go back into a church.

Even though that was over sixteen years ago, divorce is still a battle in churches today. Some churches don't want to "taint" their membership with divorcées. But Jesus wants us there. He not only wants us there, He wants us to know we *belong* there for better, no matter what "worse" has happened.

Our battle of belonging starts with belonging to body of Christ. We always belong to Him. Our families belong to Him. Our kids belong to Him. On our good days we belong to Him. On our bad days we still belong to Him. We belong to Christ whether we are single, married, separated, divorced, or widowed. Nothing we can do in a relationship on earth will take away our relationship with Him. We all leave people better or worse than when we found them. Let's strive for better.

## WorkHearter Wisdom

Jesus never stops fighting for us. He tirelessly is always in our corner. He is always welcoming us to His table. He is always standing up for us. He is fighting for the divorcées. He is fighting for the body of Christ. He is fighting for our children. Jesus can raise the dead, and His name can raise what's dead in you. He holds resurrection power and I believe it can resurrect anything. We need more Jesus and less of what world gives us to consume.

When our children make new friends, we can ask them: Do they make you a better person? Do you make them a better person? It's a challenging question to ask ourselves as well. The company we keep should be for us and not against us. Jesus is always for us and never against us, for better not worse.

## Patience of a Butterfly

There is a time for everything, and a season for every
   activity under the heavens:
a time to be born, and a time to die;
a time to plant, and a time to uproot;
a time to kill and a time to heal;
a time to break down, and a time to build;
a time to weep, and a time to laugh;
a time to mourn, and a time to dance;
a time to scatter stones, and a time to gather them;
a time to embrace, and a time to refrain from embracing;
a time to search, and a time to give up;
a time to keep, and a time to throw away;
a time to tear, and a time to mend;
a time to be silent, and a time to speak;
a time to love, and a time to hate,
a time for war, and a time for peace.
Ecclesiastes 3:1–8 NIV

Butterflies go through difficulty just to become a butterfly. The process is meant to make them stronger by squeezing out excess—what must be shed to be able to fly. They go through complete metamorphosis by entirely breaking down and have to remain motionless until they reach their new form and can fly. They transform into a total opposite of how they began. Many adult butterflies only live for a month. Likewise, Elijah had to be quiet in a cave after traveling forty days and nights in 1 Kings 19:9 in order to hear the Lord speak to him. It was an opposite reaction to his action.

In all of these seasons mentioned in Ecclesiastes, each reac-tion is opposite. When it is time to be silent, our mouth is shut but speaking opens it. When we love, our heart is open but hate shuts it. Weeping and laughing both cause our eyes to close, but for two very different reasons. We can cry both happy and sad, releasing tears of grief or joy. But in all seasons, we are transformed.

I've found in my own life that I'm becoming stronger after difficult times. I must shed the old thoughts of what I thought this time of my life would be, and I must heal from that expectation. I have to transition and be stretched from my old self to my new self. I grow from releasing what I don't need so I can fly, and through that time of healing I am renewed.

We put so much pressure on ourselves to meet our own personal goals on top of the unattainable societal goals. If we can release ourselves from that pressure, we will emerge a different creature. When we grow, we lose a part of ourselves that we don't need to be free to soar. It may be the weight of those unmet goals or expectations, or it may be simply something we picked up along the way that we were never intended for us to carry. We don't have to multitask to prove our worth. The butterfly stops being a caterpillar to patiently grow into a butterfly. Listen, mama, we don't need to do all the things or say yes to everything in expectation of something beautiful coming. Sometimes, we simply just need to stop and be still and wait for God to change us.

## WorkHearter Wisdom

Lord, help me to remember being still is holy, and there is a time for it. I know I cannot gain anything from my work alone. Help me to rid the excess that is weighing me down as a mom, as a wife, as a daughter and as a friend. Remind me today and every day that you make "everything beautiful in its time" (see Ecclesiastes 3:11).

## House Divided

If a house is divided against itself, that house cannot stand.

Mark 3:25 NIV

When my son was in second grade, our small town split into two school districts. It seemed ridiculous at the time. The county line ran right through the middle of town. For years, both county sides supported one school district for economic reasons, until one person decided to challenge that. Due to the subsequent meetings of the minds, it was decided to split into two school districts.

This influenced more than just school buildings and funds. It affected the local real estate market. One side of the county got to keep existing middle and high school buildings in their side of town while the other side kept the elementary school buildings. One side had to come up with a new mascot in addition to the logistical challenge of all the middle and high school aged students in an elementary school building. They had to start from scratch with sports and extracurricular activities. Due to drastic changes in a small town, one county suffered with drastic drops in property values overnight while across the street the other side experienced a dramatic increase in property value. Businesses were on one side or the other when it came to advertising and support.

Adults got into their own conflict, but the students were the ones who suffered from the division. The kids were the ones who should have been considered in the meetings about splitting up the schools, instead of the dollars the adults were arguing over. No one saw the fallout that would affect them for years to come when our town became a house divided.

Jesus told us a house divided cannot stand. It didn't take long for the citizens to realize the truth in this—and that the community needed to come together to support both sides for the sake of the students. Now the community is stronger because of it, even if there is a friendly rivalry between the two.

## WorkHearter Wisdom

As parents, we can't effectively raise physically, mentally, emotionally, and spiritually healthy children if we stand divided. Kids need strong support from both sides. Whether we are together in our marriage with vastly different parenting styles, or we are divorced and have trouble seeing eye to eye on our parenting strategies, the children are the ones who suffer from it. If parents can't stand together as a couple, it's imperative to stand together as parents. Children need to witness unity. A visible representation of their parents standing strong with support on both sides will help them stand strong.

As Christians, we can not let gossip or insecurity divide us in God's house. It ruins relationships and comes from a heart that is not healed by Jesus.

## The Good Side of Social Media

Is anyone among you suffering? Let him pray.

James 5:13 ESV

I've quit social media a few times. I've quit for Lent. I've quit to focus on school or work. I've taken breaks on Sundays for family time. As distracting as social media can be, and quite addicting at times, it was a welcome distraction during my time of grief over my sister's death. I had friends I had not seen in twenty years contact me on social media to tell me they were praying for me.

Every post, message, word gave me hope. It gave me hope that people cared. It's important to feel that hope and care during the dark days of anger, guilt, shame, and regret that comes with grief. I'm not exaggerating when I say I felt hugs through those posts. Especially when Brooke's friends would tag me or mention me, even if they barely knew me. I was included in their part of the story, and they were included in mine. That is how social media should be all the time: inclusive not exclusive, lifting others up, not tearing them down.

Honestly, I couldn't have been torn down more during that time anyway. I was carrying a weight that I wasn't strong enough to carry. My baby sister died from a relapse drug addiction. She fought those demons for years, and I, her big sister, couldn't save her. I was supposed to protect her and I couldn't. It is a failure I still carry to this day. Everyone has a rock bottom, and I was at mine. I thank the Lord every day for those who took time to lift me up in prayer. His love is stronger than the weight of grief. His love got directly to me on all sides through others praying for me. The good side of social media is access to a sea of strangers and long-lost friends who can support you no matter the physical distance.

When tragedy or natural disaster strikes, local communities step up on social media to spread the word quickly and gather resources. If you believe in serving in a local church and/or community and not just being a bystander or receiver, social media can be utilized the same way. Silently scrolling with no interaction is not utilizing the tool social media can be. It can be used as a good tool to be the hands and feet of Jesus.

Prayer is a great power. Sometimes, we need others to pray for us because we are tired, sick, grieving. We may not know what to pray for. The technology we have can be part of helping others when they struggle at the very moment of their darkest times. We have been given a great gift to work in others' lives that costs us nothing but brings great rewards.

### WorkHearter Wisdom

What have you experienced with the good side of social media? How can you make social media a more positive place? We can build community online if we choose to be positive and interact as a community. Whisper a prayer today for someone who is suffering—even if it's yourself.

## The Bad Side of Social Media

> Strive for peace with everyone, and for the holiness without which no one will see the Lord.
>
> Hebrews 12:14 ESV

It is not an easy task to stay at peace when there is divisive speech going on all around you, particularly during news-making events. It is even more difficult if you are on any type of social media. At times, one-sided posts fill up my news feed. I see viewpoints from both sides. I read hateful comments and deceit-filled articles on both sides. It is difficult to watch my friends and family become so divided. It's like watching your parents' divorce play by play online. No matter how much I want to speak out, I know it is a no-win situation, so I choose silence. I choose peace. I choose grace. I pray for those who twist the truth. I stand firm in my stance to keep the peace.

When social media or life takes a turn toward darkness, I try to post/think about other things. I try to distract those who can't see straight because they are so angry with each other. I believe our voice can be the most beautiful instrument God has given us to use, as it is the audible sign of life. I tried to use it to show there is life out there on the other side of these screens/life events, but by trying to produce alternatives, I inevitably consumed too much of others' voices.

Social media and television-streaming services have given

us an endless menu of consumption. But God made us to be creators—to create not just consume. If we only consume, it takes away our creativity. Our focus on creating should be to make what will withstand the test of time.

I didn't end up abandoning social media altogether, because there were many there seeking a peacemaker or seeking answers—a calm voice that said, "I see you, I hear you, and you are not alone." You don't have to agree with everyone to lend an ear and reassure them. You do need the discipline to get away from constant conflict.

Our children need an example of how to keep tempers from flaring. They need to see a calm and collected example when division is so heavily weighing on our communities. They can learn from us when we are challenged or confronted. We can use this division to teach our children how to navigate these conflicting times they are living in.

## WorkHearter Wisdom

You need a plan for peace by mediating on scripture. You will confront division as soon as you walk out the door. As soon as you go online even if you avoid social media. Even in our own home: it is everywhere. It's in the living room, in the bedroom. Our need for Jesus is everywhere. We all have differing convictions. We have a need to be proactive to combat the reactive, promote peace, build up one another and live in community-in life and online. And since we create what we consume, we must intentionally plan on creating peace. How can we plan to be creative more and consume less in order to have peace?

# WorkHearter Wisdom: Twenty Things I Wish I'd Known About the Preteen Years

1. This is the only time that your child will want to be around you on a regular basis without being embarrassed.
2. They don't need a cell phone or social media. We don't really need it either, but I digress.
3. They don't need fancy clothes, gifts, or money. They need our presence, attention and time.
4. Spend time with their friends and their friends' families. You need to know who they are spending time with now, before they are able to drive with them on their own.
5. Their favorite things will fluctuate. Don't spend too much time or invest in something that could be a passing phase.
6. Take vacations with them every year, no matter the distance or brevity. Their personalities, confidence, and physical appearance change so much in a year. A trip away with them to soak in who they are in the moment is as essential as buying them new shoes every few months.
7. Screen-free Sundays are lifesavers for your sanity. Take away tablets, TV, anything with a screen and let them be bored. Boredom breeds creativity. Join in the fast with them, I dare you. As a GenX member, I double dog dare you.

8. Applaud them and encourage them every time they help out, whether they do so voluntarily or not. Love them so loud by seeing them, hearing them and knowing them that they hear you above all the other noise. They feel love by feeling seen, safe and supported. This kind of love speaks louder than fear shame or inadequacy that evil tries to whisper. Remember 2 Corinthians reminds us "Satan himself masquerades as an angel of light" (11:14 NIV). They will easily recognize if they are ever mistreated the more they are loved.

9. They do not have any patience, and they do not forget. Do not promise something tomorrow and think they will forget. If you try to procrastinate, they will whine until you cave. Our battle of wills is weaker, I promise.

10. They look forward to time with their parents after school. They have activities planned and are excited to see us when we get home. Embrace it and relish it. This passes once they become teens and have vehicles, jobs, and independence.

11. The only audience they care about is you in this season. They will tell you long repetitive stories for as long as you'll listen. Kids want to be our audience of one and they want us to be theirs. They will even follow you or find you in the bathroom when they are little. When they are more grown, they will inevitably call you when you need to go to the bathroom and not care one bit because they need to talk to you right then. (Refer to #9). They want you to watch them do everything. They are looking for approval and reassurance from you. Be thankful they want it from you and not elsewhere. If you neglect this attention need too often, they *will* try to find it elsewhere.

12. Pray for their friends. Pray for their future spouse even though it seems in the far distant future. Let them hear your prayers.
13. Our weaknesses are not their weaknesses and our strengths are not their strengths. No matter how much they look like you or act like you, they are an individual uniquely created by God.
14. They won't remember a messy house or if your wardrobe is new or trendy; they will remember how often you spent time with them.
15. Encourage their imagination and curiosity. Let them ask you a million and seven questions.
16. Offer to help them with their school work projects. Help doesn't mean do it for them. Assist them with a helping hand so they learn to reach out to you for help when they need it.
17. Let them play outside and get their hands dirty.
18. They watch how you speak to each other. Choose kind words with your spouse. They understand sarcasm and criticism earlier than you think.
19. They will take interest in what you take interest in. Be careful those interests are positive ones for the little ones watching.
20. Make sure they know their parents are in charge and the marriage relationship takes priority. If they don't know this, they can use it against you to get their way.

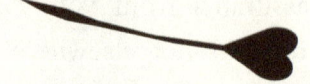

Jesus replied; "'Love the Lord your God with all your heart, and with all your soul and with all your mind.' This is the first and greatest commandment. And the second is like it: 'Love your neighbor as yourself.'"

Matthew 22:37–39 NIV

My command is this: Love each other as I have loved you.

John 15:12 NIV

## Marks We Make

Do nothing from selfishness or empty conceit, but with humility of mind regard one another as more important than yourselves; do not merely look out for your own personal interests, but also for the interests of others. Have this attitude in yourselves which was also in Christ Jesus …

Philippians 2:3–5 NASB1995

My husband loses his socks often. He only wears one color of socks so he can't say he loses one red one or blue one or even white one. He wears only black socks daily. He loses so many of them mysteriously in the dryer that he buys new ones about once a month. One day, I was stretching my legs up the wall to help my aging back muscles when he decided to try it also. He was imitating me, yet in only a matter of ten minutes or so he had made the darkest marks all up the light gray wall with his new black socks. It looked like a faded graffiti symbol. The Mr. Clean Magic Eraser can't even clean the dark spots out of the paint. My husband will pause before repeating this stretch since he saw the outcome.

As parents, we mark our lives and our children's lives with the actions we take. Some actions happen so fast we don't think about the marks we make on their lives. Waking them up gently in the morning for school or softly tucking them into bed at night are actions that set up their day or sleep routines peacefully. The mistakes we made in our lives are examples of what we try to guard our children against. Our attitudes can set the tone for our children's day and our own. Those are easy and straightforward examples. Some reminders are not visual and have a subtler way to show what to guard our hearts against. We can mark our children by our attitudes. We can mark our children's lives by putting them first and showing them they are more important than a phone call, or a client, or social media. Our care for and attention to them will leave a mark that is a lasting positive attitude.

## WorkHearter Wisdom

Our children need to feel seen. Our children need our support, and our children need to be safe. We can make this mark of love on their life by providing these things for them. A glowing mark full of light that can't be covered up because it illuminates. This is a lasting mark to leave on our children's lives.

## Sacrifice for the Sake of Others

In all things I have shown you that by working hard in this way we must help the weak and remember the words of the Lord Jesus, how he himself said, "It is more blessed to give than to receive."

Acts 20:35 ESV

When you are parenting children, you sacrifice daily for them. Parenting after a divorce? There is a lot more sacrifice. You sacrifice holiday family time, birthdays, and it is *tough*. I specifically remember I sacrificed Mother's Day one year. My children's paternal grandfather was very ill, and if I had not allowed them to be with their father, my ex-husband, they would have missed the final day of their grandfather's life. He passed away on Mother's Day. It was definitely a time when I felt better giving my time or day to my former in-laws for the sake of my children. Our children may not verbally appreciate our sacrifices, but they receive the blessing when we give it. When we sacrifice for them, we invest in them. That investment can have an eternal return.

Grandparents are a temporary gift to treasure in life. We are fortunate if they are a part of our lives into adulthood. I lost both my grandfathers before I finished first grade. My husband still had all four of his grandparents into his late thirties. I often reminded him how much of a gift that was. Both sets of his grandparents lived on the same street—almost unheard of these days—and all helped raise him while his parents were working. We will not be able to repay the sacrifices our grandparents or parents made for us. The only way we can return the favor at all is by paying it forward with our children.

Everyone says "it's better to give than to receive" and I know it's a tired saying, but there is no doubt of the truth in it. The joy you have is priceless when you see children open gifts you thoughtfully give as they have no way to return a gift to you in a tangible way. Their *joy* is the gift you receive, and joy is better than the money you spent or hours you worked to buy their gift.

## WorkHearter Wisdom

God also gave us the greatest gift we could ever receive in His son, Jesus. His joy comes from our receiving His gift, and His sacrifice for our sake. We can't ever pay back that gift—and He doesn't want us to. He knows we can't work for or sacrifice in return for His selfless gift given for our sake.

## Peace from Pieces

Now may the Lord of peace himself give you peace at all times and in every way. The Lord be with all of you.

2 Thessalonians 3:16 NIV

… to grant to those who mourn in Zion—to give them a beautiful headdress instead of ashes …

Isaiah 61:3 ESV

I have brokenness in my life; I thought I was a better version of myself when I was whole before the brokenness cracked me. Then one day, in a search for a creative outlet to just find a little calm and quiet, I pieced some broken pieces of colored glass together to make a work of art. The pieces made beautiful art, broken and pieced together in a different way. Yes—I received peace from shattered pieces. Beauty was made from broken pieces of glass that would be considered trash.

Even though my children's hearts were broken when their parents were divorced, the Lord has surely made them beautiful, each in their own way. Their hearts are tender to those who also are children of divorce. As a mother, it is difficult to know I didn't prevent some pain in my children's life, but instead was the cause of it. As a daughter of our heavenly Father, I am thankful He is making their pieces into beautiful art by healing their pain and using it to shine light on others.

Stained glass is a work of art made from broken pieces best displayed with light shining through it. We are best displayed in the same way—with light shining through us, even all our cracks. When we experience heartbreak, beauty can come from our brokenness. And the light can still shine through us. The cracks from our broken pieces allow more light to shine on those going through similar experiences we have endured. It gives us peace that we survived this experience, and peace is easily shared.

### WorkHearter Wisdom

God promises us a crown of beauty instead of ashes, a joyous blessing instead of mourning and festive praise instead of despair. He is the Lord of peace able to grant peace at all times and in every way. What does this promise mean to you? Do you have broken pieces that you can give to God so He can make beauty and give you peace? How can you see beauty coming out of a personal storm?

# Quiet Moments of Contemplation: Psalm 23:1-6 KJV

The LORD is my shepherd, I shall not want.
He maketh me to lie down in green pastures: he leadeth me beside the still waters.
He restoreth my soul: he leadeth me in the paths of righteousness for his name's sake.
Yea, though I walk through the valley of the shadow of death, I will fear no evil: for thou art with me; thy rod and thy staff they comfort me.
Thou preparest a table before me in the presence of mine enemies: thou anointest my head with oil; my cup runneth over.
Surely goodness and mercy shall follow me all the days of my life: and I will dwell in the house of the LORD for ever.

I love this passage. It was the first scripture passage I learned by heart. I would recite the entire twenty-third psalm proudly. I memorized it using the KJV when I was not yet a teenager, and it will always be my preferred translation for this psalm.

When I was fearful for my life living as a single mom, I would often recite Psalm 23 when I was going to sleep. I would recite it when I woke up in darkness to deafening silence. It was comforting, and it resonated truth to me. It is the truth I know and have lived. This truth is that God is my protector, I do not need anyone else. He forces me to rest when I am too stubborn to do it for my own good. He lets me catch my breath and shows me the right direction. I am not alone even in darkness, and I should not fear when He is with me. He provides for me and my family even when the odds are stacked against me. I have been blessed more than I could ever imagine as a struggling, broke single mom in my twenties. I have witnessed goodness and mercy in my life, and I know I will live with the Lord in eternity. Those truths do not need to say the word *thy* to have the same meaning for me. The truth will move you no matter how it is spoken, no matter what translation you choose. Truth is truth, no matter how you slice it. Truth will stay with you all of your days. This passage is a truth you can hold tightly to in any difficult season.

## Boiling an Egg Without Water

But whoever drinks the water I give them will never thirst. Indeed, the water I give them will become in them a spring of water welling up to eternal life.

John 4:14 NIV

I am a repeat offender of forgetting about a pot of boiling water with an egg in it. The pop of the egg exploding onto the ceiling and floor of my kitchen is my instant reminder, if I haven't already smelled the empty burning pot first. It happens about 25 percent of the time I boil eggs. I get distracted and lose track of time. I could blame it on the phrase I heard all my life: "A watched pot never boils." I don't watch it so it will boil.

I have a prior traumatic experience on forgetting boiling water when my firstborn was in the NICU. It was the middle of the night, I had no baby at home to nurse but needed to pump on schedule to keep up my milk supply. I was exhausted and healing from my C-section. I put the bottle parts in the water to sanitize and took a short rest on the couch. My first mistake was thinking I would remember to wake up before the water boiled out. Suddenly, I was waking up to blaring smoke alarms and the worst burned plastic smell scorching my nostrils. Our ceiling was black with smoke from the stove, leaving a visual reminder.

This is a character trait I have obviously not outgrown—

overestimating my own strength. I was too tired to wake myself up using my own strength. Other times when I boil the water out while trying to boil an egg, I'm too busy to pay attention to the egg. My husband will remind me to "not forget the egg."

We strive to outdo and multitask in our routines to get as much done as time will allow until multi-tasking becomes too taxing on our energy. We forget our shortcomings. We overestimate our ability to accomplish and underestimate our need for rest. Others recognize it when we try to pretend. If we don't listen to the warnings, we burn out like a boiling egg without water.

## WorkHearter Wisdom

We also underestimate our need for Jesus and His ability to fill us. We let time spread out too far between our bible study or prayer life. We underestimate how much we need Him daily to avoid burnout. We need reminders from others when we try to fool ourselves. Jesus told the woman at the well that He would give her a drink that would allow her to never thirst again. I can't imagine how refreshing those words were to her at that moment. This is true for us too. We will continually thirst without Jesus and the living water He gives. Lord, thank you for the spring of water you gave us. May we not lose focus on how great a gift this is.

# Tangles

"In your anger do not sin": Do not let the sun go down while you are still angry.

Ephesians 4:26 NIV

My daughter has the finest hair with so many tangles. They hide underneath and just when I think I've gotten them all out, another one sneaks in and stops the brush from moving. If it's a windy spring day, her hair looks like someone from the '80s teased it up to heaven.

Tangles grow while she sleeps, so I have to be proactive at night to keep them at bay. I tell her often that her hair has a dance party while she sleeps. I brush her hair out at night and in her sleep the tangles grow bigger—but if I didn't brush her hair before bed they would be out of control. How do I know? Because I am a tired mom some nights and neglect tending to the tangles. It's a simple task to help mediate the tangles from getting out of hand. It also helps us transition to a peaceful nighttime routine.

A peaceful nighttime routine is needed to fend off the night terrors. The nightmares start early in our children. Children want us to tuck them in at night so they sleep better. If we show them love right before falling asleep, they may have a better chance to rest. If we pray the blood of Jesus over our babies, Satan—who wants to disrupt their rest—will flee. If we are angry with our children, Lord help us to show them grace and love and not let the sun go down on our anger. Let us give them peace before sleep and protect them throughout the night.

## WorkHearter Wisdom

When I go to bridal showers, I often write this verse, Ephesians 4:26, as a word of advice to the new bride. In some ways, it also serves as a warning. I've experienced the downfall of anger growth and not addressing it before bed. It may not grow into a major dispute but it gives the anger and hurt a chance to cause a divide or a tangle in the relationship that can easily grow. Sleep may calm down emotions, but it doesn't solve any problems. We need to address strife in our relationships and take the time to tend to it before it has a chance to get tangled up and grow.

## Peace from Suffering

I have said these things to you, that in me you may have peace. In the world you will have tribulation. But take heart; I have overcome the world.

John 16:33 ESV

It seems ironic to me to read of peace and suffering in the same passage, but I can recall two times in my life where this was happening at the same time—right after my first child was born and during the pregnancy of my fourth child. When my first child was born premature at twenty-six weeks, weighing only two pounds, I felt suffering by not being able to hold him and breathe in his smell. He was in an incubator with so many tubes and wires on him. He looked fragile. Yet I had this indescribable peace. My high school best friend had just given birth at thirty weeks pregnant less than one month before. Her son was born in the same hospital, staying in the same NICU. I had visited with her and knew the drill of how to scrub and wear protective gear for visiting the tiny babies. We were both brand new moms with tiny preemie babies. Her sharing that experience with me helped me through my experience. I suffered yet again by not being able to take him home from the hospital when I left—a joyous day left empty when your baby is still there for the next few months. Yet still peace remained. I called the hospital every night to check on his weight and rejoiced with each ounce he ate that day. I visited every day and took the breast milk I had pumped for him. Throughout that entire painful process, I was at peace. He is now twenty-nine years old and six-foot, three-inches tall. He is healthy, and he blessed me with my first grandchild.

Fast forward from 1994 to 2014, I was pregnant with my fourth child and my husband was on military training orders several states away. His completion day was set for two weeks prior to the baby's due date, so 38 weeks' gestation. My history of childbirth was 26 weeks, 32 weeks, and 35 weeks respectively. I was not optimistic this fourth birth would last until my husband's return.

We had a lot going on in our family in 2014. I was put on bedrest at twenty-six weeks, coincidentally the same week my oldest daughter turned sixteen and started driving. My twenty-three-year-old son had left for Air Force basic training two weeks before to that. Oh, and did I mention that I was going to graduate school for my doctoral degree? It was quite the stressful time, to say the least. I suffered through awful morning, noon, and night nauseating sickness; I lost a lot of weight, and I missed my husband terribly. I was physically and emotionally spent barely sleeping. Yet I had this overwhelming peace. I had no need to worry in hindsight about timing or the health of my baby, since baby girl was born at thirty-eight weeks—one day after my husband arrived home after completing his training. I share all this to say: God is good. All the time. Even during the stressful times in life.

## WorkHearter Wisdom

Jesus also had to exhibit peace during His sacrificial suffering. He remained calm and prayerful. He was courageous sharing the good news from God, knowing it would lead to the end of His life here on earth. His peace during suffering brought about our salvation and in return our own chance for peace. We can have peace during any suffering in our lives, knowing that Jesus overcame all the burdens of this world to give us peace. He shared His peace with us so we can share it with others.

## Caught Off Guard

Be on your guard; stand firm in the faith; be courageous; be strong.

1 Corinthians 16:13 NIV

I don't need anyone to remind me to be on guard. When I drive, I am on guard with respect to those driving around me. This is likely due to the past experiences of being involved in a traffic accident. Driving on the way home, I look on both sides of the road for any deer that might dart out in front of my car. I do this because it's happened multiple times, especially during deer season. I hold my breath if I see one, hoping and praying it doesn't get spooked and run out in front of me. "No whammies, no whammies..."

We hold our breath through life during stressful seasons hoping nothing happens ... because we know it can. We are frozen like deer in the headlights. We don't want to be caught off guard again. We stay on guard. Being caught off guard can also happen in happy situations. If life's either going too good or not going great—*bam*! everything changes.

In Tennessee, tornados spin up out of thin air when the atmospheric conditions and pressure force a funnel cloud to touch the ground. Little to no warning is given when these conditions arise. I remember doing tornado drills regularly when I was a student in school to remind us to be ready. Unfortunately, the conditions that lead to tornados can happen while most people are sleeping. Just when we get comfortable in our homes, the storm can strike and cause damage. It's not *if* but *when* for our area when it comes to damaging winds of a tornado. We can only learn how to take cover.

## WorkHearter Wisdom

We don't anticipate the storms of life. They can come on suddenly like changing weather. We can be on guard and still not be prepared. Standing firm in our faith is most important when we are caught off guard. The courage and strength we need in difficult times comes from standing firm. Our faith gives us the strength and courage we need to take cover during any storm. We cannot go to sleep and get comfortable in our faith. Once we get comfortable, everything changes. Experience teaches us how to stand firm, take cover, and be on guard, but the courageous and strong teaching part comes from the heavenly Father.

## Birds, Butterflies, and Blooms

Preach the word; be prepared in season and out of season; correct, rebuke and encourage—with great patience and careful instruction.

2 Timothy 4:2 NIV

Three of my favorite parts of spring are the three things I missed most during winter: birds, butterflies, and blooms. They are the first clear signs of spring for me. Early days of spring bring birds singing a serenade early in the morning and throughout the day, butterflies fluttering through the air, and blooms budding on the trees and flowers. New life is abundant and visibly clear to my weary-winter eyes, nose, and ears. My senses are awakened. I appreciate them even more after a cold, dark winter season.

I can also recognize there's a flip side to these lovelies. Pollen blooms and my allergies go haywire. Birds poop all over our cars and patios. Changing seasons are difficult for my allergies and my sleep habits.

The presence of butterflies means other bugs are also flut-tering and crawling, and I do not love insects equally even though 75% of animals are insects. A question for heaven-Why Lord? (Let's be honest, I dislike bugs-mainly arachnids-more than I admire them.) They both exist together for me in spring—my dislike and annoyance of bugs and my love of all the blooms, birds, and butterflies.

In or out of our favorite seasons, something good is to be found in every season. No bugs in winter and no freezing in summer are two simple examples. We can find good in every season of life if we are patient. Good things and hard things can exist together simultaneously.

## WorkHearter Wisdom

Do you have a favorite season? Which one? Why? Can you think of negatives about your favorite season? How about your least favorite season? Do you see the positives in those? How can you compare and prepare for these ever-changing seasons of parenting?

Part 1: Spring Showers

## Missing What's Behind the Door

For nothing is concealed except to be revealed, and nothing hidden except to come to light.

                        Mark 4:22 HCSB

My husband builds homes, and the most requested walk-through punch list item before the homeowner moves in is a paint touch-up. Often there are paint scratches behind a door that has never been shut to a room during the build. The painter simply missed that spot. It never fails that the cleaner also missed the same spot behind the door so there is dust or dirt. Rarely, there may even be damage or a slight ding in the spot behind the door. It takes many eyes and several times before all these overlooked spots are found. It is part of a meticulous process in building a house. One contractor cannot possibly find every spot that needs attention.

We go in and out of doors daily, not taking much time to pause and look closely at the spots behind them. However, if you are paying hundreds of thousands of dollars a new house, you are more likely to crawl on your hands and knees to inspect every crevice your eye can see. When building a home, there are tiny crevices that can crack if precautionary measures are not taken. If it rains too much during the build, the lumber can expand and contract. Concrete can be compromised if it rains before the concrete sets up. The windows and doors can crack in small measure if not sealed properly. A house will show the cracks and areas that are compromised over time.

Building a relationship with your children as they grow can be a lot like watching a new home go up. Sometimes there are corners—or walls behind open doors—that get scratched or neglected during the busy days of life. Parenting is not a casual undertaking; details must be attended to. You can't pry, though, and you can't do a walk-though inspection, so details can be missed by us. We have to show that we care about everything—even the doors that may have been closed to us. Take heart that God is all-knowing and will not miss those details.

## WorkHearter Wisdom

How do you keep an open (and open door) relationship with your kids? Do you think it's possible to have complete trust—and yet sometimes overlook something important?

# Betrayal

Now that I, your Lord and Teacher, have washed your feet, you also should wash one another's feet.

John 13:14 NIV

The part of Jesus's crucifixion that personally troubles me the most is the betrayal. Judas gets a bad reputation for leading the Pharisees to capture Jesus, but we forget that Jesus's own brothers denied Him as God's son. Even His disciple Peter denied Him after He was taken prisoner. The only one who stood up for Jesus at the cross was the thief who hung beside Him.

I've experienced my own share of betrayal. Actions that felt like someone stabbed me in the back. My own family, friends, and even significant others have taken the trust and love I gave and returned it with hurt and betrayal. And it still stings to this day if I let my mind dwell on it.

The difference between me and Jesus is He forgave them all without question and without guilt or shame. He washed feet when He knew He was about to be betrayed. As one of His last acts on earth, He chose to wash feet of the one who would betray Him. He asked for God the Father to forgive others while He was barely breathing and in extreme pain on the cross. He pleaded with God in His dying moments on their behalf. He even forgave the man in that moment on the cross next to Him. I still can't comprehend the magnitude of all that quite yet. I used my experience of betrayal as a reason to be defensive and put up a wall against sharing my heart in the future. That's not even close to what Jesus modeled for me. However, with more distance from that act of betrayal, I have learned to be more forgiving.

My parents divorced when I was twenty-three years old due to betrayal. I had two children of my own, so I wasn't living with them. I was physically out of the picture when it happened. But I was not emotionally out of the picture. My mother and father had been married for twenty-four years. The divorce hurt me and they noticed. After some space and time, both my mother and father decided to share holidays and birthdays. To this day, we all celebrate birthdays and holidays with both of my divorced parents at the same time. It is a model of how to join together and be an example for our children, even when marriage doesn't work out. My dad recently had knee surgery, we all took shifts to help him during recovery, and my mom has indeed washed his feet.

## WorkHearter Wisdom

We live in a fallen world, so many of us have betrayal stories —and there's a good chance our children will experience it as well. Hopefully, our children will see us model forgiveness in a way they don't understand yet. We can join with others who have gone before us and lead our children in forgiveness. Jesus gave us the best example with His life. We can give our children a model of this with our lives. Father, give us another day to wash feet so our hands aren't able to throw stones.

## Enough Trouble

Therefore don't worry about tomorrow, because tomorrow will worry about itself. Each day has enough trouble of its own.

Matthew 6:34 HCSB

When Peter saw him, he said to Jesus, "Lord-what about him?"

John 21:21 HCSB

Today has enough trouble. Trouble we know about and trouble we don't yet know of. I was in a difficult course in college and two of my classmates were encouraging me with their positive attitude. Both were far ahead of me in accomplishments and job titles. I was in awe of their demeanor despite all the responsibility they had. I've never been one to be jealous of someone's outfit or car or other material things, but I do frequently envy a positive attitude of someone with so much pressure on them. I was constantly worried about keeping up with them in my coursework and striving to hit goals that would win the praise of the professors as they had.

I worried about not achieving enough and being perceived as the slacker in our graduating class. I was comparing myself to them. I didn't have the accolades in my past that they had. These days, our children worry about comparison earlier in school than we realize. The mutterings of comparison start younger and younger. If only we had a way to tell them what we learned the hard way—that we can't work hard enough to gain favor and comparing ourselves to others is useless. Our past and our future are too heavy a load to carry along with our present. Today is heavy enough alone.

Years after graduation, I learned they also felt pressure to perform and that pressure led them to make decisions that landed both of them in prison. For reasons I don't understand, they chose to conceal their shortfalls in an illegal manner. They were convicted and were consequently serving time in jail. Two people I thought didn't have any trouble later had more trouble than I could imagine! My worries were not in the same class as their worries, and they still aren't. Some of the troubles that surround us are not visible to us. And, they aren't supposed to be because we don't need to carry them. We only need to give them to Jesus.

## Workhearter Wisdom

No wonder Jesus told us not to worry about tomorrow because we have enough to deal with and carry today. We have gained wisdom that teens and young adults don't yet have and aren't equipped to carry; we know now that none of the comparison matters. The very young—toddlers—live in the moment. They don't worry about tomorrow because they know today has been tiring enough. If only we could trade them our wisdom on comparison and take their wisdom on living in the moment!

## Quiet Moments of Contemplation: Matthew 6:25–34 HCSB

This is why I tell you: Don't worry about your life, what you will eat or what you will drink; or about your body, what you will wear. Isn't life more than food and the body more than clothing? Look at the birds of the sky: They don't sow or reap or gather into barns, yet your heavenly Father feeds them. Aren't you worth more than they? Can any of you add a single cubit to his height by worrying? And why do you worry about clothes? Learn how the wildflowers of the field grow: they don't labor or spin thread. Yet I tell you that not even Solomon in all his splendor was adorned like one of these! If that's how God clothes the grass of the field, which is here today and thrown into the furnace tomorrow, won't He do much more for you—you of little faith? So don't worry, saying, "What will we eat?" or "What will we drink?" or "What will we wear?" For the idolaters eagerly seek all these things, and your heavenly Father knows that you need them. But seek first the kingdom of God and His righteousness, and all these things will be provided for you. Therefore don't worry about tomorrow, because tomorrow will worry about itself. Each day has enough trouble of its own.

I focused on the don't worry about what you will eat or drink part of this scripture for most of my teen years and into my twenties: I thought I was fat so it was the part I focused on. When I started walking every day outside I noticed how beautiful wildflowers are. It amazes me how they grow without being fertilized or meticulously pruned. Now I am at an age where I have learned that no matter how much or little I worry, each day does have enough trouble of its own. Worry is like compound interest, always multiplying and growing. But, seeking first His kingdom and righteousness will bring more return on our investment of thoughts and time.

I've learned firsthand that worry doesn't help us in any situation. I never really worried until I became a mom. It was planted in my brain as soon as they spoke the words, "You are in preterm labor. Don't worry, we will get you an ambulance." I struggled to turn back from daily worry after that. Once you know there may be something to worry about for your child, the thought doesn't let you go.

One child brings the worry like a tidal wave into your life, and with every chapter of parenting and adding more children or grandchildren, that tidal wave turns into a tsunami. The worries of today are different, but there were worries when God reminded us of the lilies and the flowers and not to worry. We created our children and we care for them. That care can produce worry if we are not careful, but God actually created us and everything around us. Since He is the God of all, even our children, we have no need to worry.

Sometimes, worry causes us to settle for less than God has

in store for our lives. When we settle, we gain anxiety instead of hope.

I think Jesus knew we would worry, but His point was also to let us know that before we even think about worrying, we need to seek Him first. If we seek Him first, all the things we worry about will be given to us. In fact, there wouldn't be room for worry if we focused our faith and energy on Him. He wants us to choose Him as He chose us.

# Missing the Intangibles

> So we do not focus on what is seen, but on what is unseen. For what is seen is temporary, but what is unseen is eternal.
>
> 2 Corinthians 4:18 HCSB

An intangible is something incapable of being perceived by the senses or being defined, according to the dictionary. My children have no memory of life without the Internet. My oldest may be the only one who didn't have TV or music streaming services growing up, although we did have cable TV. I think my generation is the last one to remember life before cable TV, music videos, in-home gaming systems, Internet, social media.

My childhood/adolescent life is intangible for all the generations after us. They will never know the feeling of being lost with no GPS or cell phone and trying to find a pay phone or read a road map. This must be the version of my parents' "walking to school in the snow uphill both ways." Today's youth don't have to record TV shows on VHS or wait for the next episode for a month or spend hours listening to the radio hoping to record their favorite song on a cassette tape. They will never know that joy, because they can download or stream their favorite song instantaneously. They have access all the time, so they take it for granted.

The Gen X generation, we had to wait. We were told to "Get over it" when life disappointed us. We had to keep ourselves busy with other things beside scrolling social media. We had to look up facts in encyclopedia book sets instead of getting instant answers from search engines. We tell stories to our children about our lives growing up and what we didn't have that they have now. We have become our parents, repeating the "when I was your age" narrative. We relive it by listening to '80s-themed music stations and playlists, or going to costume parties reminiscing in aqua net hairstyles and leg warmers. I often like to relive these days of old. A time we thought would last forever is now a memory. I think we take our access to Jesus for granted like today's youth take unlimited access to media for granted. He gave every generation the same unlimited access to Him.

## WorkHearter Wisdom

The feeding of the five thousand is one of the miracles Jesus performed that we read about. We were not there to witness it, but we have eyewitness accounts. The disciples' enthusiasm about the event has captured millions of people's attention, yet we are reminded to focus on the unseen: our experience with Jesus is more tangible than those miracles we didn't see, and is an open-ended invitation to a meaningful relationship with Him. That relationship is more important than any eyewitness account our eyes can behold. We have to be careful not to try to relive the intangibles too long or we will miss the tangible Jesus in front of us every moment of our day.

# Stretched and Pressed

Give, and it will be given to you; a good measure—pressed down, shaken together, and running over—will be poured into your lap. For with the measure you use, it will be measured back to you.

Luke 6:38 HCSB

As a mother of both grown children and one still in elementary, I often feel stretched thin and simply can't win. My older children have different needs and attention demands than my youngest child. If I take the youngest to a fun outing or trip, my older children, who live on their own now, will get jealous. If I take my "bigs" for an outing that is adult only, my little one is sad. I cannot win as a mom. That pressure is overwhelming at times. In addition to having a full load of responsibility, I often feel squished with no room to breathe. Feeling stretched and pressed is one-sided. My children, no matter their age, do not feel the same pressure by being my children that I feel being their mom.

My kids had crooked teeth growing up. None of them ever let it stop them from smiling. (Not a worry until teen years.) None of their joy was hidden. No matter how many teeth were pressing against each other or stretching wide in front, my children smiled proudly. The glow in their faces from sharing their smiles was one of the greatest gifts I could receive. They gave their gifts willingly and their smiling is contagious. What a lesson for me as a mom.

## WorkHearter Wisdom

Pressure is used to make diamonds. The lesson here for a mom is to not let any of the pressure put a damper on our days. We can't measure our feelings by pressure. We measure them by the promises God gives us. His word reminds us of how much we have already won with an overflowing bountiful measure.

## Peace Promoter

Deceit is in the heart of those who devise evil, but those who plan peace have joy.

Proverbs 12:20 ESV

My sister and mom call me a walking billboard. You want to know where the best place to eat in Nashville is, I'll give you a list. You want to know what face cream or natural cleaning product I use, I'll text you the link. Sometimes you don't even have to ask me, if I love something and believe in it, then I will tell you if you give me a window in the conversation about it. I truly want to help others find what I've found that is so incredibly great. I want to "share the love," if you will.

That said, I've recently learned that better than promoting my favorite product is to be a *peace promoter*. It's a tougher job, as it takes planning, but reaps bigger dividends. Plan peace, as the Proverbs say Solomon said. Instead of idly listening to gossip, which can be a plot to evil, I can promote a peaceful solution. It's easier to be a silent bystander when others are in an uproar about the latest scandal. It takes a little more effort to promote peace.

Jesus was a peace promoter. He gave peace freely. He planned to be at peace with everyone He encountered. He reminds us in scripture that He gave differently than the world: "Peace I leave with you. My peace I give to you. I do not give to you as the world gives. Your heart must not be troubled or fearful (John 14:27 HCSB). His peace eases trouble and fear in our hearts. He was a living, breathing, walking billboard for peace. If peace is something He was promoting, we should all be spreading the word about it. His peace is so much more than the world's version of peace.

## WorkHearter Wisdom

What is easier for you to share, rumors and gossip or peace and good news? Do you have an exit strategy for deflecting gossip? How can be promoters of peace instead of worry, doubt and fear? Do you have a way to respond with peace when a disagreement arises?

# Sight for Sore Eyes

Fear no more, Daughter Zion. Look, your King is coming, sitting on a donkey's colt.

> John 12:15 HCSB

I never understood the expression *sight for sore eyes* until I experienced it firsthand. After a deep family loss, my son graduated from his technical military training and flew home just a week after the funeral. We took a photo at his arrival outside the airport. I was dressed in sweats and my hair was pulled back in a ponytail. My eyes were swollen from crying from the loss, visibly exhausted from having a newborn keeping me up all night. My son was a sight for my sore eyes. The sight of him was soothing to my mama heart. He was safe. He was back in the same state. He was OK. So many parts of my life during that time were not OK. But my son was OK and that was enough for my sore eyes and heavy heart. I understood the expression of a sight for sore eyes.

When your children or a part of your family unit is gone, you feel their absence. When they return from being away, you rejoice and the incomplete unit feels complete again.

The people of Jerusalem were waiting for their king. Their lives were incomplete as they awaited His arrival. When they saw Him riding in on a donkey, the prophecy was fulfilled and He was a sight for their sore eyes. They had waited for so long for the Messiah. A glimpse of Jesus is just what our eyes need when our hearts are heavy from life.

Our children wait for us to show up, too, searching and scanning the room with their eyes at every school or sporting event to find their parents. Their eyes can rest when they finally catch a glimpse of their parents in the crowd. You've seen this and experienced the pleasure of being that sight for their eyes.

### WorkHearter Wisdom

How much are we anticipating a glimpse of Jesus in others or in our everyday life? Are we truly seeking the presence of Him in our children as well?

# A Deal's a Deal

He has shown you, O mortal, what is good. And what does the LORD require of you? To act justly and to love mercy and to walk humbly with your God.

Micah 6:8 NIV

I have been a part of many deals in my life. Some have been better than others for me. If I make a deal to have a foot rub from my husband in exchange for cooking dinner, that is a better deal for me. One of us usually must go first and trust the other will fulfill their end of the deal. These deals don't happen simultaneously. Who can enjoy a foot rub while cooking? When my child asks me to buy them something at the store and says they will pay me back more than what it costs with their money—which is always at home in their wallet—that is a better deal for them. Why? Because I must go first. Once they have the item, there is a chance my sweet innocent child will try to weasel their way out of paying at all for it, especially if attaining said item was anticlimactic for them and not as life-changing as they thought it would be. That's when I usually remind them that "a deal is a deal." I'm not asking them for anything they didn't already voluntarily choose to give up. In all honesty, I would most likely have not taken their money and just let them have it for being willing to hold up their end of the bargain. I'm not going to press the issue if they choose not to follow through, but I will be less likely to make the deal with them again.

## WorkHearter Wisdom

What we see as the benefit outweighing the cost is the better deal for us. God gave us the greatest gift we could never even ask for. It is life-changing. He offers it free of charge and we could never pay Him back. All He requires of us in return is to follow Jesus by acting justly, loving mercy, and walking humbly in relationship with Him. He gave us the much better deal, and we don't need to bargain for it. We all struggle to do the simple tasks God asks of us. If we try to weasel our way out of what He requires, He is not going to say to us "a deal's a deal," because it is a gift with no strings or deals attached. He only asks us to be just, merciful, and humble so we don't miss out on the rich fullness of His blessing in our lives.

## Losing Our Senses

My flesh and my heart may fail, but God is the strength of my heart and my portion forever.

                                                  Psalm 73:26 NIV

If we are abundantly blessed, we get all five senses to enjoy throughout life. If we are lucky, our senses only dim when we are elderly. Visiting a nursing home, you will notice how high the volume is on the television, because their hearing senses have diminished. I am over forty, so I have noticed my eyesight is deteriorating more rapidly than I'd anticipated.

My memory is not what it used to be either, and my teenage children have secretly used this against me. It got so bad at one point, I wanted to record our conversations just to prove I told them something they swore that I never said. I will fight vigorously to defend my communication. Once I fought a little too defensively and didn't realize my daughter was in tears until my furious rant was over. My heart failed to recognize her hurt in that moment. I lost my senses when I cared more about being right than being loving.

When we jump to a conclusion in a heated argument, we lose all of our senses. We don't see or hear the other person involved. God gives us the ability to choose our responses. There are typically two ways to respond to any situation—in haste or in thoughtful action. Haste is not preferred unless time is of the essence for survival. We can't always visibly see the results of our actions made in haste.

## WorkHearter Wisdom

God sees what we can't. With our limited vision, we can't see others' qualifications. Sometimes, things don't make any sense in our eyes. Only God can see the work in progress and appreciate it. Our flesh and heart may fail, but God is our strength.

# Hidden Treasure

The kingdom of heaven is a like treasure hidden in a field.

Matthew 13:44 NIV

When someone moves into a "new to them" house, they can easily overlook the buttercups or tulips if it's not spring yet. Depending on the season, there's a lot they might miss. Some new owners will hastily put up fences or clear brush/landscaping out, not knowing they are cutting out the flowers before they bloom. I see buttercups along the road that are all outside the fence like hidden treasure that pops up for a few weeks in early spring but is hidden most of the year.

We have two main roads leading into or out of our small town. One road runs from east to west and one road runs from north to south. Having access to any given direction in a small town makes for prime real estate. Small towns like this are considered hidden gems. Many people want to plant roots for their family here once they find our treasure of a town. We try to keep it quiet and hidden, but when it's blooming with growth, we can't continue to keep the secret. It's too good to stop the word from spreading.

Like flowers, we are going to bloom where we are planted—and we shouldn't cut out other people from our lives before they have a chance to bloom. There could be hidden secrets or unknown treasures in those people we can't see yet. Our children are like hidden treasures and worthy of the kingdom of heaven. We want to keep our children all to ourselves, but the world needs them. Once they bloom, their beauty can't be hidden.

## WorkHearter Wisdom

The kingdom of heaven is the ultimate treasure. We shouldn't want to keep it to ourselves, as it's big enough for all to enjoy. Word can spread all over about the treasure we found in our salvation. We should be shouting from the mountaintops with megaphones about what we found. Thankfully, the kingdom of heaven is not hidden from us or anyone else—it's too good to stop the word from spreading.

# Enough

Therefore everyone who hears these words of mine and puts them into practice is like a wise man who built his house on the rock. The rain came down, the streams rose, and the winds blew and beat against that house; yet it did not fall, because it had its foundation on the rock.  Matthew 7:24-25 NIV

My house growing up was always in a constant, chaotic mess. With four children in the house and two full-time working parents, there was little time for tidiness. My dad would hire a house cleaner, but then my mom would get upset with things being moved around. It didn't feel like home if it was out of order of the common mess we were accustomed to.

My hair was often a mess as well. My mom would call it a *bird's nest*. She cut it into a bowl cut when I was in third grade, and I never recovered from that embarrassing haircut. I didn't understand what she meant about the torture of tangles until I had my own daughters.

My daughter's hairstyles were not trendy thanks to their mom's lack of styling skills. In fact, my mom might have called them birds' nests too. I was lucky enough if I could comb out the tangles and knots in time to get them out the door and off to school. If I could get a brush through it, it was good enough. One year my oldest daughter saved her money for extensions. I was way out of my league during that season. I realized her natural bird's nest was nowhere near the mess those extensions would bring.

Birds' nests are made from fallen twigs, grass, moss, mud, and on and on. The birds find whatever they can carry to provide shelter and protect their offspring. They don't always build them in the best places; they are in a hurry to build quickly and start their families. Some are better than others, good not great—but good enough. Our children call us "home." We are their shelter. We are their refuge. It doesn't matter what status our home is in only what foundation it's built on. No one can tell our children it's not home if we are in it and we build it on the rock.

## WorkHearter Wisdom

What looks like a mess to us in someone else's home is providing shelter for their family. We can't judge a messy home if protection is provided. If refuge is found in it, it is good enough. If the home we provide for our children is a safe place for them to land after a tough battle of a day in school, work, or life in general, we have done our job. We may never feel like we have done enough to protect and care for our family in the present or prepare our family for the future. We have done more than enough, and we are enough for our children to feel safe, seen, and supported. Even though, there will be hard days when it seems we do not have the strength to achieve or do enough for our children, Jesus is always enough to fill in the gaps. He gave us the desire in our heart to do more and give more because He gave everything for us. But, He doesn't want us to miss the bless in the mess. Remember, this world is not our home. God is our home. As a child of God no one can tell us any different.

# Artist

He has filled him with God's Spirit, with wisdom, understanding, and ability in every kind of craft.

Exodus 35:31 HCSB

You do not have because you do not ask God.

James 4:2 NIV

In school, I wanted to be the "artist" kid. They looked cool. They had the best hair, clothes, style, and so on. Alas, I could never even get into a high school art class because I was on the college path, per my guidance counselor. Luckily, the Lord has the final word in our future, as always. With no art classes, degree, or experience except in college photography, I became a high school digital art teacher. God will place you where there is a need and equip you for that need by His standards, not the world's. He's a funny God, but He also equipped me with what I needed to rise to this challenge and enjoy every minute of it. No matter how inexperienced I felt or how inept others thought I was, it only mattered that God had given me this opportunity. Over time, my confidence built. I worked hard, took extra classes to learn different art mediums, and I felt like I was contributing to society. More importantly, I had more than one student tell me I'd helped them with opportunities they wouldn't have otherwise, which is the ultimate gift for any teacher. Because God saw fit to help me seek and navigate unchartered waters, I was able to help others. It doesn't get much better than that.

I am no longer teaching, but I still love to try new art techniques. Most recently, I found crushed glass art. It has helped heal places in my heart that I thought were unable to be repaired. Just like pieces of glass can be made into a beautiful piece of art, the broken parts of my life can be used to help others. God is the ultimate artist, and we are created in His image, we are all artists in some form or fashion. Even if no one else likes your artistic endeavor, it doesn't matter, because it's art. Art is subjective to the world, but the true artist loves every piece created.

## WorkHearter Wisdom

Education brings all types of opportunity. Because of my experience, I remain a strong advocate for quality education to this day. Education is more readily available than ever before. Don't let imposter syndrome stop you from pursuing a dream. God can do more than we can imagine. Have you ever wanted to be something you didn't think was possible because you didn't fit the mold for it? What's stopping you from breaking that mold or stereotype and pursuing a dream?

# Quiet Moments of Contemplation: Philippians 4:6–7 NKJV

Be anxious for nothing, but in everything by prayer and supplication, with thanksgiving, let your requests be made known to God; and the peace of God, which surpasses all understanding, will guard your hearts and minds through Christ Jesus.

These words never fail to calm me. You are undoubtedly familiar with them. There are other versions, with slight word changes. For example, in the NIV, the peace of God *transcends* all understanding. But how about this version, from *The Message*?

> Don't fret or worry. Instead of worrying, pray. Let petitions and praises shape your worries into prayers, letting God know your concerns. Before you know it, a sense of God's wholeness, everything coming together for good, will come and settle you down. It's wonderful what happens when Christ displaces worry at the center of your life.

It is, indeed, wonderful what happens when Christ displaces worry at the center of your life and shapes them into prayers.

## PART 2

# The Sweetness and Sweatiness of Summer

Summer is a sweet season for many different reasons and for all ages. It is also a season of the sweat and saltiness that result from our labors. And we do work ridiculously hard to be a good mom. Right, WorkHearter?

Parenting during a summer season can look like kids enjoying the endless days and mom pausing to see the sunshine while taking a much-needed break from work. Summer can and should be savored—but only after the all the labor has been done. When Christ said, "It is finished" from the cross, He'd spent His years teaching and ultimately dying in the most laborious way—for us. So that we would receive the fruits of His labor.

Lord Jesus, thank you for giving us the opportunity to work and receive fruit from the labor of our greatest life calling—motherhood. We thank you for creating time in our schedule during the busy year to feel the sun on our faces, walk barefoot, run through sprinklers, jump in the deep end, tend to a garden, catch lightning bugs and dance in the rain with our children and their joyous hearts. We rejoice in the sweetness of summer seasons of parenting as a brief bittersweet break between rapidly changing seasons. Thank you for giving us different seasons so we can appreciate every moment. Amen.

# Weeds and Pruning

He cuts off every branch in me that bears no fruit, while every branch that does bear fruit he prunes so that it will be even more fruitful.

John 15:2 NIV

This is the day the Lord has made; let us rejoice and be glad in it.

Psalm 118:24 HCSB

Pulling weeds is not any fun. Sometimes I stop as I'm walking by, or I may forget until the weeds have overrun the flowers ...and the weeds have prickles or spines that stick in my fingers. Pruning rose bushes can be painful too. The thorns have gotten stuck in my arm, hand, all over. I can wear the gloves but one thorn will stick me and I want to cuss at the bugger. (But I don't say bugger.) Sometimes the weeds or dead flowers and leaves will get into the prettiest blooms or flowers, and I accidentally cut good blooms because they are too close to the dead ones. It pains me to see a beautiful flower bud fall to the ground with the dead branch. Yet a few days later my rose bushes are blooming more than ever.

God allows us to be pruned by removing the parts of our lives that do not produce fruit. It is painful and it hurts, but afterwards we are more fruitful. Our children need the same pruning: discipline. Discipline involves recognizing the weeds and removing the parts that are not fruitful in their lives. I took cell phones, makeup, and car keys from my children at various times when they were teenagers. I take screens from my youngest in order to remove what's not producing fruit. Usually, the culprit of non-fruit is a bad attitude. It may be from an argument with a friend, they missed their wake-up alarm, their hair didn't lie right that day, or someone was negative about their outfit at school. Bad attitudes do not ever produce fruit, but they do multiply. The worst part of a bad attitude is if one child has it, the other one will catch it by being around it long enough. Like a beautiful rose bloom falling to the ground because it was too close to a dead bloom that was pruned, my children will catch bad attitudes. It's important to remove/prune those behaviors quickly before they spread. Our children are not their behaviors. Their behaviors are signals to us that there is a need. The need may be something is lacking in their ability to handle disappointment or frustration or jealousy.

## WorkHearter Wisdom

How can we keep from spreading our bad attitude? Gratitude is the first defense. When I get cranky and my attitude turns sour, I prune it with a list of what I am thankful for. We can also recognize we may be lacking a skill to handle jealousy, disappointment, or frustration ourselves. We need the skill to be able to teach our children how to manage when life doesn't go their way. How can we teach our children to be thankful even when a process hurts? We can start by being glad today for the day the Lord has made.

# Double Red Flags

There is no fear in love; instead, perfect love drives out fear, because fear involves punishment. So the one who fears has not reached perfection in love.

1 John 4:18 HCSB

The flag system at the beach in Florida is there for safety. It is posted on multiple large signs. It is intended to keep visitors and residents from the danger of riptides and/or marine life. And since we humans are so stubborn that a single red flag is not warning enough, they also use *double* red flags. The red flags are there to warn so lives are not destroyed by the disaster of trying to swim against a powerful riptide. Slogans such as "knee deep is too deep" are used to communicate caution and instill a healthy fear of the ocean's powerful waters. Still, with all the signs, every season tragedy occurs. Authorities don't have the manpower to physically remove and punish all of those who do not comply with the red flags, and the consequences can be fatal. Locals do not understand how tourists can miss these signs.

The Bible is clear on red flag warnings when it comes to those who seek to destroy or deceive. We consistently miss the signs. You don't know what you don't know. Our children will miss the signs also. They don't know what they don't know.

If it's a sign we already read or missed when we were

younger, we may have more patience or grace with them, since we also missed it. We understand how easy it is to miss a sign and fall into sin. But if it's a sign/sin that we know we would have never missed, we don't have the same patience. We don't relate the same to their mistake if we never made it ourselves. We don't understand it. How thankful I am that Jesus never made the mistakes I did, but He gives me grace abundantly; I don't have to fear He will stop loving me or punish me. What kind of love that must be—the kind of love I must strive to give, even when I don't understand. I don't want my children to fear punishment when they mess up. His love is perfect and does not involve punishment or fear.

## WorkHearter Wisdom

Sometimes we are the ones who miss the red flag signs. Grace is still given to us. Sometimes we are the ones waving the flags to warn our loved ones. Grace is still needed from us. In both instances, love cannot be driven by fear. Discipline and consequences are necessary when parenting, but punishment cannot be our driving force to warn our children. We can provide the warning, provide the love and grace when they do not heed it, but the consequences will be theirs to deal with.

# Inside Out

In all your ways acknowledge Him, and He will make your paths straight.

        Proverbs 3:6 NASB

When it comes to washing clothes, I don't mind the washing—either in the sink or the machine—and drying, either in the dryer or hanging dry. I do mind the folding and putting away of the clean laundry. I never worked in a retail store to learn that perfect fold. I can't do the military-style fold like my husband can. I can watch a YouTube video of how to fold and still fail at it when I try. Even though that technique looked easy and worked for others, it is lost on me. So I give up and just to put them away in a hurry—semi-folded and usually inside out. As a busy mom, it was not high priority so my kids would wear their clothes inside out instead of trying to fix them.

  But small children cannot fix inside-out clothes when they are younger. They have to learn the skill—and they don't even know where to start at first. My youngest will purposely select clothes to wear that are not inside out to be more independent. Or she asks for help to change the clothes from inside out. When she sees how to start on the inside of the clothing to get it right side out, it is not as difficult to repeat the task when needed.

  Over time, as adults, we learn we can't fix our visible outside issues without starting on the inside first. Our physical body issues usually aren't skin-deep and could stem from the inside. If we curse or use angry words as our first reaction to stress, it reflects the inner turmoil, frustration, and anger we hold. We need to work on learning that skill of turning the inside-out self we have right side out. Even if we have failed after attempting to do it the way that has worked for others, we can still focus on not being inside out. Try it again, honey. You can do it.

## WorkHearter Wisdom

Acknowledging that we need help is the first step. Once we learn how to straighten our paths, we can repeat as needed. Eventually, our practice will make the task easier. Never forget who is always there when we need help. All we need to do is ask, and even if we are inside-out, He will straighten all that out.

# Out of Shape

Yet you, LORD, are our Father.
We are the clay, you are the potter;
we are all the work of your hand.

Isaiah 64:8 NIV

We can feel out of shape in the beginning of summer. We go on vacation or to a nearby water attraction that requires a swimsuit and it is more apparent. Due to the season—farmers markets, fresh fruit and vegetables—we eat better. We feel trimmer as we sweat away calories in the sun, even if the scale doesn't show a monumental change. We wear fewer layers of clothing. We spend less time at school or work, so less stress. We eat less comfort food and therefore fewer calories. We're more active. The extra sun in summer gives us more of a shiny glow than our pasty dry winter skin. Eventually as we get into the season, we feel more balanced.

Our children need balance too. Fun, games, and play can have balance with some chores factored in. They learn responsibility and accountability while still having time for recreation. These character traits are needed in every season of life.

On the flip side, we can be so active and physically busy in the summer that our minds are not getting the daily dose of exercise needed to stay in shape. We have to learn balance in every season to stay in shape. Our minds feel out of shape when we don't spend time reading the Word or spending time in prayer. God created us to keep our lives in the shape of His image. We need Him daily to keep us in His hand to mold us.

## WorkHearter Wisdom

If you find yourself a little distracted, a little unbalanced, a little out of shape, get out your Bible. Find a quiet place to sit. Resolve to do it daily to stay in shape. God wants to hear from you. He molded us and knows how to get us in shape with Him.

# Jumping Into the Deep End

When you pass through the waters, I will be with you;
   and through the rivers, they shall not overwhelm you;
when you walk through fire you shall not be burned,
   and the flame shall not consume you.
Isaiah 43:2 ESV

My mom did her best to keep us busy in the summer. She worked long hours Monday through Friday. On weekends, she would take us to a local public pool for the dual purpose of entertaining and wearing us out so we would be quiet when we got home.

I don't remember if her bathing suit was one piece or two. I don't remember what color it was, or if it fit her. I was not yet old enough to be embarrassed by having my mom at the pool with me. The opposite was true: I wanted her to watch me jump into the deep end.

I'd just passed the swim test, so now I could jump off the diving board into the deep end. It looked like it was as high as a skyscraper from the water. When I walked the board, it felt even higher than that. Overwhelmed, I thought if my mom could watch me long enough to get from up there to the water, I would be OK. I was the oldest of four children, so it was a lot for her attention to be on me that long. The first time I did it, mom watched. She likely couldn't watch anymore out of fear, but once was all I needed. Her eyes on me felt like she was with me.

When we jump into the deep end of parenting, it often feels like we might sink when we try to keep swimming. Especially in those newborn days of no sleep and overwhelming responsibility, the magnitude we never had before is daunting and heavy. God the Father is not only watching us, He is right beside us, even if we don't see Him. He wades through the waves with us so we don't have to be overwhelmed. He doesn't just keep His eyes on us, He is cheering us on.

## WorkHearter Wisdom

When we begin something new or challenging, and it feels like a sink-or-swim situation, God being with us is the extra comfort we need to pursue what feels like deep water. And we'll be OK.

PART 2: THE SWEETNESS AND SWEATINESS OF SUMMER

# When Seasons Collide

You rule the swelling of the sea;
When its waves rise, You still them.

Psalm 89:9 NASB1995

Changing seasons are not smooth when seasons collide. Hurricanes happen when cold air and warm water collide. Tornadoes spin up out of thin air when thunderstorms start as warm air rises and cold air falls. Tornado season and hurricane season are unpredictable—even when the best meteorologists try to do so.

Our lives have seasons that collide with highs and lows of life too. One daughter can be celebrating new friends while another is mourning the loss of a friendship or nursing a broken heart.

The life-work balance can overlap like a collision, like wave after wave from the ocean landing on the beach. Some waves are fast, powerful, and ominous looking. Others are calm, steady and peaceful. The ocean can change in an hour, day, or week. A storm far out at sea that cannot be seen from the shore can affect how ocean waves hit . . . and someone else's tragedy far away can hit me like ocean waves, changing my mood, my attitude, my sense of hope. I've been discouraged by loss and devastation felt by strangers in another state or country. I've also been encouraged by outpourings of support and generosity from strangers reaching out to help those in need.

My daughter was away at college when a devastating tornado ripped through the entire town in the middle of the night. It was the transition from winter to spring weather that caused it to spin up without warning. She and her roommate ran out of their third-level apartment to the complex clubhouse to seek refuge when the winds were howling—but it was locked, so they got into their car to drive to a friend's home nearby. I couldn't be there or control what happened to her in those moments. I couldn't even speak to her on the phone during the storm. All I could do was trust the One who could when the waves kept coming nonstop during this storm.

I have a faint memory of being under water at the ocean with the waves coming on top of me as a toddler and I did not know how to get up. My older sister, Debbie, reached into the water and pulled me up. When I was not strong enough, she reached out to help.

## WorkHearter Wisdom

We want our children to be safe. And we know Who to trust when seasons collide or the waves hit. Tempers can flare and frustrations can turn into tornadoes without much warning in our home when feelings get hurt. Greater than any expert on earth can predict, our hope in Him will calm the storm. Even when waves don't take a break, God won't let the waves overtake us in this season. He is always there to reach out and help us.
Pray for Him to still the waters with calm transitions when the waves seem to repeat relentlessly and seasons collide.

# Living Water

Jesus answered her, "If you knew the gift of God and who it is that is saying to you, 'Give me a drink,' you would have asked him, and he would have given you living water."

John 4:10 ESV

I've been hungry, and I've been thirsty. I've been tired, and I've been exhausted. I also know what it feels like to be fed, rested, and rescued. Most of the time, the difference and responsibility lie completely on my shoulders. Decisions I've made in a hurry or committing to more than any one person can accomplish have left me empty and weary as a mom, leaving nothing for me to give.

In my haste, I abandoned reading scripture. Nothing can give my whole mind, body, and spirit rest like the peace that comes from drinking living water: staying hydrated with His words.

Water is crucial to healthy body function. All our organs need it. I once thought I was having a heart attack. I felt faint while driving and called for an ambulance. In the emergency room after the tests, they ruled out everything but dehydration. Dehydration is a common diagnosis for body ailments. In this case, lack of water caused my heart to beat out of rhythm.

Before a surgical procedure, we are required to fast and not drink or eat. But while we are under anesthesia, we are given hydration intravenously to prevent dehydration. Hydration is vital to recovery. When we need healing and we are recovering from a difficult season, we need the living water of Scripture to revive our souls. Only His word can rehabilitate us allowing our life to become saturated again.

## WorkHearter Wisdom

The gift of God's living water is vital to moms. We need it to live. It hydrates our soul so that we can recover daily. Being a mother requires taking care of others—but we must take care of ourselves too. Do not allow your living water to be depleted (and don't get dehydrated, either, mama). I have more energy and patience when I stay in scripture—it's living water vital for life and keeps my heart in rhythm. Thank you Jesus for life giving water.

## Sandy Knees and Honey Bees

How sweet are your words to my taste, sweeter than honey to my mouth!

Psalm 119:103 ESV

Gracious words are like a honeycomb, sweetness to the soul and health to the body.

Proverbs 16:24 ESV

Some of the sweetest moments in my life have included sand on my knees during the spring and summer seasons.

Honey bees buzzing around are a sweet reminder of hard work in the summer. Those bees work diligently as a team in the spring and summer for the sake of the hive. They are small and yet can produce an enormous amount of honey. How sweet it is to work together for the common good and enjoy the fruit of that season! Even though honey is sweet, it is considered a salve for its healing properties.

Sandy knees are no different. I love the ocean and if I get down on my knees to pray when I'm there and feel the grit of the sand, it not only smooths out the rough spots on my skin, but it smooths out the rough spots in my heart. I can reflect and be thankful any time I am near the beach. The tiny grains of sand are too numerous to count, but the ocean never makes a long-lasting dent in the enormous amount of beach sand.

Words given to us in scripture can be sweet like honey to taste and digest. And we were made to want God's Word: it's like having a sweet tooth for it. In turn, the Bible says our words to others are healing to the soul and body—others who need to hear grace, kindness, and courtesy, and us as well. Our life experiences can give us rough edges. Like sand smooths skin, God's Word can smooth our rough edges. We need our rough edges smoothed out to give gracious words naturally. We need honey to heal our cuts and bruises that come from life. It's amazing to think that the same God who provided honey and sand to smooth and heal, gave us soul affirming words to live by and heal us also.

## WorkHearter Wisdom

What places take you to a point of thankfulness and reflection? Have you been there recently? What hurt areas or rough edges do you need smoothed out and healed? Jesus, give us sandy knees to smooth out the rough edges in our hearts and words like honey to give others and ourselves when we need healing.

# Salt and Light

Salt is good, but if it loses its saltiness, how can you make it salty again? Have salt among yourselves, and be at peace with each other.

Mark 9:50 NIV

You are the salt of the earth. But if the salt loses its saltiness, how can it be made salty again? It is no longer good for anything, except to be thrown out and trampled underfoot.

Matthew 5:13 NIV

Being a mother does not always equate to being a good cook. I have improved over the years, but am nowhere near being a skilled professional. I do, though, know the difference between needing salt or not. I don't salt everything on my plate before I taste it, so I can savor the flavor before I decide to add salt. My best friend from high school always salted everything before she tasted it. When she quit smoking after twenty years, she was amazed at how food tasted *without* having to add more salt. Cigarettes had made her taste buds lose their taste. They dulled her senses.

That said, we can tarnish our senses with what we choose to do in our lives. My taste for healthy foods has been a process. I still love butter and bread daily, but I have more willpower to turn down sugar. My dictionary lists the word *sweet* as being the opposite of salt. I love to nourish my body with vegetables and fruit now. I crave sustenance, not junk. If I give my body what it needs, it doesn't give me trouble like headaches, stomachaches, or other digestive issues.

Similarly, if we keep our senses, we can live at peace with one another. *Salty* is a term used to describe bitter or upset. It originated with sailors beings toughened or "salty" from experience. I don't think this is what God meant by keeping our saltiness. If we keep our light shining for all to see and that light spreads, we give glory to God. Matthew goes on to say, "You are the light of the world. ... let your light shine before others, that they may see your good deeds and glorify your Father in heaven" (vv.14–16). A lightning bug (firefly) can give so much light to a night sky. Lightning bugs use all their energy to make light to attract and warn others. What we put in our bodies and on display for others to see can determine if we keep our salt and light. I crave God's Word as well. When I am starved for it because I've neglected to feed my mind, I can feel the emptiness. We can't bring glory to God if we are not nourishing our bodies and minds. We have to stay diligent to keep our saltiness in this sticky-sweet world and use more of our energy to be a light.

### WorkHearter Wisdom

How have your taste buds changed? They do, you know. Lord, please help us to recognize that bitterness is not from you. What ways can we make sure to keep our salt salty and light shining in a dark world?

# WorkHearter Wisdom: Twenty Things I Wish I'd Known About Raising Teens

1. They don't hate you. Most of the appearance of dislike teens have toward moms is self-loathing. They feel safe with you to release all their emotions; be grateful for that and keep the space safe for them.
2. They want you to show up for them. Even if they say they don't care or tell you not to, they want you there.
3. They hope you will interact with their friends and their friends' moms, but they won't tell you. You will also benefit by getting to know the adults who are raising their friends.
4. You can keep the hormonal tensions from rising by remaining calm. Don't let them push your buttons. They know your soft spots. Not everything they say or do needs a reaction from you. No reaction can be the curing calm.
5. The teen years can be fun if we have boundaries for them and for us. Electronics and social media are a distraction and can be limited for both parents and children.
6. Comparison truly is the thief of joy (Theodore Roosevelt). Don't compare your children's accomplishments, grades, attitude, aspirations to another's. Ever.
7. No matter how busy they are or you are in this season, take them on trips. They won't remember the money you spent on their shoes or clothes or electronics, but they will

remember the trips. My daughters would often talk more to me in a car ride than at home.

8. You don't have to be the cool mom. Leave that to someone else. You just need them to trust you enough to be honest with you. You can do that easily by being the loving mom.

9. They are smarter than you were as a teen. They also have access to so much more mischievous options than you did. They will figure out how to trick a GPS tracker, get around not having Wi-Fi and learn passcodes on parent permissions.

10. They are imperfect. You are imperfect. Love and grace are free and meant to flow freely back and forth. Forgive yourself when you lose it and forgive them as well.

11. Hormones wreak havoc on our previously perceived perfect children. My mom said I was an angel until I turned thirteen. I gave her some hell after that. She still loves me and wants to spend time with me, thankfully. Your teens will turn into your best friends with time.

12. Even though we all know it is not, it feels like the end of the world to them if they miss out on one special event or experience heartbreak. Remind yourself how it felt to you at their age and sympathize.

13. Admit to them when you mess up and show them what an authentic apology looks like. Forgive them when they mess up and show them what grace looks like. They can't give it to others if they don't see an example of it. Remember, you are growing up with them.

14. Their friends have more influence in their life than you realize. If you sense anything is off, don't hesitate to act on it. Trust your intuition. I wish we could tiptoe around difficult conversations/seasons, but we can't.

15. They don't know how to microwave food no matter how easy it seems unless you show them. They only know what you teach them how to do. Most schools don't teach them basic life skills.
16. They need to face the consequences of their actions: oversleeping and missing school, missing work or practice. The consequences of these are minor but if they don't learn about consequences now, it could be devastating for them as an adult.
17. Only intervene at their school, work, or sports if they are in danger, in the way of harm, or sick. Otherwise, they need to learn how to navigate these areas on their own.
18. College is not the only path. Their opportunities are *their* opportunities and *their* choices. Be careful not to project your hopes and dreams to supersede theirs.
19. They need you to understand, include, and accept them—not vice versa. It is not a two-way street now. They will be more able to reciprocate that for you when they are older and the hormones have simmered down. Just keep saying "Serenity now" to yourself.
20. Teach them how to tell unwavering truth and how to stand strong in their faith. This foundation will help them throughout their entire life, no matter what path they choose in the future.

I praise you because I am fearfully and wonderfully made;
 your works are wonderful,
 I know that full well.

Psalm 139:14 NIV

# I Want All the Fruit

> But the fruit of the spirit is love, joy, peace, patience, kindness, goodness, faithfulness, gentleness, self-control; against such things there is no law.
>
> Galatians 5:22–23 ESV

Fruit is my favorite. I prefer it over vegetables. I love all fruit. I have some ranked lower than others in my list of favorites, but I do not dislike any fruit. My favorites include strawberries, raspberries, bananas, and pineapple. I know all of them are healthy for me to eat, and they are all classified as fruit. The scripture verse does not say "fruits"—it says "fruit." Meaning, all are one fruit of the Spirit. I can't choose a fruit of love, joy, kindness, faith, and goodness, and pass on peace, patience, gentleness, and self-control because I'm full. It is all or none.

Peace is one of the hardest ones for me. If I made a list of the fruit and which one(s) I fall short on the most, peace would rank highly. Worry is the opposite of peace, and that is because worry is a mental war or conflict. It is a battle of fear on our minds, thoughts, and actions. I worry about my weight and my aging body. I spend more time worrying than doing anything different about those things like exercise and healthier eating, though.

God gave us the list of how to tell if we have fruit of the spirit. It is not a grocery list that we can shop around for. It is not a list that can be changed or revised to only accommodate our favorite fruits or current diet trend. The list of fruit of the spirit is the guide from our Father in heaven to check ourselves against before we wreck ourselves—but also compare to those we seek for guidance here on earth. Coincidentally, a few verses before the fruit of the spirit list, He gave us a list of the works of the flesh, stating the obvious. Somehow, we may have items on both lists when we take stock in ourselves. However, the fruit list is the one we need to focus on. We need all the fruit to cut out the works of the flesh.

## WorkHearter Wisdom

It is not possible to have peace while worrying. But it *is* possible to feel at peace and notice your worries have ceased. Action steps to take to protect your peace ... your fruit ... include:
- Battle your fear and worry by letting down the sword of control. Control can include winning an argument. We don't have to be right all the time, but we do have to be loving. Let it go...
- Run the race of love in all kinds of weather.
- Take a breath before speaking (or emailing, texting) and keep it kind, always. This simple pause will help protect your peace.
- Trust God and His word at all times. No matter what we go through, we have to trust His timing regardless of our current situation or the odds stacked against us. The Lord is incapable of making mistakes or being wrong.

- We have goodness when we provide for our children and when we pray for our enemies.
- If we hold our temper and our tongues, we practice the art of patience. Don't hold your bladder though-no one has patience when they have to pee. But, with temper & tongues: use restraint, do not seek revenge, and think carefully. Patience is a sign of strength and will bring self-control.
- Self-control is our ability to say no to self, to our wants. Instant gratification makes us slaves to selfishness.
- Always remember joy is a staple but it's not the same as happiness. We can have joy in unhappy seasons. The apostle Paul wrote the joyful book Philippians while in prison. Joy is a choice not dependent on our circumstances.
- ENJOY THEM: Enjoy your babies, enjoy your kids, enjoy your teens, enjoy your big(adult kids), enjoy the moments that turn to memories before your very eyes.

## Perfecting Peace

And let the peace of Christ rule in your hearts, to which indeed you were called in one body, and be thankful.

Colossians 3:15 LSB

Fear and worry and doubt can cloud my thoughts faster than cirrostratus clouds cover our skies in winter. These clouds produce rain or snow-within twenty-four hours of their appearance, covering the whole sky like a thin veil. Sometimes they're so high and so thin all you can see is a halo around the sun (or moon). I can produce worry that clouds my judgment quicker than that.

I'm proficient at worry. It doesn't take much for my mind to wander to the worst-case scenario. When my oldest daughter started driving, we didn't have GPS technology on phones yet. I asked her to call me when she arrived at and left school events. One night after a basketball game, she didn't call. She also didn't answer the phone. It was late and I was home pregnant on bed rest. I feared the worst. All the bad scenarios from school parking lot flat tire, dead battery, to highway car wrecks played like a movie trailer taking over my mind. I wanted to a be a fly in the back seat to make sure she was OK, but what I needed was peace. She arrived home five minutes later. Her phone battery had died and she didn't have a charger. (That girl never had a charger.) I thanked God internally and vocally in that moment, but I should have thanked Him earlier instead of worrying.

I overanalyze small situations until there are so many moving parts that the anthill size situation has grown into the size of an active volcano. *Active volcano* in the sense of me waiting for the opportunity to overflow with all these thoughts I've had about the situation, overanalyzing everything. One reaction I'm working on having instead is thankfulness. When I don't understand why or how it happened, I am practicing thankfulness.

Instead of asking why, I can ask *What can I learn from this?* When I'm being extra positive, I think *What am I being spared from?* Thank you, Lord. Even though I don't know, thank you for your protection. Repeating/practicing these words of thankfulness can change my heart from scattered, irrational overreaction to peace and calmness. I can breathe easier and slower, which always helps my nerves and my mood.

Who would have thought we could gain peace from practicing thankfulness? If practice makes perfect, we can strive to have perfect peace. Speaking the words *thank you* can be the path to breathing a little easier. When we breathe easy, our heart rate slows and nerves get calmer.

## WorkHearter Wisdom

What are you letting rule your heart and mind? Is it peace and thankfulness or worry and doubt or fear? As a practice, try thankfulness in your mind if you want peace in your heart. If we start and end our day with thankfulness, the worries in the middle tend to take a back seat to peace. If what we *should* do becomes what we *would* do, peace can be perfected.

# Formative Years

But whoever causes one of these little ones who believe in me to sin, it would be better for him to have a great millstone fastened around his neck and to be drowned in the depth of the sea.

Matthew 18:6 ESV

Truly, I say to you, whoever does not receive the kingdom of God like a child shall not enter it.

Mark 10:15 ESV

When I was in preschool circa late 1970s, I attended a church day-school program. I don't remember much from that year, but I do vividly remember one teaching from that school program. I was taught along with the rest of our class that the world would definitively end in 1993. Obviously, that did not happen, but I spent all my life until 1993 carrying that thought in my stored memory. To say it did not hold influence over any of my decisions would be a lie.

One lesson at one class as a child stayed with me for many years until I learned that it was untrue. It was a humbling moment for me and proved the power adults can have over children. The adult who told us that did not have to earn my trust or prove it to be true. I believed him because he was an adult in a church. It was merely spoken to me as a child during my formative years. It could have been a miscommunication, but as a child it stayed in my mind. The worst part was I kept it a secret and held onto it alone.

Children believe adults most of the time until that trust is broken. The trust of a child is precious. Jesus spoke about humbling ourselves like children. As adults we know better and think we are wiser because we do not blindly trust—but it makes us less humble.

As adults, we must be careful with our words. They carry a significant weight with them. They carry the weight of children's trust and of forming their thoughts and beliefs. Our words to ourselves and to others are not just words spoken and then forgotten; they can be ingrained in memories of children who trust adults without any needing proof. If we trusted our Lord and Savior in the same way, what a difference it would make it in our everyday lives! If we place our trust in Him, it is well placed.

## WorkHearter Wisdom

Communication is a powerful tool. Miscommunications happen and lead to misunderstandings. How can we communicate to minimize misunderstandings in our home? How can we use our words to enrich others' lives? How can we trust God like a child? Lord, I pray our children share with us any fears they are holding onto so we can guide them to trust in you.

# Final Post

> But the Advocate, the Holy Spirit, whom the Father will send in my name, will teach you all things and will remind you of everything I have said to you.
>
> John 14:26 NIV

Our first above-ground pool at our house was an expense that didn't leave us money to pay for a professional fence company to install the fence required by city ordinance and HOA rules. Our only option to comply was to do it on our own. My husband and son both got to digging holes and pouring concrete to set the posts. It was hot outside and the work was labor-intensive, even for our small backyard. My son almost cried when he set the final post. It was likely the easiest one to set after all his experience, but it was the one he remembered the most, and it gave him great joy.

When someone famous or familiar passes away, people immediately go to their social media profile in droves to see, read, or watch their final post. It could have happened yesterday or a year ago, but it is the most viewed since it was their final post. News outlets report on what's in the final post made by that person as if it was their final words.

God gave us all His *posts* to use in life as reminders and encouragement in every situation. Jesus's last *post* on the cross told us He'd finished it for us. We don't have to endure the pain Jesus experienced, but we can have the great joy from His final post. His words of reassurance before His crucifixion bring even more encouragement about the power of the Holy Spirit. He left us words of wisdom along with love as a legacy to us to live by. He also gave us the Holy Spirit. Without Him, we would be on our own. Who want's that?

## WorkHearter Wisdom

For our family, our last post is how we showed love to each other. We remember the love and words of wisdom we have been given by those who raised us. Our children, in turn, will remember our love and words as the legacy we leave for them. What parting words of wisdom are we giving our children as reminders when they leave our homes to live on their own?

# Defining Degrees

The people were amazed at his teaching, because he taught them as one who had authority, not as the teachers of the law.

Mark 1:22 NIV

For I have resolved to know nothing while I was with you except Jesus Christ and him crucified.

1 Corinthians 2:2 NIV

I worked tirelessly to earn every one of my education degrees. I obtained all of them after having children, and it took me years longer than the average student to complete them. I started my doctoral program while I was pregnant with my fourth child at the age of forty.

I used to get upset with celebrities who were given honorary doctoral degrees until I correlating this concept to motherhood. Celebrities are given a degree that aligns with their many years of experience in their field. Mothers should be given the same. Research experts have settled on ten thousand hours of expertise to define you as an expert. Mothers have double that amount of experience parenting by the time their child is age two.

We are defined as experts no matter what degree we hold. There is no degree for parenthood. It is not taught in an Ivy League university or a community college. It is barely covered in the hospital before or after you become a first-time parent.

Physicians don't teach you how to nurture or raise a child. They do instruct you on how to keep them alive.

We need to have celebrations and graduations for mothers at differing stages of parenthood. When they reach the toddler years after age two, moms should be given an "honorary" bachelor degree. When they survive adolescent and preteen years, they should be given an "honorary" master's degree. Once they have an adult child, they deserve the "honorary" doctoral degree. If they have twins, it's a double major. More multiples than that, they should have a school named after them, in my opinion! The library of knowledge a mother holds is passed on or lent to her children when grandchildren are born. They are consulted first before a doctor or friend is called when their child is sick. The help they provide is not defined by an education degree, but the life experience of motherhood ... gifted from God.

## WorkHearter Wisdom

Jesus was the greatest expert on earth but He held no degree in law. He had the authority from God that amazed those who heard His teaching. He was not defined by a degree. He was defined by his experience with our heavenly Father. He should be our first call or contact when we need help. His library of knowledge has been loaned out to us in His teachings. We have been gifted the grace from God to use when we need it. It's not what you know, but Who you know. Because, what/who do I know? I know Jesus and that's enough for me.

# Quiet Moments of Contemplation: 1 Corinthians 13 ESV

If I speak in the tongues of men and of angels, but have not love, I am a noisy gong or a clanging cymbal. And if I have prophetic powers, and understand all mysteries and all knowledge, and if I have all faith, so as to remove mountains, but have not love, I am nothing. If I give away all I have, and if I deliver up my body to be burned, but have not love, I gain nothing.

Love is patient and kind; love does not envy or boast; it is not arrogant or rude. It does not insist on its own way; it is not irritable or resentful; it does not rejoice at wrongdoing, but rejoices with the truth. Love bears all things, believes all things, hopes all things, endures all things.

Love never ends. As for prophecies, they will pass away; as for tongues, they will cease; as for knowledge, it will pass away. For we know in part and we prophesy in part, but when the perfect comes, the partial will pass away. When I was a child, I spoke like a child, I thought like a child, I reasoned like a child. When I became a man, I gave up childish ways. For now we see in a mirror dimly, but then face to face. Now I know in part; then I shall know fully, even as I have been fully known.

So now faith, hope, and love abide, these three; but the greatest of these is love.

You have heard this countless times, doubtless at a wedding or two. But just sit with this now, and contemplate it: The greatest of these is love. Always. The greatest impact we will have on our children is our love. Our love has no end. The greatest impact Christ has with us is His love. His love never ends.

## Grand Openings versus Soft Openings

> I am sure of this, that he who started a good work in you will carry it on to completion until the day of Christ Jesus.
>
> Philippians 1:6 CSB

Every time a new restaurant opens in our small town, it is swamped with all the locals who want to try the new food options. The owner will do a soft opening night or two to help the employees work out the growing pains and be more efficient. Weeks later, they will announce a grand opening when they feel ready to offer their best work to the customers. Ultimately, they will still have growing pains to work out. Wait times will be too long, food will be delivered cold, or orders prepared incorrectly. An item or two will inevitably be missing. None of this is on purpose, but it is taken personally by both the staff and customers—creating a negative experience they couldn't predict.

As a new mom, I would have needed years of a "soft opening" before presenting my motherhood skills on a grand opening date. By the time I was in a good rhythm and comfortable routine, my child would get a new tooth, virus, fear or separation anxiety. These growing pains would create a negative atmosphere between me and my child. We both would need time to start over with a soft opening. Yet again, a new season of life would bring peer pressure, learning trouble, and social struggles for both parent and child. None of it would be on purpose—just learning experiences to grow us. I never felt like I could be confident enough to reach a grand opening date. I still don't. But, God says I've always been enough.

## WorkHearter Wisdom

We will never reach the grand opening readiness of Christian life. The wait is too long. Something will always be missing on our end. We need to be gracious with ourselves. If we are comfortable and feel like we have it down pat, we are not rooted deep in our faith. God will continually carry out our growth and the good work He started in us until the day Christ returns. His return will be our grand opening. Ready or not, He is coming. Let's continue the work He started in us until it is complete by holding continuous soft opening up of our hearts to those around us and especially inside our homes and family.

# Bruised Bananas

Either make the tree good and its fruit good, or make the tree bad and its fruit bad, for the tree is known by its fruit.

Matthew 12:33 ESV

I've been guilty of purchasing bananas with all good intention of eating them before they get too ripe. The bruised ones I save for banana bread. I have noticed while using them for banana bread that the bruise on the peel does not always go through to the fruit. On the surface, the peel looked like the fruit was damaged, but the fruit, even though it was soft, was fine on the inside.

Jesus told us we will be known by our fruit. We may have bruises and battle scars that are visible on the outside, but if we are fruitful, the bruises won't affect our fruit. Even a coconut shell that is hard to open cannot reveal the fruit inside. We have to open it to see it. Our fruit is not found by our looks or body condition. It is found in our soul. We can show it to others in action, in words, in kindness and truth-telling. We can share our fruit with others by showing up, even when we feel like we are not looking our best. When our peels are bruised, torn, or disheveled, we can still show up and bring sweetness to others in their times of need by being selfless.

I have never placed importance on what someone visiting

me was wearing, or their hair or makeup condition at a funeral home or from a hospital bed. Their presence, not appearance, was sweet to me. It didn't matter in the slightest to me what they looked like. It mattered more that they showed up and considered me worthy of their visit. Even our bruises can make situations sweeter just like bruised bananas make the best banana bread.

## WorkHearter Wisdom

Can you remember a time when the presence of a loved one or even a stranger was comforting to you? How can our bruises and battle scars be used to help others? How can we be the comforting presence for our children when life experiences have bruised their hearts?

# Power of Prayer

Finally, be strong in the Lord and in his mighty power. Put on the full armor of God, so that you can take your stand against the devil's schemes. For our struggle is not against flesh and blood, but against the rulers, against the authorities, against the powers of this dark world and against the spiritual forces of evil in the heavenly realms. Therefore put on the full armor of God, so that when the day of evil comes, you may be able to stand your ground, and after you have done everything, to stand. Stand firm then, with the belt of truth buckled around your waist, with the breastplate of righteousness in place, and with your feet fitted with the readiness that comes from the gospel of peace. In addition to all this, take up the shield of faith, with which you can extinguish all the flaming arrows of the evil one. Take the helmet of salvation and the sword of the Spirit, which is the word of God. And pray in the Spirit on all occasions with all kinds of prayers and requests.

Ephesians 6:10–18 NIV

Prayer is the most powerful tool that has sustained me throughout my life. I've called out to Jesus in desperate cries for help with just a couple of words: *Help me, Jesus*. I've prayed lengthy pleading prayers that listed all those for whom I was interceding. I've prayed until I fell asleep mid-prayer and prayed when I couldn't go back to sleep. Prayer is a calming, sustaining force—even when we don't have any words for our prayers. When I'm angry about a situation that is unfair to one of my children, I pray because everything is ultimately out of my control.

As a mother, when tragedy hits close to home or even far away, it *feels* close to home if it involves children. Many public tragedies have occurred since I became a mom almost thirty years ago. Each time, I ache for the parents. I ache for the children. I ache for the loss. And these feelings used to paralyze me in fear for what could happen to my own children—until I found the power of prayer.

Being prayerful isn't a bumper sticker, social media post, or just Southern slang. It is an action. It moves through us and in us because of its power. Being in prayer is being in the presence of power.

We can move with useful effort in any situation near or far to intercede for others and to calm our worries. As a self-proclaimed mama bear, I have lost many a night's sleep fuming in frustration contemplating how to protect my own cubs. We don't have sufficient power to do that, particularly if we are trying to fight against the powers of evil or darkness. We don't even have the words most the time. He hears our prayer even when we don't speak them. He put the protective instinct in us because He has it for us. We need the full armor of God to fight those battles for us.

## WorkHearter Wisdom

So as moms we pray all daggum day. We pray in all

situations and give all requests and prayers up to God. We ask humbly for the power of the Holy Spirit to go into the dark places we cannot go ourselves to protect our children. We can start with baby steps prayers-short, simple ones where we may feel like our words are fumbled, but He knows our needs before we speak. Those prayers are powerful and will give us the peace we seek as moms of babes, littles, bigs and growns.

## When I Walk Down the Same Path

Though it is the smallest of all seeds, yet when it grows, it is the largest of garden plants and becomes a tree, so that the birds come and perch in its branches.

Matthew 13:32 NIV

I love to walk. It is my preferred method of staying active and getting exercise. And I love to walk outside—on the beach, on a trail, on my road—preferably in the mild days of spring or fall. I can't only walk in one season and avoid the rest or I'd be as big as my couch from all the carbs I like to eat. So I walk outside often in every season.

My most frequent and convenient path is on my road. We have a tree in our yard that mirrors another tree right across the road. When I walk through these trees in winter, I hurry through the unwelcoming cool shade to get back on the other side into the warm sun. When I walk in that same spot during summer, I want to linger in the shade to get some reprieve from the heat of the sun. Same path but very different seasons give different perspective and preference. The sunshine is the same but the temperature is different.

When I was going through divorce, I didn't want to linger around sappy lovesick couples or even watch romantic movies. When I was having and raising babies, I didn't want to linger in thoughts about empty nest seasons which would sneak up quicker than I thought. I remember thinking that I would not be that old anytime soon. Now those baby-raising seasons are behind me, and as someone *that* old, I miss the newborn sounds and toddler babble, but I do love to linger in nights of full sleep.

Everyone is different and has different experiences. Grief can coexist with seasons of joy. We grieve what we miss in our new seasons. I personally missed sleep the most. I missed my autonomy as a person. Then the children grew up. The joy may be small at first when the grief is so enveloping. With time, as a small mustard seed can grow to the largest garden plant and become a tree, joy can grow larger than our sorrow if we water it with a thankfulness perspective.

We can walk down the same path but have different perspectives depending on what season we are in. I see the new moms in their weary season who want to linger in the shade and sleep a little longer, and I also see their season as a time of long sunshine days of beautiful baby giggles that I would love to linger in while they sleep in the shade. Maybe as a grandparent, I will get to do just that and see the same path in a different perspective due to my experience in previous seasons.

## WorkHearter Wisdom

Even if the temperature of this season is different, the sunshine is the same. Let's all see the joy in today and linger longer in all of it.

# The Little Things

Whoever can be trusted with very little can also be trusted with much, and whoever is dishonest with very little will also be dishonest with much.

Luke 16:10 NIV

"Because of your little faith," He told them. "For I assure you: if you have faith the size of a mustard seed, you will tell this mountain, 'Move from here to there,' and it will move. Nothing will be impossible for you."

Matthew 17:20 HCSB

I remember the big things from growing up in the South—like family vacations, birthday and Christmas gifts, and long summer days of playing outside. But the little things that I look back on are what stand out in my mind as the biggest blessings of God winks and whispers.

The boring and mundane small pieces of "extra" are what I remember the most. A special drink my mom got at the gas station *just for me*, that I didn't have to share with my siblings. Five dollars of ice cream money my mom sent in a card to my kids for a treat during college. Letters from my son while he was away at basic military training. These little things were breaths of good blessings in my life.

God gives us the most memorable moments if we open our

eyes up to see them. We don't need qualifications for His word to be productive, we only need to serve Him with it. If we are faithful with the little things, we can be trusted to be faithful with more.

Several years ago, I went on a job interview for a job I was qualified for but didn't have any connections to give me an advantage over the many applicants. In faith, I prayed for the Lord's favor mentioned in the Prayer of Jabez in 1 Chronicles 4:10, because I felt I was in over my head. In a nervous panic of congested traffic, I ended up parking in the wrong parking lot, which was only for executive positions. The parking attendant was kind since I had an interview and let me in so I wouldn't be late. He's probably going to heaven. I got onto the elevator with a friendly smiling lady who asked my name and where I was from. We chatted and she eased my pre-interview jitters. As we approached the floor, she introduced herself and we both laughed as I realized she was interviewing me and soon after would be my new boss. It was another small whisper from God that he heard my prayer.

We can nickname these moments "right place right time." I've sure had my share of "wrong place wrong time" experiences, so I can identify the "right place right time" ones quickly ... and appreciate them as they grow my faith. I pray scripture over my children often. I've seen its usefulness in "right place right time" more than I can count.

## WorkHearter Wisdom

God gives us these "winks" or blessings more often than we recognize them. Even if we don't feel qualified or equipped to parent, He will send us little reminders that we are and we can use our mustard seed faith to move the mountains of our day. More often than not, the little things *are* the big things—a respite from heaven given freely to us so we can breathe easier. All we need to do is look and listen closely to these winks and whispers of the right things for Him to help us grow our faith and be trusted with the most important work of motherhood. What we think are little things are needed to be trusted with bigger things. The right things, big or little, will be easier to see and hear without the congestion and noise from the wrong things.

# Speak Life

The mouth of the righteous is a fountain of life …

Proverbs 10:11 ESV

As iron sharpens iron, so one person sharpens another.

Proverbs 27:17 NIV

Lying in a hospital bed in extreme pain will teach you a few things rather quickly. You will learn how rapidly the pain can make your head spin and body feel faint. You will learn how important a good nurse and doctor can be in moments. If you need surgery, you also need someone to stitch you back together. You learn how out of control you truly are in this life. You also learn that small talk is cheap. Chitchat is not welcome when you are sick or in pain. There is no time for it. Health care workers don't sit bedside and talk nonsense gossip to their patients. It wouldn't help heal the patient at all. Their presence is comforting and any encouraging words about remedies are a relief, knowing they have ideas on how to help you feel better.

My kids all went through their own seasons of sickness. There were times when prescriptions or rest didn't give them the healing fast enough. Their discomfort became my discomfort. When my kids were sick, I wouldn't talk to them about the weather or what a celebrity was doing in their personal life or a controversial social media post. I would give them comfort of a cool towel for delirium of a fever or a warm snuggle with them for the discomfort of cold shivers. I would care for them by making meals for nourishment. I would give them a Band-Aid for their scrapes or wounds, speaking words of love to them, reminding them that "Mommy is here." I would ask what they needed to feel better, hoping I had what they needed. When their choices brought pain to their lives, I was point person trying to stitch their wounds with constructive loving guidance.

The Bible tells us that the mouth of the righteous is a fountain of life, and that Jesus is the bread of life. It is the nourishment we need for our daily lives. It is also what our children need. If we don't give them life-giving words, they will seek it elsewhere. Just like our children come to us when they are not feeling well or have made poor choices, we can point them to the life-giving words in God's book to turn to when their hearts are troubled. In return, my children have helped me have a positive outlook during troubling times. We can sharpen one another by knowing God's word.

We can choose to speak life into others' lives every time we open our mouth. Even if someone is not under the weather, all of us are hurting in some way. Chitchat, small talk, and gossip will not encourage or build them up. Small talk does little to help others—that's why it is described as "small." Speaking life into others, though, is big talk. Big talk or encouraging words of Jesus and His righteousness give life to the hurting. It is transformational, making a big impact. Entertainment doesn't give life. Entertainment distracts. Let's resolve be righteous fountains of life to our children.

## WorkHearter Wisdom

A fountain needs water to work properly. For us to speak life, we need to be filled and overflowing with the living water of God's Word. We need to listen before we can speak. We need to hear what is needed to feel better. The Holy Spirit whispers and shouts at us in life-giving speech. He cheers us on with big talk to speak life into our lives. We can use His teachings to do the same and show His love to others.

# What If

> Now faith is the reality of what is hoped for, the proof of what is not seen.
>
> Hebrews 11:1 HCSB

As I get older, I'm learning that I can't always trust my eyes. Public restrooms are an area where this is becoming more prevalent for me. In all types of lighting, it gets harder to trust what I think I see in the bathroom stall.

I bring this up because when I started to work with teenage youth ten years ago, they would not believe anything unless they saw it with their own eyes. They had grown up learning that what others say isn't always true, so they relied more on what they saw. If they saw it happen, they believed it. As you can imagine, this can be challenging when teaching about a God we cannot see. During that time period, I heard Billy Graham speak about the wind. He explained it so eloquently when he said, "I've never seen the wind ... I see the effects of the wind, but I've never seen the wind." What a way to explain the effects of our Savior to a generation of youth who can't trust what they don't see.

As a teacher, many times my heart was broken by the behavior of a student. I've had it broken in both good ways and bad. In good ways, I watched youth step out of their comfort zone to share Jesus with another student in word and deed.

Then, I got to see the effects those brave students had on others. I saw a few even voluntarily bow their heads during the moment of silence, sing and dance in praise to the Father in a school talent show, and lend a helping hand to another student who was struggling. I've also seen the anger, bitterness, and hurt from a student who had a heart-wrenching home life lash out in anger at another student or teacher—projecting their pain onto another when it was too much for them to carry alone.

Whether their behavior was positive or negative, it never ceased to teach me how much these youth needed to know about the Lord. Many of them would ask "What if ..." as in "What if this happens because I don't conform to peer pressure?" and "What if I don't know what to say?" I would always add one word to their *what if*: God. As in "What if God ..."

In contrast to my eyes becoming weaker and failing me as I age, my faith has indeed become stronger from seeing my own "what if" turn into "what if God"— He is What Is always showing up and doing something I didn't expect. I see the effects of His hand as clearly as I see the effects of the wind. My faith has grown from these experiences because our faith is what we hope for and proof of what we can't see.

### WorkHearter Wisdom

When have you been afraid to do or say something because you are relying on your own sight? How can you overcome that fear by relying on what you can't see? How do we help our children not be afraid of the unknown? And, how do we help them say "Even if, I will still trust Him" and believe it?

## Almost There

I am sure of this, that He who started a good work in you will carry it on to completion until the day of Christ Jesus.

Philippians 1:6 HCSB

But do not forget this one thing, dear friends: With the Lord a day is like a thousand years, and a thousand years are like a day. The Lord is not slow in keeping his promise, as some understand slowness. Instead he is patient with you, not wanting anyone to perish, but everyone to come to repentance.

2 Peter 3:8-9 NIV

I have always been a planner for the sake of efficiency. But everything I tried to plan in life, in work, in travel never worked out like I thought it would. Why, I wonder. I've wanted to make the most of my time. I had trips planned out. I had my days and weeks of daily life planned out. I'm not saying planning is bad, but I was starting to feel anxiety for upcoming events when they were around the corner because of the dread I felt when my plans always seemed to fail. The dread felt like being in the back seat of a long car trip or on a long flight anticipating the "almost there" feeling with sweaty palms trying to rush the journey itself to get to the destination. When you arrive or land, you breathe with relief, only to do it all over again when the trip is over. I would have trepidation about the event/date and then feel relief when it was over. The relief was short-lived when another event was upcoming. I had this "almost there" anxiety about what I was doing. The controlling feeling if I could get there in a rush through *my* plan, I would be able to breathe. I always felt like I was almost there.

Traveling with kids is not for the weak. One common ques-tion on a road trip asked by littles and teens is "Are we there yet?" or "How much longer?" and our parental response is, inevitably, "We are almost there." We know how much further but all our kids need to hear is we are almost there—even if the *almost there* definition is really a couple hours away. They don't need those kind of details, just our reassurance that we are going in the right direction and will arrive in due time. We know once we arrive it will all be worth it, as the destination is the best part yet to come.

**WorkHearter Wisdom**

Working on a project that is not finished but continually needs tweaking- that is us. We are made in God's image—but He is still working on us. We don't need to be efficient or know the details, because He knows the best can still be yet to come. In my life, I found nothing hurried or rushed is from God. None of Jesus life, ministry or death were rushed. Listen to Him closely: when you ask how much longer, see if He whispers to you, "Almost there." He always has the better plan, so we can rest in knowing that if it doesn't work out, He will take care of us in those moments. He goes before us and walks along with us patiently carrying us every step of the journey.

# Perfect Salad Dressing or Bag of Mixed Chips

In the same way, let your light shine before men, so that they may see your good works and give glory to your Father in heaven.

Matthew 5:16 HCSB

I only had one salad dressing choice and preference growing up: ranch. It was delicious and versatile. I used it on salad, pizza, bread, vegetables, chips, and so on. As I ventured out into trying new foods, I discovered Italian dressing and vinaigrettes. I loved them also. When I started dating my husband, he always ordered his favorite French Catalina salad dressing. I had tried it before and liked it on occasion, but it was not my first choice.

When our budget was tight, it didn't allow us to order separate meals at a restaurant. We split our meal to save money, and it usually came with one salad. We had to order both ranch and French on the side so we could split. One day he decided to be adventurous and mix them together. We instantly discovered the perfect salad dressing. We called it Franch. It reminded me of when I was in elementary school and brought my lunch from home with a mixed bag of chips included. I loved cheesy chips of all varieties, and I mixed them together to make my perfect bag of chips. Later

—or unbeknownst to me, earlier—someone else at Frito-Lay had the same idea and created their Munchies line. The mixed versions of similar or opposite tastes are some of my favorites. Same goes with music—I also enjoy music collaborations that have more than one genre. Some musicians I would have never heard if they had not collaborated with the genre I was listening to.

In the same way, we are created in God's image with different gifts. One of our gifts is our light. It is our duty to let our light shine on our good works to show His glory. If my friend gives her time and talent to a good cause, I want to join her and give my gifts. I want that light to shine as bright as it can. We become the perfect salad dressing or blended mixed chips collaboration when we join together and shine brighter together for Christ as a result.

## WorkHearter Wisdom

What an honor and privilege it is to shine bright for Christ. He gave us the ability to be lights and beacons in a dark world. Let's not compare whose light is bigger or brighter. We will never look the same outwardly but we all have the light inside to show the world whose we are for His glory. Let's blend together to bring the light to more people.

## Wrinkles and Eyesight

> Why do you look at the speck in your brother's eye but don't notice the log in your own eye?
>
> Matthew 7:3 HCSB, Luke 6:41 HCSB

Growing older is never as apparent as when your eyesight starts getting worse and your wrinkles increase. It happens at the same time. I see this as a form of God's mercy. We cannot see our own wrinkles as clearly as others can. I used to notice that elderly women didn't rub their foundation in on their face. I wondered why. Did they get in a hurry? No, they couldn't see it. I saw it clearly, so I wondered why they couldn't. Until I experienced it, I didn't understand. It was easy for me to see others' imperfections clearer than they did. I had younger vision and a different perspective.

God's mercy on our eyesight is similar to the perspective of our past failures. He allows those to blur with time, so we can focus on positive thinking instead of negative thinking. Now, when I'm looking at myself in the mirror, it seems as if the room is always too dark to see my eyebrow hairs that need to be tweezed. At least, I blame the light, not my age, of course.

Similarly, we are quick to assume we clearly see others' sins and it takes more effort to see our own. We need to look past imperfections in others and ourselves equally. As wrinkles and eyesight deterioration go hand in hand as we age, so does the removal of the plank in our life before we can see a speck in another's life.

## WorkHearter Wisdom

What has changed in your hindsight as you look at your life? Hindsight is hard on mama hearts, but you have to forgive yourself and move forward. What can you look past today in your own life or someone else's ... to see you/them the way God sees you?

# Sticks and Stones

That is why, for Christ's sake, I delight in weaknesses, in insults, in hardships, in persecutions, in difficulties. For when I am weak, then I am strong.

2 Corinthians 12:10 NIV

No foul language is to come from your mouth, but only what is good for building up someone in need, so that it gives grace to those who hear.

Ephesians 4:29 HCSB

When I was thirteen, I broke my nose during a softball game. I missed catching the ball with my glove, but my nose caught it. My nose was shattered in hundreds of pieces. I got blood all over everyone who came near me. The plastic surgeon had to look a photo of me to reconstruct it, as I was unrecognizable. I broke another bone-my wrist- the next summer on a four-wheeler by running it into a tree in our front yard. Both of those breaks were equally painful, one required a cast to heal and one a surgery to repair. I lost sleep with both and it took time to heal, but those bones did heal. I don't feel pain from them anymore or even have a feeling of scar tissue or numbness in them. No one can see these scars. Some scars heal better than others.

Sticks and stones may break my bones ... but words will pierce my heart. My daughter Sky had a strawberry hemangioma when she was a baby, and strangers would often ask me what was wrong with her. It was harmless, so

I would laugh and say nothing to let them know it would go away with time. Over the years, some I loved and those who didn't even know me have said some words that pierced my heart; their words were not harmless and stuck with me. We often build walls that seem comfortable to keep others from hurting us and letting our scar tissue from the wounds stay numb. My heart has scarred places where it's been wounded. If I'm not careful, those piercings can produce bitterness. I've been told I have a tender heart/thin skin. And I get it: our cuts can bleed our bitterness onto others and our words can pierce more than any stone. I'd rather have a stick or stone thrown at me than a bitter word that pierces. Those wounds caused real pain and those scars take more time to heal.

Fortunately, God was present with me in each part of that pain, and He put my heart back together like it belonged-stronger in a protected spot to keep it tender to the needs of others without fear of scars or numbing. I hope my heart can stay tender because I know unhealed wounds can impact my role as a mom. If I let my heart harden, I won't have empathy for others or their situation. I know God will stay with me in the healing.

## WorkHearter Wisdom

What parts of our heart have been pierced by others' words? How can we keep from becoming bitter and passing that bitterness onto others? How can we protect our children from others or even our own bitterness? When others ask what's wrong with us as Christians, remember Jesus can laugh and respond for us. In Him, we are stronger.

# Nicknames

A good name is more desirable than great riches; to be esteemed is better than silver or gold.

Proverbs 22:1 NIV

If you have siblings, you likely have a nickname for them—and they for you. I remember being somewhat jealous of my two younger sisters because of a nickname they had for each other: Gurgie. It came from a funny moment when my baby sister fumbled her words to say girl and cookie at the same time. They laughed and called each other that for years. One day, I told them I was feeling left out, so they included me. Even though I wasn't part of the memory of that moment, they allowed me to join in the nickname club. I felt included. Family has a way of always letting you feel included when the world excludes you by choosing a name for you. This felt even more special to me when my baby sister passed away at the age of thirty. Over time after she passed, I found cards and other notes from her that I had forgotten about and all were signed Gurgie. It's funny how a nickname can bring you closer to someone—like an inside joke. My husband and I call each other sweetie; make of that what you will.

My dad gives everyone nicknames. Sometimes they aren't the most positive ones. He puts contacts in his phone as their nickname, he writes it on birthday cards, and calls them by that nickname for life. For instance, my son, who is now twenty-nine years old, was bald until he was two. And to this day, my dad's nickname for him is Baldy.

I know at times others who dislike us give us unfair and mean nicknames. These nicknames are hurtful and can stick like glue. We can shame ourselves and give ourselves a negative name—such as stupid, dumb, naive, unwanted. Jesus gave His disciples nicknames and terms of endearment, at times even calling them by other names. He called Judas "friend" right before He was arrested. Our heavenly Father also gave us nicknames and terms of endearment in His Word. He calls us Beloved, Child, Son, Daughter, and so on. All His nicknames for us are positive ones, so would we ever call ourselves anything negative? He also gave us many names we can call him: Yahweh, Abba, Father, Alpha and Omega, El Shaddai, and so forth. The terms of endearment are vast. He is a true friend to us, and He never uses hurtful or shameful nicknames for us. God doesn't want us to give ourselves those either, no matter what season we are facing. He has already named us as His.

## WorkHearter Wisdom

What nicknames have you been given? Do you call yourself negative names? It's time to stop calling yourself a negative name—either self-imposed or given by others. What's a positive name from the Lord you can begin to call yourself today?

# WorkHearter Wisdom: Twenty Insights into Youth from a Former Church Youth Group Volunteer

1. Youth want to be with other youth during these formative years, even if it's youth group at church. If they are grounded, I recommend considering church activities so they are not totally isolated.
2. Watching a movie at church they have already seen multiple times is not a waste of time, especially if they invite a friend to go with them. It's less intimidating to someone who hasn't been to church to attend a fun youth group activity.
3. Church youth groups will likely always need volunteers and money for snacks.
4. Youth trips are exhausting for the volunteers; they do not get any sleep.
5. Youth camps bring multiple life decisions and your student can be forever changed.
6. Time away from home will allow them to appreciate all you do for them—because youth leaders/camp counselors are *not being their parents* while they are away from home.
7. Pack their suitcase the first time they spend the night at camp or trip away from home. They will undoubtedly accidentally forget to pack something important if you don't, and camp leaders may not be able to get it for them

(i.e. deodorant, sunblock, hats, shampoo, socks, and so on.).

8. If they are allergic to food or have a vegetarian diet, it may be wise to pack their snacks and some food. Youth trip food stops usually consist of gas stations, pizza, tacos, or chicken fast food establishments.

9. Let them bring a friend to church every time they ask. Whether you have to pick them up or let your child drive them to church, it could change their life for the better.

10. The pastor or youth pastor/minister is not going to be the only one who shares Jesus with them. If they have a profession of faith, it doesn't matter who was the catalyst or how qualified. Only the Holy Spirit saves, and that's all that matters.

11. The world will battle hard for your child. When they are acting the most unlovable, love them back the most. If you don't, the world will offer them acceptance/what they perceive as love instead.

12. Youth group-age students all want one thing: to be *known*. Youth group leaders can't know them if they don't attend any youth group Bible study, service, or events.

13. If they don't belong to youth group, make no mistake—they will find another group to belong to, and most likely it will be a group that doesn't confront or challenge them like a church life group.

14. There is no perfect church. There will be scandals big or small. Whether you hear about them or not is another issue. If your child tells you something, believe them first and ask questions second.

15. It is not punishment or discrimination if your daughter is asked to wear a one-piece swimsuit to a church summer camp. They are asking all the females to do the same, including adult leaders.

16. Lock-ins for youth group are exactly what the name means in every sense. They are locked inside a gym, fellowship hall, or other large room. They will be tired, hungry, mentally overstimulated, and annoyed when they get home. Let them sleep/rest. No questions are necessary for twenty-four hours for them or the leaders.

17. Youth group music may not be anything you care to listen to and that's OK.

18. Be prepared to pick up your child if they get sick at church, or any outside church event. Youth group leaders cannot leave the ninety-nine for the one in this case. If they are hurt, be prepared to drive to urgent care or hospital to meet them. Even if they have your permission and insurance info, *for your child* this cannot be phoned in.

19. Youth leaders are not perfect. Don't expect them to be, and don't allow your child to idolize them, either, for the same reason.

20. Youth leaders may not know you by first name, so don't be offended. If they know your child, that is who they need to know. Their calling is not with you, it is with the youth.

Let us not become weary in doing good, for at the
proper time we will reap a harvest if we do not give up.

Galatians 6:9 NIV

## Distinguishing Differences

Be alert and of sober mind. Your enemy the devil prowls around like a roaring lion looking for someone to devour.

1 Peter 5:8 NIV

And no wonder! For Satan disguises himself as an angel of light.

2 Corinthians 11:14 HCSB

Walking outdoors is good for my mental and physical well-being. That is, until I hear a strange sound on the walking path and can't see where it came from. Everyone knows there is a difference between squirrels, skunks, and snakes. All will make the same noise along a walking path—snapping twigs or crunching leaves. The difference is to be able distinguish the danger. One is more dangerous than the others. All are distractions when you are trying to walk for exercise.

The pitter-patter of furry feet can be frightening when I am walking alone. Squirrels are looking for and storing up their food; they're considered a nuisance but mostly harmless. They are simply a distraction. Skunks are the most understood. Skunks are near-sighted and will be more scared by you than you are by them. They can create a stink, but that is simply an unpleasant smell. Snakes are potentially the most dangerous of the three. That is, they can be, but not all species are. Snakes are primarily the sneakiest.

All three play a vital role in our ecosystem and are underappreciated for their roles. Squirrels provide food sources for other animals and help with forest regenerations by saving food (nuts and seeds)—spreading it around and sometimes forgetting about it. Skunks help limit rodent and insect populations from growing too large. By limiting the rodent population—which hosts ticks that may be carrying the Lyme bacteria—snakes in turn help reduce Lyme disease.

All three of these S's will viciously defend their babies via different means: squirrels fight, skunks spray, or snakes bite. As parents, we will also defend our children. We can be relentless in our fight to prevent our children from coming near what we perceive as danger. But are we teaching our children how to recognize differences in danger?

## WorkHearter Wisdom

As Christians we can be guilty of categorizing the dangers of associating with different people groups or religions. Some may seem to be a harmless nuisance, simply a distraction. Others are unpleasant and may cause a stink for the church. Often we group other religions and people groups as dangerous and exclude them all—when only a few may potentially be dangerous. Then, this raises the question of who are we? Are we distractions or nuisances in our church or community? Are we causing a stink? Or are we guilty of being closer to the dangerous slippery slope of sin biting into our lives than our fellow brothers and sisters? Let's look at ourselves to ensure we are not the dangerous ones.

We have all been called according to His purpose. Are we taking responsibility for that calling and purpose in loving Him or are we just distracting, causing a stench, and getting closer to danger than to the purpose He has called us? Remember, in God's Word, the snakes themselves were not as dangerous as the disobedience of God's children. It's a distinguishing difference of what can happen when we don't trust in God's provision.

# Freshly Squeezed

The farmer sows the word. Some people are like seed along the path, where the word is sown. As soon as they hear it, Satan comes and takes away the word that was sown in them. Others, like seed sown on rocky places, hear the word and at once receive it with joy. But since they have no root, they last only a short time. When trouble or persecution comes because of the word, they quickly fall away. Still others, like seed sown among thorns, hear the word; but the worries of this life, the deceitfulness of wealth and the desires for other things come in and choke the word, making it unfruitful. Others, like seed sown on good soil, hear the word, accept it, and produce a crop—some thirty, some sixty, some a hundred times what was sown.

Mark 4:14-20 NIV

When I want to enjoy some lemon in my water, I try to be careful not to squeeze out the seed too. Sometimes I'm so focused on not letting a hidden seed pop out into my cup, I accidentally squirt lemon juice into my eyes—or someone else's. I've been the parent guilty of allowing my toddler to taste a lemon, only to watch their puckered-face reaction. It's the little joys of parenting that make the best memories and keepsake photos.

I know there are fancy gadgets to squeeze lemons, and I do have one at my house but I don't necessarily carry it in my purse when I travel or eat at a restaurant. It doesn't matter if I have the right tool or not, though—the seeds will come out. Because lemons have seeds in them. They are embedded in the fruit and when they are squeezed they will fall out naturally.

If we are living with our children day in and day out, our seeds will fall out naturally when we are squeezed. We could be squeezed by running out of time to get to school or work and frustratedly yelling for our children to put on their shoes and get in the ever-loving car. Why can't they just put their shoes on like a normal person? Or we could be squeezed by exhaustedly waking up nightly to reassure our child that the nightmare that tormented their sleep was just a dream. We can be squeezed in our marital relationship and accidentally spill some of that sourness onto our children.

We have to watch what seeds falling out are being sown and what juice is spilling over when squeezed. Our negative talk, cursing, and anger can fall out naturally when we are squeezed during tough seasons. These seeds are easily sown like weeds, but we want fruitful crops instead of thorns and weeds sown into our children's lives. Luckily, it only takes a little sugar to turn sour lemon juice into sweet lemonade. We can be a little sweeter to our children when they can't decide which shoes to wear. We want our seeds to be sown on good soil. The foundation of our soil is our love and a soft heart.

### WorkHearter Wisdom

God gives us guidance in Galatians on the fruit of the spirit we want to have—like gentleness, peace, kindness, self-control. The best practice I've found to help with fruit of the spirit is daily thankfulness and gratefulness. I try to start and end the day by thanking God for what I have, being grateful for what He has given me. Everything I have is His, even the children I call mine. I thank God that I have been trusted with challenges and children to teach and enjoy. Even on the tough days when I don't feel thankful, saying the words *thank you* (even begrudgingly) can change my thoughts and hopefully eventually squeeze the seeds of thankfulness enough to fall out naturally. Those are the seeds I want to be sown with love.

## My Ways Are Not Your Ways

> For my thoughts are not your thoughts, neither are your ways my ways, declares the LORD.
>
> Isaiah 55:8 ESV

The theme verse in my marriage is Isaiah 55:8. My husband and I don't do anything the same way. He is obviously doing things the wrong way, but I still love him dearly. Joking. He makes a complete mess of the kitchen and leaves the egg carton and butter on the counter long after he's finished cooking. I won't even start on the milk carton. He never turns off a closet light. I have some shortcomings too long to list, too. I mostly miss the bathroom trash can and constantly drop things without effort: I was apparently born with a sight/distance challenge. I don't always flush since I'll be returning momentarily. We differ from the direction of the toilet paper roll to folding clothes to cooking, cleaning, and parenting.

Michael will let our daughter have five more minutes of screen time to finish a movie she's watching, which will put her up past her bedtime. I will be firmer when it comes to rules and keep her at an early bedtime because my intrusive thoughts know what the night takes the morning makes. We can be at odds, but our differences can balance us out. His ways are not mine and my ways are not his. If I am not dealing with a parenting task in the best head space, he will balance me out, and vice versa. We may have our own ways of parenting, but we both have the same objective in mind: to lovingly raise our daughter.

My husband and I also agree that our daughter needs to learn about Jesus and His Bible teachings. We have to make this a priority on both fronts. It's not a place either of us can waiver. Kids will try to find out who is the weaker parent when it comes to rules. We both stand firm in screen-free Sundays. We both believe in Christ and His teachings. We both have weaknesses and mistakes that are obvious to our intuitive daughter. Kids know we are not perfect but love us anyway. And, if we parent right they'll know they are loved back.

## WorkHearter Wisdom

God's Word points out that His ways are not ours and our ways are not His. Isn't it amazing that He loves us anyway? And it's even more amazing that we know we are loved even through all of our different ways. That is a truth we can agree on and welcome into our thoughts.

# Voice In Our Head

> We demolish arguments and every pretension that sets itself up against the knowledge of God, and we take captive every thought to make it obedient to Christ.
>
> 2 Corinthians 10:5 NIV

I remember most of the voices in my head growing up were from adults. Teachers, parents, grandparents would repeat phrases enough that they echoed in my own thoughts. Sometimes we need a voice outside our own head to say "Don't do it." Even more so, we need a friend, brother, or sister to come alongside us to show us the truth. Their actions speak louder than any of the voices in our head. If we partner with a life-giving friend, we can demolish the untruths and take those discouraging voices captive.

The voice in our head is not always friendly. Even though the evil one cannot hear our thoughts, attempts to control our thoughts will be made. God did not give us demeaning thoughts. He gave us uplifting words of love and encouragement. If the voice in our head is talking down to us, we must discern how God spoke to us. He speaks to us lovingly with positive affirmations and encouraging reminders of who He created us to be and how much purpose we have in our lives. God has to continually remind me that he equipped me with everything I need to accomplish my greatest purpose of raising my children.

## WorkHearter Wisdom

How often do we listen to the negative voice in our head recycling words we heard from others? We can keep confident in the voice of our creator by repeating his words as a reminder of our true identity in Christ. Our children need to hear affirming words from us on repeat as well. Whether we like it or not, our words will echo in their minds for many years, even after we have left this world. When they hear our voice on repeat, let's make it count and be positive.

## We Don't Grow Without Being Tended

At least there is hope for a tree: If it is cut down, it will sprout again, and its new shoots will not fail. Its roots may grow old in the ground and its stump die in the soil, yet at the scent of water it will bud and put forth shoots like a plant.

Job 14:7–9 NIV

Tendency is defined as an inclination toward a particular characteristic or type of behavior. Tendencies can also be defined as a predisposition to think, act, or proceed in a particular way. I have a tendency to start a garden strong in the spring, then forget to water or tend to it as the weather gets substantially warmer outside.

As Christians, we have a tendency to allow our faith to guide our actions, but even our faith needs to be tended to. Soil in a garden needs to be tended to remove weeds. Weeds are food for grub worms. Grub worms are food for moles. It doesn't take much for the worms to feed larger menaces in life.

Moles can mess up a yard but they wouldn't be there if they weren't being fed. The problem is in the soil.

Fears feed doubt, but if starved doubt grows faith. What we feed the doubt is what it grows into. If we starve it out and not allow it to flourish, we can stop it from growing. If we don't feed the bad thoughts or the fears, doubt can't grow. Misperceptions and gossip can spread like wildfire that start out with a small spark. They can mess up a life without much thought or even watering, as scripture says that even a scent of water can bud and put forth shoots like a plant. We can't even give evil a sniff of water. We have to starve it out of our life. Our hearts are the soil that needs to be right.

A study in New Zealand on hydraulic coupling found that trees around tree stumps can help the stump continue to live through their root systems. Job spoke of this in the scripture. There is always hope for the roots in our children's lives even after they leave our homes if we tend to them and their hearts are right with the Lord.

## WorkHearter Wisdom

Let's choose to water our children with the crops of hope and faith to put out any fires of doubt. Let's not grow weary of tending to them when the days get heated. Let's show them how to snuff out and starve the doubt that causes weeds to grow in our hearts and minds. Let's light a fire and kindle that fire into a flame of faith with deep roots that spreads out across our lives into the lives of our children.

# Facing Resistance

> Submit yourselves, then, to God. Resist the devil, and he will flee from you.
>
> James 4:7 NIV

My daughter consistently worked hard to become pretty good at the game of soccer. She was small but mighty and held her own against fierce competitors. All that work and time learning how to finesse the ball-handling skills was no match for a coach who held a grudge against her, not for any particular reason. He didn't hold a grudge against any other player but her, and we never figured out why. She was the strongest player on the team. It may not have been personal at all and simply his coaching method, but it crushed her spirit and she began to dislike the sport. She learned quickly in that situation that life isn't fair. She fell but she got back up. She also grew in maturity. She faced resistance and came out stronger. It took a lot for this mama bear to resist the devil and not take up a discussion with the coach. In the South, we call these "come to Jesus" meetings. But I digress. My small but mighty "fancy feet" held her own without any help from me.

Our spiritual growth faces resistance daily. The closer we attempt to walk with Jesus, the more challenges life brings our direction. The devil doesn't care about us if we aren't getting close to Jesus. If we are weak, he will not even bother us. The devil will let us go about our happy-go-lucky lives without a single interruption from him until we get stronger. But when we resist, he will flee. Sometimes, this strength is shown through our children as a reminder for us to submit everything to God.

## WorkHearter Wisdom

The Bible is full of stories of faithful servants who were facing resistance no matter what they did. They loved the Lord and still struggled with the devil's persistence. Nicodemus was one who couldn't stand up to the resistance, but Peter did. Peter may have fallen down for short period, but he got back up. Peter came out stronger in his faith after facing the resistance and submitting to God. We have the hope that we, too, can face the resistance and come out stronger. Glory!

# Quiet Moments of Contemplation: Isaiah 43:18-19 CEV

**The Lord said:**
Forget what happened long ago!
Don't think about the past.
I am creating something new.
There it is! Do you see it?
I have put roads in deserts,
streams in thirsty lands.

Don't keep brooding over old history, over the past. You cannot change it. The message here is to *look forward*, toward the new day and the new way God has prepared ... for you. Consider this. Our past can creep in our minds and take over our thoughts, which eventually and quietly take over our actions.

I know my actions have hurt my kids and when they were working through their hurt, they tried to hurt me back. You know why? That's what hurt people do—they hurt people. Praise God we are not defined by what we have done. We are defined by what Jesus did for us. There is nothing we've done in the past that cannot be redeemed by God. He can put water in dry land. I've tried too hard and failed even harder, but my past is a dead plant that I don't need to keep watering with my time, energy, or thoughts. My failure can be viewed as success if I accept it, use it as a learning experience, vow not to give up, and keep moving forward to try again with something new. My future needs the water to grow fruitful. I can put down my past by letting go of what someone said or did. The Holy Spirit will harvest the seeds I plant in my thoughts today. When we mess up as parents, all we can do is look up and move forward. Looking back on mistakes will only help if we learn from it and pave a new path in our attitude. We can't change the past, but we can create a new future with God as our focus. The best part of my history is HIS STORY.

# Let Me Unlock Your Prison

> You, my brothers and sisters, were called to be free. But do not use your freedom to indulge the flesh; rather, serve one another humbly in love.
>
> Galatians 5:13 NIV

As children, situations can put us into a box. Even if the box is only in our mind, we grow into adults who stay in that box from our childhood. Being the oldest sibling in our home, I was often put into the responsible and successful category box. I was the caretaker, babysitter, driver/chaperone, and on and on for my younger siblings. When I left home at nineteen, I immediately became a mother at age twenty. Thus the responsibility box continued, although I thought I was free.

When I got divorced, not just once but twice, I once again felt free and simultaneously that I had let my family down. I was supposed to be the responsible, dutiful one. The label I was given was now no longer true for me. Judgment from others outside my family felt like people were locking me away in a prison. Their words added locks onto my life that I thought would never be removed. I felt like my decisions had locked my identity into a prison cell box. The prison was in my mind. I thought I'd never be a good person again. I was labeling myself a failure. Trying to parent when you feel trapped in failure is no way to be a parent.

Both of my younger sisters sensed I was struggling. Their words helped me, each in their own way, to escape from that mental prison. The only constant through my life of marriages, heartbreak, divorce, all my children, and other life milestones, were my siblings and my parents. I've had great friends but none who were present for all of it. Some friends only existed with the marriage relationship, some friends lived far away or were going through their own struggles. Not even my church family was there for all of it. The freedom I gained from my sisters in those dark moments was exactly what I needed at the time. God knew He could use them to give me what I needed to live free from labels and shame so I could be the mom my children needed.

## WorkHearter Wisdom

As God's Word says, I was called to be free. And in that freedom, I am to serve others in love. When someone tells me their marriage is failing and they yearn to be free, I share the devastation and sadness I experienced. I also share the redemption from God I have now, which is the true freedom. I never want them to think I'm a proponent for divorce—the damage it does to all of us is lasting—but I want them to know that God does not love them any less. Even when we don't agree with someone's life choices, we can't lock them into a prison with our words of judgment. They are padlocking themselves up enough on their own. We need to help them be set free. Whose prison can you help someone unlock today?

## Pride Comes Before the Fall

Before a downfall the heart is haughty, but humility comes before honor.

Proverbs 18:12 NIV

My first in-service as a teacher was scary for me as an introvert. I had to finish my two weeks' notice at my former job, so the first in-service I could attend was intended for another school's faculty. I had missed the one intended for my future colleagues due to my work commitments. The worst part of an in-service for any new teacher is the part where the instructor asks you to pair up. This is even worse for a new teacher who doesn't know a soul in the room.

I remember wondering if I could sneak into the bathroom or if this was going to take longer than that, when at that the very moment of this thought, the instructor told us to *choose wisely* because they would be our partner all day. So I stood up and made my way across the room, looking around for anyone who hadn't paired up yet—and saw kind eyes looking at me through the sea of faces. He must have known he hadn't see me before, and that I was lost. His name was Barry. We paired up and did the exercises. I started out acting as if I knew exactly what I was doing, and I didn't need help until he saw right through that too. Had I kept that attitude, I would have surely fallen on my face.

After lunch, I decided to get real. I told him I was terrified of failing. I told him how I got to this point. The job I left that paid twice what my teaching salary would pay. I was worried of making a mistake by following this dream, but I was more worried about doing a disservice to my students. He humbly told me in no uncertain terms that after many years of teaching, he still had those same fears. Even if he didn't mean it, it was such a relief! I wished he could have been a teacher at my school, but once again, the Lord knew better. Later that summer, he was offered the job as my supervisor in the district. I got to see him on a regular basis, and he was always kind to me. He knew my fears, and he continually encouraged me every time I saw him. He asked me for help with projects. He was the reason I was able to make it through that first year. I'm glad I stayed humble and didn't try to be prideful. I don't believe our work relationship would have been as beneficial if I had kept my fears to myself inside my own bubble-wrapped introverted world.

## WorkHearter Wisdom

When we swallow our pride and show our vulnerability, we can potentially gain far more than we give up by humbly sharing or giving to others. How do we show our children an introvert can open up to others with rewards that outweigh the risks?

# Walking the Beach

When hard pressed, I cried to the LORD; he brought me into a spacious place.

Psalm 118:5 NIV

When my sister Brooke died, I cried a lot every day. It was hard to hold it back. Then I thought I needed to be tough for my family and hold back my tears. It was like I built a dam holding in all those tears. I couldn't find a space open and big enough for me to unload of all the sadness I was carrying. That year was tough enough but holding those back made it tougher.

My husband and I had planned a month getaway at the beach for that December. It was our "we just had a baby and you've been gone for six months" trip, planned well before my sister passed in August. How much more God knew, putting this trip in our hearts, that I would need that trip after holding back my grief.

The ocean has always been a therapeutic place for me. It was the only place I felt I could release all my tears walking on the beach alone. As I walked, I passed many faces. Typical beach walker etiquette is to say hi or at least smile at passersby. I was a blubbering mess, with my head heavy from all those tears I'd held onto. So I looked down at the sand, thankful for the warm summer sun on a winter day drying my tears.

God still got my attention when I thought I saw my sister's same footprint. I was listening to her playlist and "Comeback Story" by Kings of Leon came on. The lyrics that resonate with me go like this: "I walk a mile in your shoes and now I'm a mile away and I've got your shoes." It's tongue in cheek, but makes me laugh like my sister always did. I knew the One who gave her a sense of humor and who gave me that laugh in the midst of tears that day was one and the same. I walked miles on that beach and I did truly have my sister's shoes as I had packed her beloved flip-flops. My sister didn't have an earthly comeback story with her battle of addiction, but I think she gave one to all of us left here on earth. I came back from the walks on the beach lighter from releasing the tears I had held onto. I return frequently because a piece of my healed heart still lives there since I poured it out there with all those tears that day.

## WorkHearter Wisdom

God gives us space to cry out when we feel pressed or have held in our emotions for too long. Sometimes we need to give our children space to feel their emotions during tumultuous times. We want to be near them and help them process, but space is sometimes exactly what they need. Let them cry out to God when it feels heavy and He will lighten their load. Our job is to teach them this resource is available to them and to remind ourselves it's there when we need it too.

# Babies and Blue Hairs

Show me, LORD, my life's end and the number of my days; let me know how fleeting my life is.

Psalm 39:4 NIV

When you have a baby, age is calculated at first by days, then months, then years. We post photos of babies when they are 2, 3, 4, 5, 6 days old. Then we move to weeks, 2, 3, 4 weeks old, Then we move on to months. We stop counting the days and spread out the milestones they hit with each passing day. We start out realizing how precious a day is in their calculation of age, but eventually it gets easier to translate ages by numbering years.

Every time I had a newborn baby, I was amazed by how bold the senior citizens—blue hairs—were. In public places and at my church they would touch and kiss my baby. After my fourth baby was born, the first time we took her to church she was six weeks old. A lady I've never met kissed her on top of her head like an anointing. A bit shocked, I saw it as a tender moment and no harm since my baby didn't get sick from it. I got the impression that these two, so far apart in age, were so close to Jesus at the same time. Like they knew a secret no one else did. It was almost as if she whispered to the baby about Jesus.

It showed me that it was important to see my 101-year-old

grandmother, Cutters, and take my newborn baby to her. It wasn't easy, since I was nursing and travel to her was a three-hour drive. No matter how difficult it was, I knew it could be the last opportunity. Ella Gray wasn't even two months old yet, but watching them together it was as if they had an inside secret. My grandmother passed away a couple of months later, three weeks after my sister's passing. I'll never regret that trip.

Time is a thief and a gift simultaneously. The time that my babies were newborns passed quickly but so did my sister's and my grandmother's final days. My baby sister was only thirty, definitely too short a life. Even though my Cutters lived a long life, time with her seemed too short. When I sat with her, time went by a little slower. I wasn't in a hurry, and I was at peace. I believe these babies and blue hairs share the secret to peace. They aren't in a hurry to go anywhere. They are content sitting with their loved ones as long as we allow them. It's a milestone if they eat or sleep. We have a lot to learn from babies and blue hairs. They both number their days for different reasons but in the same appreciation of how fleeting life is. We only get one life to live and the blue hairs know those babies are just beginning so there is no hurry.

## WorkHearter Wisdom

The verse above also appears with the verse that follows: "You have made my days a mere handbreadth; the span of my years is as nothing before you. Everyone is but a breath ..." How often do experienced moms remind the new moms how quickly the days will pass and all we have are the memories of diapers and sleepless nights? How can we keep the pace of appreciating all the days of parenting a little bit slower to adequately take it all in?

# Counting What's Lost

> Now to him who is able to do immeasurably more than all we ask or imagine, according to his power that is at work within us, to him be glory in the church and in Christ Jesus throughout all generations, for ever and ever! Amen.
>
> Ephesians 3:20–21 NIV

As I mentioned, my first child, Blake, was born twenty-six weeks premature. He weighed two pounds, four-and-a-half ounces. That half-ounce was such an important detail to remember. Ask any mom of a preemie and they will tell you every quarter or half ounce their baby weighed.

Here's why: he couldn't go home until he weighed at least four pounds. I called the NICU every night to see how much weight he'd lost or gained. If he gained a fraction at all, I went to sleep joyful. If he lost weight, I went to sleep crying. He was in the hospital for two months and eight days.

While he was there and I was home, I did the only thing I had any control over as his mother: I pumped breast milk every three hours. Believe me, an ounce of breast milk is an accomplishment when you first begin. No one prepared me for the pain I would feel when my milk came in with my first child. I was glad to be able to use that pain to provide my baby with nutrition. I could have slept through the night while he was in the hospital, but I woke to the discomfort like clockwork, knowing it was time to pump. I had a freezer full of breast milk. I was so proud of what I had accomplished. After some time had passed, upon delivering some milk to the hospital I learned from the doctor that Blake's stomach was unable to digest it. He recommended I discontinue it and use predigested soy formula instead.

I was beyond upset. I had done everything by the book in my first pregnancy. I gave up caffeine. I changed my diet to eat many fruits and vegetables to have a healthy baby and he still came early. Now, as I was trying to be the best first-time mom I could be—when I couldn't even hold my baby yet—I was told to dump my breast milk. Devastated is an understatement. I didn't know donation organizations existed, and we only had one freezer. Those hours spent in the early morning hours pumping and praying for my baby seemed like a waste.

But … they weren't. I was only counting what was lost and feeling the blow to my pride. I forgot to see how that time focused on my baby helped me survive the time without him being home yet. It also reminded me that this new formula would help him gain weight. That was the goal. Even if I couldn't help him reach that goal, I loved him and wanted what was best for him. I had to put my ego aside. I couldn't get any of that lost time or sleep back, but I could look forward to the day my baby would be home with me. That goal was worth keeping track of.

### WorkHearter Wisdom

We don't gain a thing when we focus on what is lost. When we are self-seeking, we are not loving. In all matters of raising our children, we must practice patience and kindness. Our pain is never in vain, our wounds are not wasted. By Jesus wounds, we are healed. Glory Hallelujah! I learned from experience, God can more with one drop of breast milk, than I could do with a freezer full. Don't count what is lost; instead focus on what is gained because Trust Him to do immeasurably more than we can ask or even imagine.

## Lunch Ladies

Two are better than one, because they have a good return for their labor: if either of them falls down, one can help the other up. But pity anyone who falls and has no one to help them up.

Ecclesiastes 4:9–10 NIV

When you go through a breakup or a divorce, the mutual-friends situation can get sticky. Some friends will not know what to say, so they keep their distance to avoid the awkward. Others will take a side and then feel guilty about the other party. Yet divorce can be the time you need friends the most to pick you up out of your self-pity. It's the same as a marriage: in any relationship, you get what you put into it. There are times that you need to carry more weight. That heavier weight will make your friend muscles stronger.

When we were planning our twenty-year high school reunion, my friend (who was also a class officer), dropped out of the planning all of a sudden, no reason or excuse. She said *I can't do this right now*. My first reaction was frustration. I only saw the extra weight her dropping out that I would need to carry. She not only wasn't able to help plan it, but she didn't attend the reunion either. We did a lot of planning and she simply didn't show up. I let my ego get the best of me and never asked her what happened.

Then I decided if I wanted friends, I had to be one. I invited her and two other classmates to regular lunch dates. I stopped keeping track of who last contacted whom or who put forth more effort in keeping in touch. I found out, after two years of lunches, her mom had passed from ALS. They had received her mom's ALS diagnosis the day my friend dropped out of our planning committee. Talk about a gut punch. If you only see your side of the story, you will stay in the blame game and lose friends. I could have lifted some of her burden if I'd asked instead of assuming. We stay in touch more now—having lunch with other ladies in our graduating class—and I personally think we have grown up a lot together and separately. We are the "lunch ladies." We realize more now how short our time is. There's something special about being with friends who knew you before life got so complicated; spending time with them heals a broken part of me that they didn't break.

## WorkHearter Wisdom

There is not enough time to play games with people we love. We need to pick each other up. I make time and look forward to lunch with these ladies. Lunch is an easy way to get back into the friendship game—or start off with coffee if lunch is too taxing on your time schedule. There is always time to have lunch or coffee somewhere on the calendar in order catch up with old friends and remind you as a mom that you were young once. If you have a friend that pops into your mind for no reason, give them a call and see if you can reconnect.

## Everyone's a Fan of Someone

As She stood behind him at his feet weeping, she began to wet his feet with her tears. Then she wiped them with her hair, kissed them and poured perfume on them.

Luke 7:38 NIV

I was a typical fan girl in the '80s and '90s. I had magazine photos of teen heartthrobs taped up on my bedroom wall. I saved every dime I got to go to concerts to see my favorite bands. I was envious of their gifts and blessings. I didn't see my own blessings and gifts that had been bestowed on me. My gifts were not the same as those given to these stars—somehow their gifts seemed special. Over time, you realize not everyone is a fan, but everyone is a fan of someone.

My mom is one of my biggest fans and cheerleaders on earth. She is the one who speaks louder than the critics. She offers praise when others complain reminding me how I should be encouraging to those I fangirl over. My dad, on the other hand, is not known for giving out compliments. When I was in high school I got selected for football homecoming queen. It was only a fifteen-minutes-of-fame deal but the video my dad recorded will always be a reminder of his unmeditated, spontaneous praise. He shook the video camera in disbelief up in the air while it was still recording, so all you see is the sky, because he was so proud. In the background, you hear him cheering, "Way to go, Michelle!" followed by his response to someone in the audience, "Yes, that's my daughter." No matter the outcome, I believe he would have been cheering me on. Even though the applause from the crowd was temporary, affirmation from my father will be what remains in my memory. Like my father, I'm guilty of not giving enough spontaneous praise.

Our children get enough criticism from us and others all the livelong day. Let's amp it up to make the positive side more balanced so they aren't so shocked by our extravagant praise.

Parents know how easy it is for the haters to extinguish the fire in someone rather quickly. That's why parents will shout so loudly at their children's sporting events. We need more fans to fan the flames of encouragement, so it spreads like wildfire.

Jesus had some haters in His life and some cheerleaders. Some would shout His name in admiration while others would call Him names that should not be whispered much less shouted. The woman who wiped His feet with her tears and hair was so glad to be in His corner as one of his biggest fans. This woman was considered a sinful woman by the Pharisees, and they immediately mocked Him because He allowed her to touch Him. He forgave her many sins, canceling her debt and the labels the Pharisees had given her.

### WorkHearter Wisdom

My favorite mental image is one that suggests Jesus dances over us and sings to us with joy as our cheerleader in heaven. Jesus is not a fair weather fan. He cheers for us in every season even when we feel like our team can't catch a win. I want to be more like Jesus to those who need it and let them know they have a fan. I want my children to know I'm in their corner cheering them on as their biggest fan without any accomplishment required, especially when life throws hard punches at them. Everyone needs someone in their corner singing over them with love, canceling out the noise of the haters and clapping louder than the naysayers. Close your eyes and picture Jesus dancing over you and cheering you on today.

# Knowing the Difference Between Windows and Doors

But anyone who hates a brother or sister is in the darkness and walks around in the darkness. They do not know where they are going, because the darkness has blinded them.

1 John 2:11 NIV

Windows and doors open and close. It's key to know the difference between the two in life. Windows don't stay open all the time. Neither do doors, but one is not like the other. When my youngest was a two-year-old, she had a short window of time as it got closer to bedtime before she became so restless that I was unable to speak to her rationally—and the door would slam shut on our window of calm at bedtime.

Opportunities in life can have small windows of time as well. Doors can be the entrance or exit into or from situations or seasons of life. It's usually best to go in through the front door, but when we get comfortable the back door is unlocked and open. When we let our guard down, it's easier to let things slide as we get comfortable. Businesses use back-door entrances for employees only because they are trusted and have been trained. They have an investment in the company. These back doors are usually not in well-lit areas of the parking lots or alleys, so it's not good for customers to have access to back-door entrances.

My husband, a builder, always puts a camera up at his new homes by the back-door entrance. He has learned over time that more people will check to see if the back door is unlocked rather than the front. Since it's darker on the back of the house than the front where the streetlights are, one can assume trespassers are not there fumbling in the dark out of curiosity alone. So he puts surveillance there for an added layer of protection. People often leave the back door of their homes unlocked when they feel safe, but the back doors of our hearts should remain guarded against hatred toward others.

## WorkHearter Wisdom

We should protect the back doors of our minds and hearts by always keeping an eye on them. If you let down that guard, anything can come in through the back door, like hate or thoughtlessness into our thoughts and actions. If an opportunity is trying to come in the back way as a workaround or to skip necessary steps, it may not be the best opportunity to entertain. If we slip up and let our guards down on our heart, hate can cause us to fumble around without light when we are blinded by darkness.

# Breath of Heaven

The wind blows wherever it pleases. You hear its sound, but you cannot tell where it comes from or where it is going. So it is with everyone born of the Spirit.

John 3:8 NIV

All scripture is God-breathed and is useful for teaching, rebuking, correcting and training in righteousness.

2 Timothy 3:16 NIV

Summer in the South brings heat and humidity. Breathing becomes labored when the air is hot and heavy. We hear reports of people having heat strokes often in our area. The heat index is a gauge of safety when cooling off is critical.

In my experience, I look for breaths from heaven in every season. In winter, the snowflakes falling feel like a breath from heaven. In fall, the autumn leaves turning bright colors are a breath of heaven. In spring, it's a gentle rain and in summer a cool breeze. Summer is when I welcome the wind.

Winds of change in my house are not as welcome. Sometimes, a change happens so quickly I get whiplash looking to see where that attitude or snide remark originated from. Did it come from their hunger, their lack of sleep, or a result of my own sarcasm?

I am also guilty of being a little moody without knowing

where my mood came from. My husband has even responded with *Where the heck did that come from?* But he didn't exactly say *heck*, hence no quotations. The word he did use is precisely where it came from—the pits of hell. To which I responded that I indeed felt like I was in said pits of hell. I needed heaven to breathe on me in that moment and change my heart.

## WorkHearter Wisdom

God breathes into our lives in every season as a reminder that He is with us no matter the weather. Our hearts will change often—like the seasons of change that happen in our homes. We need a breath from heaven to cool off our heated spirits when the winds of change blow through. God breathed into scripture because we will need to use it to teach, rebuke, correct, and train ourselves and our children.

# PART 3
## The Finality of Fall

When leaves change colors and fall to the ground, it signals a change in seasons that we can see. Watching our children in this season is beautiful and bittersweet at the same time. If we don't stop long enough to appreciate the beauty changing before our eyes, we'll miss it—just as the leaves don't linger once they start falling from the trees. Even peacocks shed their stunning feathers in fall. Their season of shedding is to allow time to replenish energy needed to grow the new feathers.

Fall is not the season to wait. It is the season to pause to appreciate our children before they graduate from high school, leave for college or military service, get married, have their own children. All of it goes by in an instant. "Babies don't keep" comes from a timeless poem by Ruth Hulburt Hamilton that reminds us it's ok sometimes to ignore chores and distractions that scream for our attention. Psalm 90:12 says "teach us to number our days carefully so that we may develop wisdom in our hearts" (CSB). Our life is fleeting like the falling leaves of autumn.

Fall is my favorite season because it doesn't force you quickly into change. It comes in quietly and gently transitions you into a different season of life. I welcome fall with open arms like a long-lost friend I haven't seen in a year.

Father, please help us see the beauty in change before it is final. End of seasons are tough for parents and children alike. Thank you for walking alongside us and allowing us to witness the visible changes in the work of raising our children. It goes by quickly, but we have a lifetime season pass to watch all of it as their biggest fan. Teach us to linger a little longer with our embraces and stare at the beauty of our children's eyes as the gift it is. Grant us peace to trust in you through the days of change. Give us wisdom to know when it's OK to let them go and start their next chapter. Amen.

## Class Reunions

Each of you should use whatever gift you have received to serve others, as faithful stewards of God's grace in various forms.

1 Peter 4:10 NIV

I've been out of high school thirty years now. When I see a classmate or hear about something going on in their life through social media, I feel proud and cheer for them. Somehow, even if I don't have their gifts, I celebrate them because I knew them way back when. We grew up together and I feel connected to their story, even if we don't see each other now. They knew me before I had kids or got married; they knew me young. And even though time has passed, this connection brings us together to reminisce. We had a small graduating class, and even smaller turnouts make it for our class reunions.

I've been married twice before and when I hear about a win for my kids' father, I celebrate in my mind with them, because we also grew up together as young parents. We are from the same generation, GenX, so we get the same jokes and pop culture references.

As a mom raising my kids starting when I was twenty, I grew up alongside them too. They still remember me young and I remember them young, even as we age. My firstborn, Blake, does not call me regularly but he will take the time to call me when a celebrity he knew I appreciated passes away. When Prince died, he said, "Mom, I'm just checking to see if you are OK?" Prince passed away on my son's birthday. He called me when Matthew Perry, star of *Friends*, recently died also. *Friends* season one began when Blake was born in 1994. That show was a welcome weekly laugh and retreat from whatever my new season of parenthood brought for the first ten years I was a mom. We didn't have streaming services then so we had to wait for the next episode. Can you imagine? We planned our lives around our favorite shows. When I got pregnant twenty years later and was on bedrest, I watched it all again on nightly reruns. My son knew it was a favorite because he grew up with me.

When a celebrity passes away, we feel like we knew them from watching them go through a very public life. And in some ways, we grow up with them. The funny ones who always make you laugh or the talented ones who make you sing can feel like a friend you know, because they shared their talent with you. But did we share our gifts with them? The gift of salvation is usually my first reflection. Did anyone share the gift of salvation with them? Seriously.

## WorkHearter Wisdom

We are all growing up together, because we all get just one life. As Christians, we receive gifts from our heavenly Father and ours are no less than anyone else. Our gifts are given to us to share God's grace with others to lead them to Christ. Let's cheer each other on and make sure our class reunion in heaven is record-breaking. And, play 80s music today.

PART 3: THE FINALITY OF FALL

# Empty Nest

You prepare a table before me in the presence of my enemies. You anoint my head with oil; my cup overflows.

Psalm 23:5 NIV

Two things that leave the environment looking empty when they are gone are holiday decorations... and tree leaves. Nature is a reminder of empty nests, children going to college or getting married. Only God can fill our emptiness.

If you are in the empty nest season, try to remember all the hobbies or tasks you were putting off until you had more time. Keep yourself busy with those activities, *not* following their social media or tracking their GPS location. If they are close enough to visit weekly, take them to lunch or dinner. Food is the love language of most college students. Pair the gift of a meal with the quality time of your presence. Write them letters.

My mom loves to write all my kids letters while they are in college. She gives them a manifest of the daily happenings of the week in our extended family and puts five dollars for ice cream in the envelope. It's a smart move to include cash—knowing they will be looking forward to her next letter. This covers the gift love language. Mom also wrote to me at college, but I didn't get the five dollars. Go figure with these grandparents! All her grandkids write her back, telling about their college happenings.

The lifeline of a pen pal is a lost art that we can revive. In a way, it's much better than a text or an email since students can take their time to respond when they have a free moment and do so in a reflective way. Later, looking back on old letters can remind you how full your cup is even when your home seems empty.

## WorkHearter Wisdom

We all have our favorite seasons of life: parenting, waistlines ... Appreciating all the seasons we are gifted to be a part of will help the transitions of joyous celebratory seasons to sad gloomy seasons. Often we need a reminder to remember that only God can fill our emptiness.

## Puzzle Pieces

No discipline seems pleasant at the time, but painful. Later on, however, it produces a harvest of righteousness and peace for those who have been trained by it.

Hebrews 12:11 NIV

When it comes to assembly, I've done my fair share as a self-proclaimed non-handy parent/adult. I am usually missing a tool even if the package includes an Allen wrench key. Inevitably, every single time there will be missing pieces. I have been guilty more than once of trying to make a piece fit because it was available. I knew it wouldn't fit, but I still tried so I could be done.

Disciplining children is like a puzzle. Some children need quiet time to reflect, others need toys/electronics removed for a time. The pieces for each child are puzzling. What works for one will not faze another. When you start parenting, reading books is helpful to give you tips, but they are not the absolute resolution. It takes some trial and error of trying different practices to complete the puzzle. Some solutions don't fit your child and won't work.

Life doesn't show us the whole picture of the puzzle. We have to find our missing pieces. We also need to guard ourselves against the pieces that don't fit. When I can't see the whole picture because I am missing some of the information, the best thing to do is ask for help from our heavenly Father.

## WorkHearter Wisdom

All of life is a puzzle. Sometimes we try to make pieces fit that do not belong in our lives. Children will attempt to allow parts that are beyond their years into their lives. It is our job as their parents to block those attempts. If it doesn't fit into what is best for them, even if it's a new shiny puzzle piece that their friends have, we must be the ones who say no. No is a complete sentence.

# Recognition

Religion that God our Father accepts as pure and faultless is this: to look after orphans and widows in their distress and to keep oneself from being polluted by the world.

James 1:27 NIV

Give proper recognition to those widows who are really in need.

1 Timothy 5:3 NIV

As moms, we don't get enough recognition. Many of the mundane tasks are so routinely done, they don't get recognized unless we are absent from the home. I can make pasta and cake every week and my children will eat it every week without complaint or compliment, but if I skip, of course, they will complain. Jesus doesn't get the recognition He deserves. Many of the sacrifices and teachings He gave us go unnoticed until we feel His absence in our lives.

We are called as followers of Christ to look after the widows and orphans. They have an absence in their lives that we are commanded to fill. Orphans are missing parents/family. Widows are missing their spouse. They deserve the recognition and attention to their needs, but they are often overlooked and disregarded. We think they will take up too much time, effort, or resources. Yet God gave us everything we have and we will always have enough.

Recognition of what Christ has done in our lives is often attributed to luck, coincidence, or something else. Yet Jesus is the one constant we can rely on and the one who deserves all the glory for our good lives. There are not enough thanks for His living sacrifice.

It is possible to have too much of a good thing in life. Too much of this world will pollute our lives. Too much Italian food, cake, or alcohol can make us ill, but Jesus is *never* too much. Those without Him are orphans without a heavenly Father.

## WorkHearter Wisdom

God gives us chances to share with the world. He also advises us to look after those in need, and in religion not to pollute ourselves with the world. Jesus is how we keep from allowing ourselves to be polluted. It is on all of us to help our children understand how important looking after orphans and widows is to the God we serve. He called us up to help with the absence they feel.

# Broken Record

> If anyone thinks he is religious without controlling his tongue, then his religion is useless and he deceives himself.
>
> James 1:26 HCSB

I wish I'd recorded my young kids' voices. The times they were the most repetitive that I thought were annoying. The times they said *mommy, mama,* and *mom* on repeat. I was tired at the time of hearing over and over: "Are you ready?" "Mom, watch this!" "Will you play with me?" "Hold you" and "One more hug." They don't say these phrases when they get older. They don't think we are watching them anymore. All the repeats I took for granted I miss now.

Younger kids constantly want the reassurance that their parents are watching. They continually check their parents' eyes. Then, almost overnight, our children turn into teenagers who do not want any of our attention. They don't want our questions and they definitely don't want to talk to us. We can blame it on hormones, we can blame it on their underdeveloped brains, we can blame it on all the lip service we gave them all their childhood, we can even blame it on the rain. (A little Milli Vanilli reference there. You're welcome for the broken record now playing on a loop in your mind.)

Meanwhile, as moms we turn into broken records with our

children. We repeat the same phrases and questions until it sounds like the record player is broken. But they don't outgrow wanting our attention. Our teen children still want us watching them even if they don't tell us or act like it. Teens want us to make sure they are fed. They want us to see them roll their eyes at us. They may not listen, but they watch us.

We should know God is always watching even as we age. Even in the pain, even in the dark, even in the glory days. He's not distracted. He's got His eyes on us always. We grow numb to His presence when we repeatedly sin. We ask for the same prayers in our petitions to God. Our repeated requests for forgiveness may be broken records but His love, grace, abundant mercy, and constant seeking a relationship with us will not break.

As tough as it is, we can find small wins with our teens in our relationship with them. If it's providing their favorite meal just to get a few kind words from them, it's a win. If they don't roll their eyes at us for a day, it's a win. Howbeit small, it's a win just the same. The little wins will help mend the gap created by those often-tumultuous teen years. Those small wins turn into big ones later in life. All the times we kept from losing our temper and causing a larger rift in our parent/teen bond will be big wins and grow our relationships stronger.

### WorkHearter Wisdom

Teens will push you to the edge of your limits. Parenting this age group is not for the weary or the weak. The calmer you can be—controlling your tongue, as James tells us—during those moments of their pushing your buttons because they know them well, the quicker the disagreement will diffuse. Teens will rise to the level that the parents rise to when it comes to temperament.

## Leftovers and Hand-Me-Downs

And when they had eaten their fill, he told his disciples, "Gather up the leftover fragments, that nothing may be lost."

John 6:12 ESV

I didn't like leftovers or hand-me-downs growing up, yet that's what my family could afford. As a kid, I wanted the freshly made dishes to eat and the new unworn clothes to wear. I didn't stop to realize that despite growing up in a leftover-eating, hand-me-down wearing household, we were rich. We were rich in love.

We have memories that will never go out of style or turn cold. My dad worked several jobs to save up money to take a vacation every year. One of my fondest memories is that we always took vacations. We only went out to eat at restaurants on birthdays. With a household of six, it happened six times a year and on vacation, so it was always a treat. I wouldn't trade a single hand-me-down or leftover dinner, which simply enabled our family vacations or birthday dinners, with their priceless memories. Nothing was wasted during those times, and I am grateful for that.

As a wife and mother, your day can seem like all that is left for you is leftover and hand-me-down moments to yourself. A hand-me-down moment is one you don't own first or even get the best wear out of. It may be a dinner shared with your spouse talking about his day at work. It could be a nightly bedtime routine with your kids trying to calm them down so they can sleep better. After all this, you could be totally depleted with nothing left to have for yourself except the memories of the day. In these times, when the days are long and the nights are short, remember nothing is wasted here either. The richest memories of your marriage or the ones your kids have about childhood could be the mundane ordinary daily life moments that make room for their milestones.

I find it easier to accept leftovers and be satisfied knowing they were mentioned by Jesus. When we grieve lost time and lost moments that we can't get back, He reminds us of the crumbs. We may only have morsels of time left for ourselves at the end of the day, but that means we were full all day long. Our productivity may not have been full in what we had planned, but in our family's day we filled them up.

## WorkHearter Wisdom

Note that in the scripture above, Jesus even added to "gather them so that nothing may be lost." Even our leftovers have worth. Some days all I have left is a sigh of relief that the day is over and I survived it, or a small prayer of thanks. What can we do with what time we have left today? What memories filled up our day? What memories do you have now of times long past?

## In Spite of Circumstances

Give thanks in all circumstances; for this is the will of God in Christ Jesus for you.

1 Thessalonians 5:18 ESV

Thanksgiving is the best day for me to be thankful and give thanks for everything in my life, because we are all sitting together with full bellies and warm hugs. I didn't realize how much of an art form being thankful was on all the other days of the year. A much more daunting task is giving thanks when my I find a nail in my flat tire, or it starts raining on my head carrying in groceries, or my children are being disrespectful, or I'm in pain from having sprained an ankle. That is, until I started to think about *everything* differently. The bigger picture is hidden from my view, but I can imagine why I got a flat tire to avoid a more dangerous situation, or appreciate the rain that is watering my flowers, or take the time to find out what is bothering my child, being thankful they are safely at home with me. I also remember how thankful I am for being able to walk without discomfort when I've healed.

God knew we would need the reminder to give thanks in all circumstances. Thankfulness is a state of mind and an action that we need help with practicing. Practice makes perfect, right? We can become better thankful children by practicing the art of thankfulness. Going through the alphabet thanking

Him for something that starts with each letter or counting your blessings instead of counting sheep at night are two simple ways to practice. Waking up to thanking Him for sleep or the sunshine outside our window is a great way to start your day. In times of struggle, finding just one thing to be thankful for can be your practice. It can change your mood, your attitude, and your outlook.

We can teach our children this practice to keep with them the rest of their lives. Even if we aren't with them, they will have an action plan in thankfulness. God didn't give us the reminder as a parent to discipline us. He gave it to us to help us and our children. His will is *for* us and not against us.

### WorkHearter Wisdom

Can you imagine having a perfect spirit of thankfulness? Wouldn't that mean we have fully grown into God's will? Consider this too: How have you witnessed a thankful heart despite unfortunate circumstances?

## Quiet Moments of Contemplation: Isaiah 40:31 NIV

But those who hope in the LORD
will renew their strength.
They will soar on wings like eagles;
they will run and not grow weary,
they will walk and not be faint.

Parenting a newborn, new teen driver, or even a college freshman living away from home for the first time is tiring. I felt like a new person once my babies slept through the night. It was short-lived as then came the teething nights. After that, we entered the night terrors stage, then the teen years, then the child living out of your home—which feels like breathing with one lung—and now I am blessed with the night sweats. Sleep is a fleeting gift with shorter visits that come less often. When I hope to renew my strength in the Lord, I have more energy to face whatever the day may bring.

Think about it, WorkHearter. Center your hope in the One who knows you, and contemplate ... soaring.

# All Four Seasons

For everything there is a season, and a time for every matter under heaven.

Ecclesiastes 3:1 ESV

I have four children in different ages of life. They are always in and out of different seasons. Right now, as a parent, I have a child in each of the four seasons simultaneously. My oldest and only son is in the season of spring. He is having lots of first experiences in his adult life. He has a full-time job. He has his own apartment. He is a new dad which means I am a new grandmother. He is trying to learn best how to be on his own and pay his bills. He's making a lot of mistakes with the pruning process of adult life and learning some valuable lessons. My oldest daughter is in the season of fall: she is taking all the knowledge from her K–12 education and college and learning how to change into an independent adult, like the leaves of fall. My teenage daughter is in the season of winter. She is learning how to navigate through the cold-hearted hormone years and wade through the bitter teenage years to find her own identity. My youngest daughter is in the season of summer. She is always embracing adventure and wants to be independent. She still skips everywhere she goes instead of walking. Her favorite season is summer because she can play outside all day. She reminds me of the sunsets of summer after long days of playing outdoors.

When they were younger, even as babies, I could not imagine them at the ages they are now. It's difficult as a parent to know how to help or support all of them in different phases of their lives. The scripture God gives us in Ecclesiastes reminds me that there is a time and a season for everything. I've noticed some of these seasons repeat in my life with my children, especially the most difficult ones. It is comforting to know that I can take my experiences with a difficult season and learn from them for the next time. It is also comforting to know these seasons are temporary and fleeting. The comfort this brings to a mama heart is needed now more than ever.

No matter the season, we must show them how to depend on Christ. The only constant is change and He is more worthy of their dependence.

## WorkHearter Wisdom

Different seasons bring different challenges that require different comforts with our children. Warm blankets are welcomed in winter but not in summer. Just when we get comfortable in a season of parenting, it changes. What season of parenting do you find yourself in now? How have you learned from the first experience as a mom?

# Workhearter Wisdom: Practical Tips for Undistracted Cooking/Baking/Cleaning

As a parent and/or household manager, juggling multiple hats at the same time can easily cause distractions that take us off task. I have found some simple and practical ways to keep me focused at least for a short time:

- Set up a short music playlist for doing these tasks listening to music. My friend Ginny uses "The Eye of the Tiger" method as a song timer goal she sets to tidy up a room. She has twins so we trust her.
- If music is playing, getting distracted by social media and losing track of time is less likely to happen as easily. Or listen to a podcast.
- If waiting for water to boil, use the time to organize a kitchen cabinet or silverware drawer. Put up or remove things from the pantry during this time. Staying in the area and same room will keep you from forgetting how much time has passed waiting for water to boil.
- Clean the kitchen before cooking. It's easy for me to say I will clean as I go along, but then I get distracted. Starting off with a clean space and empty trash can keeps the distractions/frustrations down.

I lift up my eyes to the mountains—
    where does my help come from?
My help comes from the LORD,
    the Maker of heaven and earth.

                                      Psalm 121:1–2 NIV

# Identity Crisis

> So in Christ Jesus you are all children of God through faith, for all of you who were baptized into Christ have clothed yourselves with Christ.
>
> Galatians 3:26 NIV

I wasn't exactly sure of the day and time I went from *Mommy* to *Mama* with my first child until I watched a home video that showed the moment he started calling me Mama. He was only four years old. I would still be Mommy to my baby daughter, but to my oldest, I would be called Mama until that title turned to Mom. Now he calls me Mimi because I have a grandson.

Our seasons of identity and names we are called can be short or long. It doesn't matter how long we have a certain identity as a parent … or as a daughter, sister, wife, or even an employee. What matters is that we don't forget who we are in Christ. We can put our identity in our work accomplishments, our job titles. We can put our identity into being a mom raising our kids, or as a wife taking care of our homes.

Then, when that part of life changes and we enter a different season, we feel like we don't fit into that role or title anymore. It happens to all of us including our children. As young adult, they will enter mid-life and have their identity crises. All of our lives, our bodies continually change. Eventually, all our hair turns gray, unless we dye it.

Eventually, all our kids will leave our homes to start their own seasons of adulthood.

We go from mom to mother-in-law to grandmom, titles that all fit a particular season but don't quite feel right at first. It is like trying on a new outfit or one that is not comfortable and doesn't always fit perfectly at first. All these shifts in changing seasons of our life as a parent can contain small identity crises. We ask ourselves questions quietly:

If I'm not a stay-at-home mom, who am I?

If I'm not a full-time worker, who am I?

If I'm no longer a daughter due to my parent's death, who am I?

If I get divorced and am no longer a wife, who am I?

We did this growing up, but we don't remember it. We go from carefree kids to hormone-ravaged adolescents to newlyweds and first-time moms. It's all normal. No matter the season change, we remain children of God. Our identity in Christ does not change.

## WorkHearter Wisdom

Through it all, we are clothed in Christ Jesus and that is the most perfect fit. When our children don't know how to fit into their new seasons of life, we are the ones who can show them the identity they have in Christ is going to fit every season of their lives. And ladies, I have the answer to all the questions above for you: You are the precious daughter of the King. No matter what you do or don't do, you will always be that to our heavenly Father.

# Things We Keep

Finally, brothers and sisters, whatever is true, whatever is noble, whatever is right, whatever is pure, whatever is lovely, whatever is admirable—if anything is excellent or praiseworthy—think about such things.

> Philippians 4:8 NIV

Space in our lives isn't meant to be filled with items, clutter, or worry. Space is meant for margin. All the clothes, knickknacks, and items we hold onto after their useful life thinking they may come in handy one day are only good for collecting dust. We fill our empty rooms with stuff because we have the space. None of that stuff is doing us any good.

The space stuff takes up isn't just physical space. Living with emotional and mental clutter doesn't give us the peace of mind we need to focus on Jesus. A cluttered mind doesn't give Jesus room to breathe into our thoughts. *He* needs room and space to grow. We should set aside space that is meant for Jesus. Space that is meant to grow and not shrink as we fill it with good thoughts.

Letting go can give us the space we really need. We can let go of things we don't have any business holding onto. Things we keep or hold onto—bad memories, stuff, regrets are the toughest to let go of, but we can do hard things.

The name of Jesus alone can raise up what's dead in you. Letting go of one can cause a domino effect of leading to others ceasing to take up space within you.

## WorkHearter Wisdom

Some of these things we must let go of are either in our heads, our hearts, or our homes. Stuff that is too heavy for us to carry and doesn't allow space for us to grow in a positive way. No one asked you to hold onto it. We don't need to. Be encouraged sisters to lay it down and keep/hold our thoughts on whatever is true, noble, right, pure, lovely, admirable, excellent or praiseworthy. When Jesus said he finished it, he meant it. We can't do anything to make it unfinished. So, let it go.

How can we help our children let go of the tough stuff if we can't do it ourselves? What do you need to release from your thoughts/life to live more freely?

## Give and Take

Oh, taste and see that the LORD is good! Blessed is the man who takes refuge in Him!

Psalm 34:8 ESV

As mothers and wives, we give and give. It's not a stretch of the imagination to say that in general we give and give and our children innocently take from us because it's our job to take care of them. I've learned as a mother of four that I have to *take* for myself. I have to take time for myself, and I have to take it when I have nothing left to give.

My top three free takes are: Take a nap, take a shower, and take a walk. When I am empty and do not have anything left to give, taking one or all of three of these will give me what I need to be able to give again. I cannot pour from an empty cup. The power of a nap, a shower, or a walk to fill me up after tiring days or trying times is underestimated.

If none of those work, it is usually a desperate situation and I need a bonus: a snack. Snacking is an art form for moms. We have to snack quietly and in a way that no one else (children, husband, dog) senses we are going to enjoy a snack. I pride myself on being a sneaky snacker. So if the three takes don't do the trick, I make a snack. These easy takes are a refuge for my weary self.

Scripture talks about how good the Lord is. He is a refuge.

We can all learn from taking refuge more often. We can take shelter from our distress in God Himself. *Take* is used in this scripture as an action verb, so we can freely take it. In our daily life of give, scripture says we can be blessed if we take refuge in Him.

Our children need us to be their earthly refuge. They will take more than they give, and we should be OK with that. We will do the same with the Lord and He's OK with it too.

## WorkHearter Wisdom

A nap and a snack for changing your outlook is not a new concept. It can help our attitude as well as our children's. God did this for Elijah in 1 Kings 19 when he prayed to die —gave him a nap and a snack—twice. Have you ever been so depleted that a snack, healthy or indulging, turns the whole day around? When have you sought refuge and how did that rescue you? How can we practice this and demonstrate rescue to our children?

# Singing Off-Key

Let the message of Christ dwell among you richly as you teach and admonish one another with all wisdom through psalms, hymns, and songs from the Spirit, singing to God with gratitude in your hearts.

Colossians 3:16 NIV

Speaking to one another with psalms, hymns, and songs from the Spirit. Sing and make music from your heart to the Lord.

Ephesians 5:19 NIV

So what shall I do? I will pray with my spirit, but I will also pray with my understanding; I will sing with my spirit, but I will also sing with my understanding.

1 Corinthians 14:15 NIV

I do not enjoy math. It is a necessity but it makes my brain hurt. I know how the basics—add, subtract, multiply, and divide—but knowing how to do it and doing it well or with ease are two different scenarios. It's like singing a song. I can know the lyrics and melody to the song, but I am off-key. I think I sing well in the shower, listening in my head, but when I hear it on playback using my ears, it is not the same-the math is not mathing. I know there is math involved in music—octaves, key and time signatures, measures, meter—and I'm sure that is why I am no good at it.

I love to bake, but math takes all the joy out of baking. I learn recipes and use the eyeball measurement method instead of measuring cups. When I start a recipe, I don't pay much attention to the size of the bowl. But my least favorite household chore is dishes, so I will use every tactic I know to keep from washing an extra dish or utensil. When I realize the bowl is not big enough for the ingredients, it's too late. I've fully committed to using this bowl to prevent extra dirty dishes. I've lost the rhythm of the recipe. My bowl may not be big enough, but my determination and dedication is. As you can guess, when the mixers get going, I end up with an even bigger mess outside the bowl. I meant well by trying to make something from the heart for my family, but I got the measurement wrong and made a mess. I was baking off-key or out of rhythm, but I was doing it from the heart.

I cannot sing but I still try. If only I could eyeball my way through singing better/on key. I'd even settle for being in rhythm. I can't even clap on time! The Bible reminds us that singing well and doing math well are not necessary to give our hearts to God. We just need to try ... and give it from the heart. We may be off-key or we might bring a smaller bowl than needed. We will receive more than we give and probably always need a bigger bowl for the blessings He gives.

## WorkHearter Wisdom

How often do you receive messy gifts from your children presented with beaming eyes full of pride? They try so hard to handmake gifts for us. Think about how precious these thoughts and gifts for others are coming from the minds and hearts of our children. How can we receive these gifts with gratitude?

# Traditional Education in an Untraditional Way

> I will instruct you and teach you in the way you should go; I will counsel you with my loving eye on you.
>
> Psalm 32:8 NIV

I used to be a jerk to my mom. She bore the brunt of all my teenage angst. She had to put me out of the car many times, making me walk home due to my hurtful words misdirected at her. I would have never spoken to my father that way (or I wouldn't have been able to walk comfortably). Mom always turned the car around and came back to pick me up, thanks to my siblings' pleading on my behalf. Of course, my stubborn self would say no when she circled back to ask me to get back into the car. She kept her loving eye on me no matter how much I lashed out.

She had to be biting her tongue trying to absorb my angst in those moments. Those closest to us are often first or last to recognize this: we lash out where we feel the safest.

I learned from her traditional example not to permit this with my children. Our kids will at times act like jerks. I recognize they feel safe enough to direct their big feelings toward me, but I do not absorb their angst. I redirect it lovingly. If I remain calm, the situation diffuses faster. I pick up a lot by learning how to ask questions. I do not yell (anymore). I do not join in with their choir of slamming doors. Listening intently and becoming keenly aware of what is happening to them or how they are feeling in the moment is my continuing education as a parent.

## WorkHearter Wisdom

Communication is key to our relationship with our children. A basic ask of "What is really going on?" or "Who else are you mad at besides me?" is often the starting point to turning the car around. If we open our eyes to see that our kids are walking alone or in the wrong direction, we can pick them up and help teach them. We all want to be the parent that they feel safe enough to get back in the car … rather than get out.

## Harvest Festivals

So we're not giving up. How could we! Even though on the outside it often looks like things are falling apart on us, on the inside, where God is making new life, not a day goes by without his unfolding grace. These hard times are small potatoes compared to the coming good times, the lavish celebration prepared for us. There's far more here than meets the eye. The things we see now are here today, gone tomorrow. But the things we can't see now will last forever.

2 Corinthians 4:16–18 MSG

Then he said to his disciples, "The harvest is plentiful but the workers are few. Ask the Lord of the harvest, therefore, to send out workers into his harvest field."

Matthew 9:37–38 NIV

Every fall, we have a harvest festival in our small town. As a younger kid, I equated these festivals with fun games and face paint. As an adult, I realize there is more than just harvesting produce involved in various booths at these festivals, which are scheduled around the harvest moon. A so-called harvest moon signals autumn, and it appears full for a few days at the same time each night. This bright moonlight was often helpful to farmers who harvested their summer crops well into the evening, and gave us the concept harvest moon.

Many local artists use the festivals to showcase their work. Music, art, and handmade crafts are parts of the showcase. The ability to view what took many days, weeks, months, and even years for the artists to create is taken for granted by those walking by without appreciating the time involved in the work. The artist puts their hard work proudly on display, hoping to share it with the world. Hours of music practice honing their craft, and hours of molding materials and pieces into a work of art. They are proud not only because they finished the work but because no matter how difficult it was, they didn't give up on it. Similarly, farmers who struggle to produce a harvest have obstacles like rodents, weather, and bugs that infest their crops. They spend long hours tending to their crops relentlessly not giving up. They know if the crop has any life left after these trials, tending to it can still reap a harvest.

Jesus had compassion on the crowds who sought Him for healing from sickness and disease. He did this because He knew that those proclaiming the good news were fewer in number but the harvest would be plentiful as long as He, the Lord of the harvest, responded.

This reminds me of how much time as parents we put into raising our children. We are relentless. Only a parent can calculate the hours of sleepless nights, days of missed school, work, or sports due to illness, and weeks of vacations or road trips spent in the short years of their childhood. No one but me, for example, can tell you how much my child has grown—as I will gladly tell anyone about my six-foot-tall son who was a two-pound baby at birth. I was falling apart many days when he was a preemie with colic, but I did not give up on being his mom. Those days were extremely hard. My only goal each day was to keep him from crying for hours at a time and, eventually, see him smile. Today, I hope to see his smiling face once a month if I'm lucky, but it's a work of art I appreciate. Our children are the harvest, but they are also called to grow to be the workers. It doesn't take perfection to point to Jesus. It only takes a willingness to work.

## WorkHearter Wisdom

We proudly put our children on display, hoping to share with the world the work of art they are ... but we forget how much of that art is a reflection of us as a parent. They are a celebration we worked up to for many days, weeks, months, and years, never giving up on them. More so, how much they (and we) are a reflection of our Creator in heaven. Every wrinkle, scar, and stretch mark I have to show after raising my babies is a unique work of art that only I have—and a sign that I didn't give up. I have no trouble being proud of the work of art in my children. I am still working on being proud of the work of art I have become throughout my life. I see the imperfections but I can't quite see what God sees in me. And yet—God is proud of me as His work of art, just as I am proud of my children and the works of art they are.

# Flash Point Held Captive

"In your anger, do not sin": Do not let the sun go down while you are still angry, and do not give the devil a foothold.

Ephesians 4:26-27 NIV

See to it that no one takes you captive by philosophy and empty deceit, according to human tradition, according to the elemental spirits of the world, and not according to Christ.

Colossians 2:8 ESV

*Flash point* is defined as the lowest temperature at which vapors become combustible, burst suddenly into action, ignite when exposed to flame. I learned about it in a photography darkroom lab and with chemicals used in a lab. I can still smell those chemicals to this day if I think about them. They permanently singed my nose hairs. Flash point can also mean the point at which someone or something erupts into significant action.

Stress can cause our bodies to erupt into significant action. If we feel sick, we rest and hydrate to feel better. If we sense an emergency, we act before thinking. If we get angry, we say things we regret and often act out in sinful ways. When we allow the devil to get a hold, a foot, a toe, a toenail, in our life, he will not let go. If he finds the most vulnerable place he can attack us, he will attack us repeatedly to take us captive.

We've all been held captive by something. Our thoughts can hold us captive by worry or fear or regret. We can relive different scenarios in our minds that hold us captive. Rules and guidelines can hold our children accountable but also captive at the same time. Time limits can hold us captive. There is only so much time in a day. We should be capturing that time by holding our children's hands. Those are the thoughts that will last long after their hand outgrows mine. Hold onto what's right and what will last.

We don't have room to hold onto the good if we are too busy gripping the bad. If you let go of the thoughts that hold you captive, you will be open to hold onto what's right. Let go of what doesn't matter. Life is too short to hold onto what doesn't last.

## WorkHearter Wisdom

Jesus in His goodness will withstand the test of time. No matter the season, *Jesus Christ is the same yesterday and today and forever.* Hold tightly onto that fact in the face of captivity and it will set you free. Let's resolve today to let go of anger and deceit so we can come to our senses in the freedom of Christ.

# Muscle Memory

The tongue that heals is a tree of life,
but a devious tongue breaks the spirit.

> Proverbs 15:4 HCSB

My husband was a personal fitness trainer for the YMCA when we first got married. He would often speak about muscle memory and how quickly it returns when you start exercising again after a hiatus. No matter how long the hiatus was or how much loss of muscle occurred, the muscles quickly showed definition again if you consistently stuck it out. Holding our tongue when we really want to snap back a smart-aleck response can produce a muscle memory that we will often need multiple times with our children. We will also need it for those who are teaching, coaching, or mentoring our children. The tongue is a muscle that needs practice with restraint to have the muscle memory to be used for healing. It has power to heal or destroy those we speak about.

No matter how well we know a song or how many times we have sang the lyrics, we all mess up at least one line. Our minds wander during the familiar parts and our mouths and brains don't always remember in the right order, especially if the chorus changes a line or two. Bible memory verses do this to me when I memorize one version and another translation is used. I get hung up on the difference and don't finish the song or the scripture. I let my mind focus on the mistake or the disconnect between my mind and mouth. Muscle memory helps some, but it's slower with the passage of time.

As we get older, muscle memory doesn't always kick in fast enough. And that's OK. We need to lean in to slowing the busyness and the multitasking giving ourselves more time to think before we speak. We should allow ourselves grace in aging: glasses, notes, lists, wrinkles, gray hairs. I love snowflakes in my hair but not gray hairs. When we notice others' appearance is different, we don't always need to speak about it. Insecurity spreads insecurity.

### WorkHearter Wisdom

Maybe our friends see our grays like the beauty in a snowflake: designed intricately and fleeting—and they'll be sure to say something nice about it. We all need to focus more on healing words instead of wounding words that come from our own woundedness. Our muscle memory for kind words may be slower but the memory is still there. It may take a tamer workout to get moving as we age, but the memory of what we need to do will come to us. Let's resolve today to pause longer and choose healing words when we speak.

# Students Will Confront Your Bias and Fear

And you belong to Christ, and Christ belongs to God.

1 Corinthians 3:23 HCSB

When I first became a teacher, I worked in a school that had drastically different demographics than the school I had attended in high school. I was from a small town, but now I worked in an inner city. I was thirty years old, but I was naïve. I thought I needed to prove myself as a new teacher—and I did this by pretending I had it all figured out. I didn't eat lunch with the other teachers or try to make friends for fear they would see me as a fraud with no traditional education training—only life/work experience in the field I was teaching.

I came into the job with biases about teachers and students. I thought kids who dressed "emo" were troublemakers. I didn't understand why they insisted on wearing all black, even including black makeup. Until one day, one of my best students began to dress this way. She was quiet and didn't have many friends, but she was an excellent student. I asked her why she decided to join this group of friends, and she responded, "They accept me and I just want to belong somewhere even if I have to pretend to like dressing in all black." All of my bias was confronted. She joined this trend and group to be accepted. They accepted her when no one else did. She wanted to belong to a group.

We all just want to belong. I wanted to belong as a teacher, so I began by holding in all my fears and doubts to pretend like I had this teaching thing figured out. Even though I wanted to be accepted, I chose to eat alone in my classroom during lunch so no one would figure out I was winging it being a teacher and ultimately drowning. I fell on my face daily in front of my students—but they were kind when I messed up. Once I realized that my students were more like me than I ever thought, I decided to put myself out there with the other teachers. Even though I (and my teaching style) was different, they accepted me. They helped me and gave me a place to go for help.

They gave me a place to vent when strategies didn't work. They gave me advice on what worked for them, reminding me they had been first-year teachers once as well. I needed them to lift me up. I was drowning in a job I didn't feel prepared or qualified for. I wouldn't have survived the first year without the help. I felt like I belonged not because I was qualified but because they accepted me as I was and helped me along the way push through my struggles.

## WorkHearter Wisdom

Our children will seek to find a place to belong. As parents, we want them to always know they belong in our family no matter the struggle. We want them to belong to a group that provides support, accountability and challenges them. As an introvert adult, I find it hard to do small talk with lots of friends in a group. Although I wanted to have many friends when I was younger, now I yearn for deep meaningful relationships with a select few that challenge me and provide accountability. The difference is—I know where I belong. We belong to Christ and once we realize that, it doesn't feel like we have to pretend.

# WorkHearter Wisdom: Twenty Tips from a Former High School Teacher

1. Your kids act differently in the classroom that they do at home.
2. Your kids act differently in the hallway than they do in the classroom.
3. Your kids act differently outside of school than anywhere else.
4. Your kids are looking for any group in the school to fit into. They want to belong.
5. Extracurricular activities cost time and money but they keep most students out of trouble.
6. Clubs and trade/vocational classes are valuable and not a waste of time. If you don't believe me, compare the student debt and income of a recent college graduate to a student who became an electrician, plumber or mechanic.
7. Coaches are not all created equal. Teachers are not all created equal. They are also not all bad. Don't let one negative experience negate all the good people working for peanuts.
8. School lunches, even if they are free, are not enough to feed your child. They are hungry before, during, and after school. Teachers need more snacks (and feminine hygiene products). These two essentials students ask them for can take all their extra cash.

9. Instill your family values and the words of Jesus in your children. If you don't, someone at the school will teach them their values.
10. Your kids will forget to tell you everything that was announced at school. They don't listen to announcements. Think of yourself at a work meeting.
11. The only way to keep an eye on your student while they are at school is to volunteer for the PTO/PTA. As a bonus, you will be able to see the teachers act up at the faculty meeting when the PTO sponsors the snacks.
12. Please don't text your child during school unless it's an emergency. If you ask them how their day is going, they will only ask you to pick them up or bring them food.
13. Don't get upset with your child if they hold their poop all day at school. Bathrooms in high school are not always safe. I've seen many fights break out in the bathroom.
14. Encourage your kids to participate in fun school dress-up days. They will be boring adults soon enough.
15. If you buy your child something expensive and allow them to take it to school, they will either lose it or it will get stolen. Keep it at home no matter how much they beg, because they will be crying once it's gone.
16. School supply fees are not always required but suggested or requested. A teacher cannot force you to pay a fee if you don't have the money to pay it. There are federal programs that help.
17. If you do have extra funds, pay for another student's supply fee or field trip. Teachers don't make enough to pay those, and they will not plan something if everyone does not get opportunity to go.

18. Children can pray and bring their Bible to school. Period.
19. School administrators deal with discipline 90 percent of their day. They will likely not greet you with a smile, as their days are tough. If they don't know you by name, don't be offended—take that as a win.
20. Attendance is important. It will prove even more important with post-secondary education or work later in life. If your kid didn't go to school that day, don't let them go to the game that night.

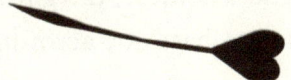

Jesus answered, "It is written: 'Man shall not live on bread alone, but on every word that comes from the mouth of God.'"

Matthew 4:4 NIV

## Only Job with No Training Is a Mom

Train up a child in the way he should go: and when he is old he will not depart from it.

Proverbs 22:6 KJV

For if the willingness is there, the gift is acceptable according to what one has, not according to what one does not have.

2 Corinthians 8:12 NIV

In high school, I had to fight to earn a spot on the trade school bus. School counselors thought I didn't belong on the bus to shop class due to my college path of education. The bus was reserved for those who couldn't or didn't want to go to college. I wanted to take a shop class so desperately, I told the school counselor to change my education path. Suddenly, a spot on the bus opened up. Trade school students get more hands-on training in vocational/career technical courses than students do in traditional college path classes. It was an amazing way to learn that was not from a textbook.

When you become a mom, there is not a beginner course you can take beforehand, and there is no prerequisite. There is not a hands-on course you can take while it's happening. There are so many books to choose from, but you will not know which one to pick up to read until after you've experienced motherhood. It is the only job all professions will pass through—every doctor you've seen had a mom. Every teacher had a mom. You are thrown into a new job as a mom and it's 100 percent hands-on. You are not ready for what this challenge brings, no matter how much you study or try to prepare in advance. God equips us when He calls us to motherhood. None of us are ready but if we are willing, God will equip us to finish the work.

I've had many jobs in my life, and many of them gave awards of merit or reviews for promotions with a title. The measure of those recognitions was tied to my identity as an employee. It took me years to realize my worth was not tied to my work at a job. While pursuing my doctoral degree, I went to campus for a class wearing a catheter bag less than two weeks after giving birth. It was rough, but I thought I had to attend to keep my 4.0 GPA. The professor gave me a B grade because I missed another class due to illness. I physically could not have worked harder in that class, but I still didn't earn the A. How ironic is it that I thought hindering my recovery postpartum by working hard when I felt terrible would help me measure up? Now I realize I have a more valuable title as a mother than any job or grade could give me.

## WorkHearter Wisdom

And yet even my parenting work is not indicative of my worth in the eyes of Jesus. My worth is defined by Jesus alone—and nothing I do or don't do will change the value of my worth in Christ. Do you know your worth? Do you know your worth is not determined by your work?

## Growing Pains

Therefore we do not lose heart. Though outwardly we are wasting away, yet inwardly we are being renewed day by day. For our light and momentary troubles are achieving for us an eternal glory that far outweighs them all. So we fix our eyes not on what is seen, but on what is unseen, since what is seen is temporary, but what is unseen is eternal.

2 Corinthians 4:16–18 NIV

A woman giving birth to a child has pain because her time has come; but when her baby is born she forgets the anguish because of her joy that a child is born into the world.   John 16:21 NIV

And the good news must first be proclaimed to all nations.

Mark 13:10 HCSB

When pregnancy stretches the uterus, those growing pains are truly painful—but you see the fruit of that labor when a baby is born. When you start a small business, the late nights, weekends, and working early mornings just to break even is painfully tiring—but the end result of success can be seen if you persevere. When kids grow into adolescents, growing pains are described as painful ache in the legs, even though researchers state that growth is not proven to be painful.

A dandelion is a plant that grows in all fifty states of America. From the root to the flower to the leaves, every part is edible and nutritious. What we call a weed, if harvested can be used for tea. So you can call it a weed or an edible plant, depending on your perspective. Dandelions spread easily and widely. They grow without effort. It's as easy as making a wish while you blow on the flower. If part of the root is injured on a dandelion, their long taproots can produce multiple shoots. So pulling this weed can signal several more to sprout up. The parachute of a dandelion can distribute its seeds for miles.

Just as every part of the dandelion is useful, so are the growing pains we have in life. It was painful to go through pregnancy and labor pains, but once the painful part is over, we do not have to fear it ever again. Pain signals change, and all the pain from growth we experience can have purpose. None of our pain is wasted.

We may have growing pains over our changing bodies as we age, but our children have those same pains. We may have growing pains in our businesses or jobs but our children have those same pains with our changing schedules and work demands. We may have growing pains in our homes but our children are feeling those same stretches in school, online, and in social friend groups. Our relationships with our children will stretch and have uncomfortable growing pain seasons, but we can show them how to grow with those pains to see a beautiful end result.

Our children are our dandelions. They are resilient with every stage of growth, even if it's momentarily painful. As a mom, much of their future is unseen to us. As a parachute of a dandelion can spread for miles, what we grow in our children can spread far and wide. What we can do is establish strong roots to fix their eyes on Jesus and spread the good news about Him to all nations.

## WorkHearter Wisdom

How can we navigate the growing pain seasons of transition with our children? Prayer is a good place to start. After that? Talk to another mom—one that is going through the same season or one that has been through it already. Remember, the pain is never wasted. What can we do today to show our children they have a far reach for the kingdom no matter how small? How can we help our children learn how to spread the good news to all nationalities?

# Full Circle

The Lord will fulfill His purpose for me. Lord, Your love is eternal; do not abandon the work of Your hands.

Psalm 138:8 HCSB

One of the most difficult times for me as a mother is to watch my child make the same mistake I made. Parenting experts say we have to let our children make their own mistakes. I agree with their logic, but when you know what the outcome of that mistake is, because you have lived it firsthand, it is difficult to watch their consequences play out.

I was young, single, and pregnant. I would not change my decision to become a mother once I was faced with that decision. It was tough. Money was scarce, and I learned the hard way how to live on my own and raise a baby. I would have preferred my children wait until after marriage and maturing before becoming parents, but my oldest faced the same life decision. It's not easy to be young and a parent, but he is a wonderful father. I was in no way ready to be a grandmother, but I get to watch him be a loving and responsible parent. I'm sure my mom wasn't ready to grandparent when I became a parent either, but I'm blessed to have a grandson to spend time with. In a way, it all came full circle.

As a mother, it is so difficult to pray for your kids in their tumultuous seasons of life, when you really want to just fix it. This verse helps me to remember that all things work together for the good of those who love God, because we have been called to be mothers to these children. It brings me comfort to know that difficult times can be worked out by my Father in heaven and brought full circle in His time.

## WorkHearter Wisdom

Do you worry your kids will make the same mistakes you did? How can you pray for God to reveal the good in those mistakes? How can you remind yourself of the good God made from mistakes you made?

## Quiet Moments of Contemplation: Matthew 6:19–21 NKJV

Do not lay up for yourselves treasures on earth, where moth and rust destroy and where thieves break in and steal; but lay up for yourselves treasures in heaven, where neither moth nor rust destroys and where thieves do not break in and steal. For where your treasure is, there your heart will be also.

I have watched those who work hard get great rewards, but I have also watched those who worked little gain reward on the backs of others. Money or lack of money has been a concern for most of my life. It has caused worry. It has caused heartache—until I figured out money is not my treasure.

As disciples of Christ, our treasure is not monetary rewards. Our treasure is in heaven. God gives us a glimpse of treasure in our children. It is crushing when your children tell you they don't need you anymore because they are making their own money—as if all we provided was money for them. Yes, we did provide funds for their clothing, food, shelter, education, and so on, but more than any of that we provided love. Love is the treasure in heaven. It is the only currency. How guilty are we of telling Jesus we don't need Him when we fear, doubt, or worry—as if the cost of His love and sacrifice was not enough of a treasure for us?

In Ireland they have a saying: "You'll get your reward in heaven." Sometimes it's something a mom says to a child she is comforting out of some childhood disappointment. Later she says it with a twinkle in her eye to that same child, now a teen, who is unhappy with the events of his day. The meaning is the same, and echoes these lines: Your treasure is in heaven. Nothing here can compare, so don't fret, dear one.

## Worry and Want Go Hand in Hand

Cast all your anxiety on him because he cares for you.

1 Peter 5:7 NIV

Take delight in the LORD, and he will give you the desires of your heart.

Psalm 37:4 NIV

All day long he craves for more, but the righteous give without sparing.

Proverbs 21:26 NIV

I have two hands and I can hold two things at a time. Many times, worry and want are what I hold onto. I worry and I want at the same time. When I want to keep something, I worry about losing it. When I want to get something or achieve a goal, I worry I won't be able to complete it. I never really knew worry as a daily habit until my first child was born. The worry came simultaneously upon hearing his first cry. My worry-free days ended with his birth.

We want the best for our children—and so does our Father in heaven. We worry they won't make the right choices and receive the fullest blessing. The difference is God doesn't worry. He guides us lovingly, and He trusts us. He doesn't want us to worry. How do I know? He repeated the sentiment in His Word. We still break His heart when we don't trust Him in those moments, but He doesn't bring it up again and He doesn't want us to, either—including reminding our children about times when they broke our hearts with their decisions. Ask the Lord to go before them. He will go first.

## WorkHearter Wisdom

If we prayed as much as we worry, there would be nothing to worry about. When we stop worrying and start praying, it changes lives. Making Jesus Lord of our lives is believing not only in His wisdom but also in His divine authority. Worry is the plan to destroy your joy—and the power of prayer takes back the joy of your life. Worry is making a costly down payment on a problem you may never have. Keep that down payment and pay it forward in prayer.

Part 3: The Finality of Fall

# Unfamiliar Territory

Jesus answered, "I am the way and the truth and the life. No one comes to the Father except through me."

John 14:6 NIV

Graduating high school from a small town and going to college away from home, you are thrown into unfamiliar territory. To familiarize myself with the new area, I learned new roads, new places to go, and how to get along with new people. I learned the way around campus on foot to time distance between classes. I didn't have GPS back then, so I relied on a paper campus map to help me find my way. It wasn't as useful at night with no light to see the map.

My kids' first route to master when they learned how to drive was the route home. They did have GPS but they also liked to use landmarks. When it was dark, the landmarks didn't look the same. They couldn't see as well without daylight so they relied on GPS to speak the directions to them.

Jesus said He is the way, the truth, and the life. There is not another way to God the Father. Even with GPS, landmarks, daylight, headlights, tour guides, we simply cannot take the route to heaven without Jesus. If we take a shortcut or try another path we think is faster, better, more efficient, we will get lost. Parenting experience can provide life hacks, but there is no hack to life without Jesus. His way is familiar and honest and full of life. His way of life should be the most familiar route we take on our daily journey as parents.

## WorkHearter Wisdom

In life, we simply can't know or learn the way to be better parents without Jesus's guidance. *He* is the only way. We also can't speak truth to our children without Him. Whether it's too hard to be honest or too tough to discipline, we can't do it alone. It's even harder to see the light or give love without Jesus, who is all these things. We can't truly live and have an abundant life without knowing and following Jesus.

## Peace from Permission

> Ask and it will be given to you; seek and you will find; knock and the door will be opened to you.
>
> Matthew 7:7 NIV

My daughter is in college, and she is dedicated to working in the architecture studio long hours. Her work ethic is unmatched. She spends so much time on work, she rarely gives herself time to rest and have some fun. She acquired this dedication to work and inability to balance from both of her parents, who are self-employed and bring work home.

As her parents, we didn't give ourselves permission to rest, take a vacation, and truly disconnect from work, so she didn't have that example to live by herself. Each time someone gave me permission to take my time it was a gift with no tag, card, or fancy wrapping paper. Permission is a freeing concept. When you have permission, it takes away guilt, shame, fear. It's much like grace. Give children grace more than they ask for it. Give it so freely that there is some left for you too.

If no one has told you today or this week or this month, I give you permission to pause. You have permission to pray. Permission to fall down at the cross and lay down your mistakes. Permission to rest your soul as long as you need. As you ask Jesus for grace, it will be given in abundance.

## WorkHearter Wisdom

If we as adults in our own wisdom still need permission, how much more do our children need permission to pause? If we give ourselves permission, we can show them they can have permission ... to say no, to cancel on tasks that are too taxing, and to rest.

## A Mothers' Intuition

My sheep listen to my voice; I know them, and they follow me.

John 10:27 NIV

I have taken some trips away from home without my kids. But even in their absence, I would hear someone else's child say "Mama" just the way my own did. It sounded so familiar I had to look twice to make sure my own child didn't *somehow* get away from home to where I was.

Mother's intuition can recognize need in another child's voice when they cry out to their mama, even if that child isn't ours. Sometimes we hear it before they are even finished speaking. We recognize it because it is familiar, and we hear the same love in their child's cry.

I think Jesus's mom would have recognized Him when He was talking on the road to Emmaus (John 24). I think she would have heard it before the first word was completely uttered. A mother's intuition knows our children better than anyone else. We recognize little warning signs, even when our kids try to act like everything is fine.

## WorkHearter Wisdom

Jesus recognizes us in that same way when we are lost or when we get lonely. He recognizes our voice when we cry out to Him. We learn to recognize Jesus in the way He recognizes us. We recognize the familiar and loving response within ourselves. We need to show our children how to recognize the love of Jesus by showing it to them firsthand. The love of Jesus has to become so familiar to them that it is easily recognizable. Our kids won't recognize Jesus if they don't see a reflection of Him in us first.

# Close Calls

Jesus answered him, "Truly I tell you, today you will be with me in paradise."

Luke 23:43 NIV

Growing up in a small town with no internet, cell phones, or obvious mischief to get into, we created our own mischief. We had some close calls with racing cars down the street, sneaking out of our homes, and making numerous questionable decisions. I shudder to think about the number of close calls I experienced in a matter of moments during my tumultuous years.

We may be able to count the close calls we know about, but there are many times we have been protected that we have no idea about. Close calls are not all negative. Jesus gave the criminal who hung with Him on the cross the most positive close call. He told the man he would be with Him in paradise.

We get close calls to be around and minister to others in the name of Jesus. I believe we are a breath away from anyone in need and if we just reach out to those around us, we can be the close call they need. Our children need us most when they are having a close call. We want to be the ones they reach out to during those moments. We need to talk to them about trust and possibly using safe words to pick up the phone if they are experiencing a close call. We need to drop everything and come to pick them up, no questions asked. We need to give them grace to be honest with us when they make a mistake. We need to show them they could not disappoint us. We want them to know they can come to us when moments matter. We are all one close call away—bad or good—from a lifesaving situation.

## WorkHearter Wisdom

When was the last time you had to answer someone's close call? Were you available to give that call a safe place to land without questions, shame, or guilt? How can we show the grace we need when it's too close for comfort?

## Divorce Does Not Define Me

I am the light of the world. Whoever follows me will never walk in darkness but will have the light of life.

John 8:12 NIV

I have been divorced. Divorce is a dark part of my life and my history; it has affected me but it is not a definition of me or who I am. Although I was a participant and it didn't just happen to me like a car accident or a life-altering disease, it left scars and numbness no one can see or feel but me. I feel the consequences of it along with my children. It inconveniences no one else as much as it does us.

Outsiders think they know the details of my divorce and who was to blame. They use shame in word or deed to remind me of it. The dictionary defines the word *definition* in two ways: first, a statement of the exact meaning of a word; and second, the degree or distinctness in outline of an object, image, or sound, especially of an image in a photograph or on a screen. There is no mention of a person or identity in either of these.

Divorce does not define a person or their life. It is merely an outline or a degree of one aspect, a snapshot image of a time in a person's life. It could be one chapter or a few but not the entire book of life.

## WorkHearter Wisdom

Our mistakes leave scars but don't have to leave us in the dark. We can walk in the light of life that is Jesus. We aren't defined by our mistakes, scars, or even our accomplishments. Nothing (No thing) can define us. Jesus chose to keep his scars so even our scars can be used. We are not defined by moments that leave marks on our life, we are defined and redeemed by Jesus and His eternal mark of salvation. He defined who we are (His) not because of anything we did or didn't do, but because of what He did.

# Rich

> Command those who are rich in this present world not to be arrogant nor to put their hope in wealth, which is so uncertain, but to put their hope in God, who richly provides us with everything for our enjoyment.
>
> 1 Timothy 6:17 NIV

Growing up, we were not among the wealthiest families in town. We had what we needed and we used what we had. We learned young to use what's in front of you. If you can't find a knife, use a fork. If there is no fork, use something else. In my house, we couldn't wait on washing a dish or utensil to eat if we were hungry. In a house with several siblings, you learn to eat fast or the meal will be gone. We were quite the animals when it came to food consumption, but it did teach me a lesson about tools. Tools are not what makes the recipe taste better. If you are hungry, it's the nourishment that counts. The time involved in process and the ingredients in the food are valuable.

When I got my own house, I enjoyed buying tools and kitchen gadgets. I loved having a tool for every type of recipe right in my very own kitchen. I felt wealthy to have a corn scraper and not have to use a knife to make fried corn, or an apple peeler slicer to avoid cutting my thumb trying to peel an apple. But the value was not in those gadgets I could now afford. It was in the joy of cooking for my family.

I have always had trouble asking for help or even accepting help offered without asking. I tend to lean on myself more than others. Multiple surgeries and illnesses have forced me to humbly accept help over the years. I knew I needed it and gladly accepted it even if I didn't really have a choice. My family and I still needed to eat, but I was not able to provide in those recovery days. I was certain I needed help. When you are sick, there is not much better than a delivered meal that you didn't have to cook for yourself or your family. I didn't care if they had the right utensil when they prepared the meal in those moments of my desperation. I was nourished and that's what mattered. God richly provided for my need.

## WorkHearter Wisdom

God knows what we need and when we are in need. He gives more than a little help. We only need to accept it. We have a choice to be arrogant and put hope in our own tools or put our hope in God to provide. His provision is much richer than any tools we have or think we need.

# Wearing Out Your Welcome

The God who made the world and everything in it is the Lord of heaven and earth and does not live in temples built by human hands.

Acts 17:24 NIV

And how can anyone preach unless they are sent? As it is written: "How beautiful are the feet of those who bring good news!"

Romans 10:15 NIV

Getting to church or the gym is only half the battle. After I get ready, mentally arm wrestle my kids to get out of bed and get ready in time to go to church or school, I normally rush to make it to service or the gym on time.

Once I'm there, there are a few things that make me want to leave. Coincidentally, these things exist at both places. When I walk into church or the gym and I see a clique of people hovering around the machines at the gym or door entries at church, I feel like an outsider. If there is no room to walk around the track or all the machines are full at the gym, I don't see a place to fit in. If I can't find a seat at church, I feel the same way. Sometimes, I feel this way before I even set foot inside the building if I can't find a place to park. At both establishments, unwelcoming stares are a deterrent to keeping me present.

Churches and gyms have a great deal in common. All of us can belong there and we can always go in our current condition. We are all there to get better. That's why it should be the most welcoming door to walk through. All we want is for everyone to get better by being there.

Pain is often what happens in churches or gyms ... or it can be the reason most people go there. If you suffer an injury, physical therapy requires you to exercise through the pain. If you have a heartbreak, you may seek church to ease or work through your pain. We grow after experiencing pain. Our muscles and joints get better and grow from the painful soreness following exercise. Our joy grows bigger after heartache, remorse, guilt, and shame. Babies growing in their mother's bellies cause painful ligament stretching to make room for them to grow bigger. Mothers take the pain for the sake of their child. If we experience growing pains in our churches, we take the pain for the sake of the child of God.

Whatever membership we take, remember God is not confined to a building built by human hands. He is the creator and Lord of all. He can get to anyone anywhere. If someone can not physically get to church, we are to take the church to them. We can do this by ministering to those in prison, in the hospital, in a funeral home, or someone in pain in general.

## WorkHearter Wisdom

We are all called to spread the good news of Christ so others can hear and be able to call on Him. God doesn't require membership to belong to Him. He only requires a willing spirit to be part of His family. All those who call on His name will be saved. All we need to do is be willing to be sent and trust Him with the rest. He is waiting to welcome you—and we can make sure our children know He welcomes them also, no matter their age or ability. We will never wear out our welcome in His presence.

# Finality of Fall

Therefore, as God's chosen people, holy and dearly loved, clothe yourselves with compassion, kindness, humility, gentleness and patience.

Colossians 3:12 NIV

Of all the seasons, fall is the most predictable in the South. We see leaves changing colors, smoking tobacco barns, and fall festivals. It begins officially at the autumnal equinox around the end of the third week of September.

We mark our seasons on the calendar to know the beginning but don't know the end. Driving through our Tennessee hills, the changing leaves fall with the wind and cover the ground. We know from experience the leaves will fall and winter will settle in shortly. Even though we know fall will end with the last leaves, we don't know the exact day. It lies somewhere between the first day of fall and first day of winter but in the South, they are roughly three months apart. Fall is a season that never wears out her welcome, and it seems to go by too fast every year.

The last day is final whether a day is designated on the calendar or not. Winter comes early some years with barren trees, and the finality of fall becomes real quickly. It always makes me wish I had taken more time appreciating the changing leaves before the last day of fall. Like a peacock takes time to grow a train full of impressive feathers, as mothers it takes us awhile to recognize our children growing too fast.

My children all had "last days" growing up. There were last days of naptime, last days of snaggletooth grins, last days of wearing braces, last days of elementary, last days of middle and high school, and last days of my picking out their clothes. With my girls, it was last days of battles over clothes. My style was not in sync with their style, and I couldn't keep up with the trends. Last days were only noted on the calendar when it came to school years. The last days of transition over to a new phase were not warned or anticipated until just like that it was over. Like our final fall leaves, I watched my children change a little over time … but then a lot all at once. And at the same time, I mourned the end of the season (most of the time). Over and over again, I wished I had spent more time appreciating the season of their life before it changed. Just like my sadness at the end of autumn, I mourned the season of parenting. Remember to treasure the season while you are in it. In every season, clothe yourself with compassion, kindness, humility, gentleness and patience. Those will remain in style no matter the season.

## WorkHearter Wisdom

God watches us change daily and—like the fall leaves that bring tourists from all over to watch leaves change from green to crimson red, fiery orange, or bright yellow in the fall—He is watching us with awe. He appreciates our changes and knows that even when a season is over, another one is beginning in us.

## Taste Buds

Give us today our daily bread.

Matthew 6:11 CSB

Like newborn infants, desire the pure spiritual milk, so that you may grow by it for your salvation, since you have tasted that the Lord is good.   1 Peter 2:2 HCSB

For the word of God is alive and active. Sharper than any double-edged sword, it penetrates even to dividing soul and spirit, joints and marrow; it judges the thoughts and attitudes of the heart.

Hebrews 4:12 NIV

I disliked the flavor of broccoli and sweet potatoes until my twenties. I didn't like avocado until my thirties. All are now some of my favorite foods. My taste buds changed—but also my mindset changed. I changed my mind from thinking these were yucky foods to knowing they were healthy, flavorful, good foods. If I'm being honest, I never really gave myself a chance to enjoy them when I was younger. I did what my kids do and barely tasted a tiny sample before turning up my nose. My palate was not refined.

Green vegetables like broccoli and Brussels sprouts along with green fruits like kiwi and avocado were disgusting to me as an adolescent for the simple fact they were green. The comfort foods I liked were bland foods that were familiar. In my early twenties I discovered how delicious broccoli could be cold in a broccoli ranch salad, then hot in a cheesy casserole, and I have not looked back. A decade later I tasted an avocado in a newly presented way—with a mandarin orange. The complement of another ingredient made these greens not just taste edible but delicious to me. What a treat I would have missed if I never tried them with a new ingredient added!

It's like a new friend complementing a friend group who thought they had enough friends, or someone bringing a significant other along that makes them feel more comfortable. If we are not open to new opportunities, we can miss out. Conversely, we can be reluctant to change and will stay in a toxic relationship or endure more than we should due to its being familiar even if it's bland. Even misery can be comforting if it is familiar. Instead, we should be open to learning something new to grow our palate. We are not to be comfortable in our spiritual growth. Like a ripe avocado tastes good once we give it a real try, God provides us with spiritual milk to grow in us if we give His word a chance to nourish us. We must open it and be open to it. Each time we read it, our thoughts and attitudes change.

## WorkHearter Wisdom

Our taste buds may change. Our seasons of life may change. One thing that will never change is God's Word. It is the daily bread we need to survive the day, the season. It is alive and active. No matter the time of life, our hunger for guidance only God can give should always be savored and allowed to grow.

# Worthy of It All

You are worthy, our Lord and God,
to receive glory and honor and power,
for you created all things.

*Revelation 4:11 NIV*

But if we walk in the light, as he is in the light, we have fellowship with one another, and the blood of Jesus, his Son, purifies us from all sin.

*1 John 1:7 NIV*

My kids have a bad habit of throwing away silverware. They find it easier to throw it away than wash it or they forget it's on the paper plate when they don't pay attention and toss it into the trash. This leads to me buying more silverware, so it costs me money. I know they don't always do this on purpose but it happens, nonetheless. It's a resource they take for granted. When silverware is dwindling, they assume more will appear in the drawer like magic.

How guilty are we as children of God that we assume God will put more tools into our drawer when we throw them away accidentally? He gives us all tools to get through life, and we casually toss them aside without appreciation. We keep our Bibles on the nightstand but they turn into a decoration and get dusty when we don't open them as frequently as we should. We don't pay attention and end up wasting our time on nonsensical activities. Time is our most precious commodity, and we don't spend it in God's Word enough. He is worthy of it all. He is worthy of our time. He is worthy of our attention. He created us. He created our children.

## WorkHearter Wisdom

How can we blame our children for wastefulness if we ourselves are wasting our valuable resources? Our children see how we spend our time. They see the dust on our Bible. They see us entranced on our cell phones. They are worthy of our time and our attention. If we show them their worthiness, they will not look for it to be echoed by others. God did not go into the homes with blood on doorframes in Exodus 12:23 to see if those inside were worthy of saving. Only the blood of Jesus makes us worthy. We are covered by the blood. Spending time in God's Word and putting aside earthly praise to rightfully give God the glory will be a witness to them that He is worthy in our eyes and in our lives. Lord, help us to show our children your worthiness.

## Secrets We Keep

How, then, can they call on the one they have not believed in? And how can they believe in the one of whom they have not heard? And how can they hear without someone preaching to them? And how can anyone preach unless they are sent? As it is written: "How beautiful are the feet of those who bring good news!"

Romans 10:14–15 NIV

I kept many secrets from my parents as a teenager. Secrets I thought would get me into trouble or secrets I thought would keep them from worrying. Either way, secrets were kept. My reasons didn't matter as much as the secret itself. One time, I jumped into a rock quarry pool because an older schoolmate dared me to. Even he didn't think I would do it, but I wasn't going to pass up a dare. I was scared but did it anyway, and I did survive so I thought there was no harm in not telling my parents about it. When my parents found out, I was grounded to keep me from attempting to enter that dangerous environment again. It wasn't the environment that was dangerous, it was the dare and my inability to pass it up. Telling my parents this secret may have saved me from further danger.

My baby sister had a secret disease of alcoholism and addiction. After many treatments and rehabs, the final time she kept her relapse a secret from us it killed her. What we didn't know, killed her. Some secrets we keep can kill us if we keep them to ourselves and don't get help.

Jesus isn't a secret in the South. Most people I know have heard His name, prayed to His name, or said His name in vain. There is a reason this part of the country is called the Bible Belt; Jesus is not a secret here. You will not travel far before seeing a church billboard or other visible signs of Jesus's teaching. In other parts of the world, there are remote villages who have never heard of Him. To them, He is a secret. They don't even know they are lost. In some parts of the world, it is also dangerous to teach about Jesus. The secret of Jesus should never be a secret at all. Sharing the story of Jesus is lifesaving. It is the greatest gift we can give and greatest true story ever told. The greatest problem we face is the lost. He is the good news and solution everyone needs.

## WorkHearter Wisdom

Jesus isn't dangerous and shouldn't be kept a secret. Quite the contrary! We should share Him with everyone—especially with the generation we are raising. Like being a mom, we don't know always know what to do until we know. We know to always point to Him. How will the other parts of the world be reached if we keep the secret to ourselves? Our children could be instrumental in reaching those who are lost. It is our duty to spread the good news so all can hear.

## The Best Boss

"You have heard that it was said, 'Eye for eye, and tooth for tooth.' But I tell you, do not resist an evil person. If anyone slaps you on the right cheek, turn to them the other cheek also."

Matthew 5:38–40 NIV

I've been fortunate to have more than one best boss. I had one that breathed life into my spiritual life by requiring all employees to attend a Monday morning devotional. I had one that trusted my judgment completely, even when she knew I might be withholding some information. But another *best* boss actually gave his best in life and death and after—just like Jesus did for all of us.

I mentioned him in a previous post as the man I met at my first in-service as a teacher. As a new teacher, I got a classroom with minimal supplies, outdated textbooks, and no computers. My supervisor had been appointed a few weeks before school started. His first order of business was to ask what I needed. He even told me, "I want you to be successful, how can I help?" It wasn't lip service, he really meant it.

The best boss was the best because he meant what he said. He was sincere. He truly wanted to help me do my best. He would also ask me for help with artistic ideas he had for his granddaughter. He valued me as an artist. That meant so much to me. I never got the chance to tell him how much. He died suddenly on a Thursday afternoon in a fatal car accident. A student driving the other car was at fault and not injured. However, his wife decided not to pursue charges. She knew her husband would not have faulted the student. She knew his heart, and she honored his memory.

He'd made such an impact, his coworkers at the central office asked if they could distribute his workload for a few months after he had passed. They couldn't bear to see him replaced just yet. This continued for almost a year. His colleagues would rather do more work than see their friend/mentor replaced. It made me question the cliché that we are all replaceable in the workplace. His legacy lives on in the form of an annual scholarship for students in the school district. One of his former students named a street after him in a new residential development and he has a memorial ball field in his name. Even though he's gone, he's still helping and serving students, which is what he lived for anyway. He was different and that made him remarkable.

## WorkHearter Wisdom

What leader/boss/role model has positively impacted your life? How can you continue their legacy of influence? Have you told them how much you appreciate them? We can all seek to implement the ways of an inspirational leader, whether we had an experience with a great boss or not. Jesus was the epitome of inspirational leader and His life is remarkable. When we are tempted to retaliate against those who come at us or our children, all we can do is let the Spirit lead us to be different from the world and really mean it. Let Jesus be the boss of your heart today.

## Traveling Companions for Life

For if they fall, one will lift up his fellow. But woe to him who is alone when he falls and has not another to lift him up!

Ecclesiastes 4:10 ESV

Keep on loving one another as brothers and sisters.

Hebrews 13:1 NIV

Friends come and go, and even extended family members can drift in and out of your life. Siblings—brothers and sisters—are for life. Whether you are one or ten years apart, you share a home and parents together. Those memories of childhood are strong and formative. The only ones with you throughout the ups and downs are your siblings. Love them or tolerate them, they are there through thick and thin as your traveling companions for life. Your brothers and sisters travel with you on family road trips, holidays, family reunions, funerals, weddings, and celebrations. They travel with you through most of life's defining moments.

We took family vacations every summer always in a car on a road trip. We also traveled by car to our grandparents' homes every holiday. We spent many hours in a small space with lots of frustration and laughter. Only my siblings know what "hang it out the window" means. Those same companions have remained constant in my life. We all live in the same town. My siblings walked with me down the aisle, more than once, and sat with me after my divorces. They helped me move when my marriages failed. They also held my hand at funerals when time seemed to stand still and not move at all.

When we move away from family, we often look for friends who become like family to us. If we are born with siblings, we may gravitate toward those who remind us of our siblings. For only children, friends are the siblings they never had. If I hadn't had siblings, I wouldn't have learned the meaning of sibling rivalry. I wouldn't have tried to one-up my younger sisters playing soccer when they started. (I did not one-up them, by the way since they both played at the college level.)

I also wouldn't have heard the song "Give Me Jesus," which to this day remains one of my favorite songs. It reminds me to give them Jesus—my kids, my husband, my friends, and my siblings. My baby sister is safe with Jesus now. I'm not sad about that. But I'm sad that I didn't fully appreciate the gift of having her as a sibling. I was ungrateful and took her for granted. It hurts a great deal because the loss was so great.

As parents, we can instill appreciation for siblings with our children. We can help them foster friendships that will last a lifetime. As Christians, we have numerous brothers and sisters in Christ to travel with us through life.

### WorkHearter Wisdom

How can we best nurture the relationships with our sibling companions and foster love in our children for their siblings? How can we—who may know them best—help them up when they fall? If we don't have siblings in our family, what a gift we have in our brothers and sisters in the family of Christ to help us when we fall. How can we lean on our siblings in Christ when we are struggling?

## What We Pass Down to Our Children

Be kind and compassionate to one another, forgiving each other, just as in Christ God forgave you.

Ephesians 4:32 NIV

The child will not share the guilt of the parent, nor will the parent share the guilt of the child.

Ezekiel 18:20 NIV

Parents often pass down mannerisms, physical characteristics, and personality quirks to their children. All these traits given to us are a part of our history. I have passed down my snort laugh to one child, my need to make lists to another child, my dimple to one of my children and my stubbornness to another child. Each one of these characteristics have been with me most of my life.

There is also shame in my past. It hasn't been present my entire life, but if I'm not careful, I will unintentionally pass shame down to my children. That is a burden they are not equipped to carry. The familiar phrase "the apple doesn't fall far from the tree" resonates for me, reminding me how easily we can drop shame onto our children. Shame likes to be shared or passed onto others. If it's shared, we tend to think ours doesn't feel as shameful.

I am not athletic and was rarely first pick for the school intramural sports teams. One year, on a basketball intramural team, I was passed the basketball in front of our entire middle school audience. I decided to take my shot and made the basket. Unfortunately, it was for the other team. My team was embarrassed, and I was teased about that for years. I felt shame because the teasing continued long after that game, even though it really didn't matter the next week. As trivial as the incident it sounds, I never played intramural basketball again. A middle school moment sealed that decision.

Our children can experience shame in school settings from teachers and/or other students. My daughter was in second grade when she first experienced shame at school. Someone in her class decided one day that her eyebrows were too close together. She was in tears asking me to pluck her eyebrows at the age of seven. That person passed their shame onto her like a basketball player passes a ball to another teammate shooting their shot and making a basket at her expense.

One of the places I didn't anticipate I would experience shame was at church. Churches are communities that help us heal, grow, and learn from our mistakes. Not all churches are created equal, though, and I was shamed publicly for my divorce. My daughter witnessed this and carried it—*my* shame—with her as a young child. She was innocently on my team. Instead of missing the shots of shame directed at me, she got passed a ball of shame by being on my team.

## WorkHearter Wisdom

Kindness and compassion go much further than shame ever will. Shame stops goodness and mercy. Shame falsely says

Jesus didn't do enough by dying on the cross for my past to be redeemed. Shame is not helpful. And since it is not helpful, Jesus doesn't want it in our lives or the lives of our children. We must be careful not to pass down our shame onto our innocent children who have nothing to be ashamed of.

I have been guilty with each of my children of passing on my expectations and my fears to them. If I see a spider or a snake, I will teach them to be very afraid because I am afraid. If I work hard and accomplish many goals, I will expect them to do the same. As parents, we are aptly accused of living vicariously through our children. It is part pride and part shame.

Lord Jesus, take the shame from us and our children. Show us your kindness and help us to show compassion to others as you did to us.

## Fathers and Daughters

Carry each other's burdens, and in this way you will fulfill the law of Christ.

Galatians 6:2 NIV

One of the hardest parts of being a daughter of aging parents, in this case my father, is watching him struggle to walk. When he started using a cane, I had to come to grips with the fact that he was aging. His appearance aged over the years, but he still had a youthful attitude. Recently, seeing him not being able to walk with ease was the kicker for me. I watched my grandmother not be able to walk without a cane, and thought it was normal for her age. However, watching my dad age has been more difficult to accept. I look at photos from as recently as five years ago and he seems so much younger. And I know he only gets one life to live same as me. I am anticipating the grief of a time I don't want to anticipate.

As kids growing up watching *ourselves* change, we seldom realize we are also watching our parents grow up until they are older; we look back on photos from a time they seemed old, yet now they look so young in them. Watching the man who walked you down the aisle at your wedding, taught you how to drive, the strong man who worked multiple jobs to support his family, struggle to go up a step gives a daughter a helpless feeling. He is stubborn and will not easily accept help. As his daughter, I inherited that stubborn character trait.

My dad is blunt and doesn't always think through his thoughts before speaking. You may say he's a little rough around the edges, like me. He was raised rough and rowdy in rural Kentucky. He fought, got in trouble, but he was the baby and my grandparents had lost an older son, so he was spoiled. He didn't think before he spoke. He went into the military and served in the US army. He didn't get much better at holding his tongue there either.

He's rough around the edges—but the edges keep him from getting harmed by others. Compliments put both of us off, we usually think someone is up to something. Kindness is odd to us because we don't regularly receive it. But as I watch him knowing he needs help and won't take it, I am reminded of the idiom, "The bigger they are the harder they fall." He's the hero in our family and has big shoes to fill. My daughter feels the same way about her dad. She loves her father and he is her hero. That is a heavy burden for any one man to carry. Burdens cause us to fall when they get too heavy. My dad always says, "Everything falls, I don't know why." I know why-to show us we all need help.

## WorkHearter Wisdom

We are called to help carry each other's burdens. We all need a little help even if we are stubborn, even if we don't want to be a burden or seem weak by accepting help. Have you ever pushed through when everything is falling apart although you knew you needed help? Could help have eased your burden? Lord, bring to mind those not readily apparent who we can assist today to lighten their heavy load—and help us to remember you have called others to help us carry our burdens too.

PART 3: THE FINALITY OF FALL

# Everyone Wants to See a Miracle

"Unless you people see signs and wonders," Jesus told him, "you will never believe."

John 4:48 NIV

Everyone wants to witness a miracle. They want to cheer it on and be a part of something wonderful. There are miracles all around us every day that happen but are not recognized. It's a miracle we wake up every morning with so many factors against us. The enemy throws every dagger at us and brings up every battle scar we have from past mistakes. It's a miracle that flowers bloom in the spring after the bitter cold of winter.

We are miracles in the eyes of our Savior, even if we don't believe it. And God gave us tiny miracles to watch—front row center—while they grow up. We don't deserve the miracles of our children, but He gives them to us freely. All we have to do is open our eyes to see them. We think we want to see the larger-than-life miracles of walking on water, turning water to wine, or multiplying food to feed five thousand. We forget the everyday miracles right before our eyes.

It's a miracle a seed can turn into food with water and sunshine. It's a miracle an addict who makes it through the night can choose to wake up sober in the morning light. A miracle can be a job offer that we thought impossible. A miracle can look like marriage surviving betrayal and hurt or a teenager learning how to say thank you. Miracles are all around us. We just need to open our eyes and see them. We don't need miracles to believe in the promise of heaven. There are glimpses of heaven in our homes every day in the eyes and laughter of our children—if we only look.

## WorkHearter Wisdom

My son is a miracle baby who survived being born at 26 weeks. My oldest daughter is my rainbow baby miracle conceived after a miscarriage. She married another rainbow baby and now have their own rainbow baby, my granddaughter, after suffering multiple miscarriages. My middle daughter is a miracle that survived many pregnancy complications and hospitalizations. It's a miracle I got pregnant with my youngest daughter at a geriatric age. I forget the miracles in my life since it didn't feel newsworthy happening to me. My kids are ranked high up on my list of every day miracles. What miracle did you see today? Keep a list of daily miracles and review it with your kids at the end of the week. Make a game of it like a scavenger hunt. You may surprise yourself with how many are present when we start to seek them out.

# Imitation

For you have been called for this purpose, since Christ also suffered for you, leaving you an example for you to follow in His steps.

1 Peter 2:21 NASB1995

*Imitation is the sincerest form of flattery* echoes in my mind any time my children get frustrated by one of their siblings taking their clothes or copying their choices. My mom used to repeat this phrase when my items went missing, and I found my younger sister wearing them. I thought she looked silly trying to wear my clothes that were obviously too big for her. No way I took it as a compliment like Mom suggested.

Fast forward to present day, and we are all trying to imitate what we see on social media. Parents and kids alike are influenced by accounts they hope to imitate. Parents may be influenced by strangers or well-known elites. Teens are influenced by the celebrities they follow online. There are so many edited versions of posts and filters on photos used that it's difficult to discern what's real or imitation. Some pick and choose which parts to imitate. The biggest influencers have the largest following and get paid for sponsored ads in their newsfeed promoting all sorts of products—purchasers are simply imitating the influencer.

We could be imitating Jesus as the sincerest form of flattery. He didn't use filters or edit His teachings. I don't want to imitate all areas—like sleeping on the ground outside or walking everywhere I go like Jesus did—but I do want to imitate Christ in His real love for the unlovable. I want to imitate Christ in His empathy for the hurting. I want to imitate Christ in spreading the good news to as many who will hear it. That's *the* influencer I want to follow.

## WorkHearter Wisdom

How can we imitate Jesus in today's world and teach our children to do the same—as He is the greatest influencer of all time? How many followers would Jesus have on His social media channels today?

# Quiet Moments of Contemplation: Isaiah 30:21 ESV

Whether you turn to the right or to the left, your ears will hear a voice behind you, saying, "This is the way; walk in it."

We all make mistakes. Big ones, little ones. God's chosen people had been captive for so long that they forgot who to trust until He reminded them. Sometimes there's so much going on—and so much competing commentary about what's going on—that it's easy to get confused. And that's when it's easy to make mistakes.

I have many memories of being lost before cell phones and GPS. It was the worst feeling to have no idea which direction to go and trying to find a pay phone to call my mom for directions. I was scared, panicked, and got disoriented navigating in circles going nowhere. All I wanted was someone to tell me which way to go. How loved are we that God gave us direction and we will not under any condition be lost again! We can trust Him. Even if we're lost, frantic, confused … if we listen to God, we won't get lost.

Our children look to us for direction. The only discernment we need is to point them to Jesus in all circumstances.

## Ones We Miss Most

Dear children, let us not love with words or speech but with actions and in truth.

1 John 3:18 NIV

I have missed many of my children's sporting events due to my job duties. I missed almost every one my oldest daughter's volleyball games due to traveling for work during her senior year. She didn't always play, so I didn't think she cared if I missed them. She took shots but missed many of them. Even though I didn't think she cared if I was there to see her miss, I was wrong. I think back to my senior year of high school, and I remember those who showed up for me and my events. Those faces were comforting to see in a crowd of strangers. They brought me calm. My parents rarely told us they loved us with words. They showed us. I was fortunate to know my family loved me whether they showed up or not, but the showing up for me proved what I knew to be true. Those were the good old days for me.

The moments we miss aren't the prettiest ones wrapped up in a shiny bow. The people we miss most aren't our prettiest relatives. They aren't the perfect family members or friends. They don't speak the most eloquent words or have the highest degrees. The people we miss most when they are gone are the ones who knew us at our worst and always showed up. It didn't matter how they were dressed or the type of car they drove. It only mattered they were the ones who tried their best and who showed up. They were the ones who loved us so much we felt a hole in our heart when they left.

The ones we miss the most filled us up with so much love that we couldn't hold it in and it overflowed. When all the love overflowed, we felt the loss because we can't give it back to them once they are gone—and that creates a void. But we can give it to others who need it and may not have anyone who showed up for them. We can show up in action and in truth for our children and give them so much love that it fills them up so they can love others.

## WorkHearter Wisdom

What little things do you remember most growing up? What little moments are your favorite memories of your children? Our favorite memories are not the big planned out celebrations or speeches in life—most likely they are the routine sometimes mundane moments of daily activity where a laugh, hug or a smile was needed more than any words. Let's show up today for our children and smile, hug, laugh and love them like there is no tomorrow and treat every day like the good old days.

## PART 4

# *The Weary Days of Winter*

Winter is a vacation time for many who only take off during the holidays. It is also a time of rest for those who work outdoors during the long days of the growing season. Winter provides a time for the soil to rest, a time of hibernation for some animals, and unfortunately a desolate time for those who are alone and not getting outdoors as much.

This season is also a time of increased sickness, such as the flu or a cold, so hugs aren't given as freely. Less contact with others can prove lonely when you don't have many people to spend time with.

Parenting during a winter season with a child can also prove lonely even with some grief mixed in. Adult conversation and connection is vital to companionship. I ask a lot of "Why's?" in winter. Why is it so cold? Why is it so dark? We can prepare for the cold, dark days during the other seasons in order to survive, storing away morsels of wonderful memories during the growing seasons and breaking them out as needed—like the tomatoes grandma canned in late summer—during winter.

That said, winter in the U.S. brings reasons to gather, too, like Christmas and New Year's Eve and Day. We may be growing or sowing during winter seasons but we don't have to be thriving. So it's a mixed bag, winter.

Lord, give us rest on weary days. Help us regain our strength and fill us with warm hearts in the cold, lonely season of winter. Remind us you are working when we are at rest and we can rely on you fully. Please give us glimpses of spring shining through these dreary days. Help us to remember who we are in you when we feel like our identity outside of being a mom is fading. Break our hearts for what breaks yours so we can realize our purpose and gear up for that work.

> He says, "Be still, and know that I am God; I will be exalted among the nations, I will be exalted in the earth."
>
> Psalm 46:10 NIV

## Rest Does Not Equal Laziness

Sweet is the sleep of a laborer, whether he eats little or much, but the full stomach of the rich will not let him sleep.

*Ecclesiastes 5:12 ESV*

Let my soul be at rest again,
for the LORD has been good to me.

*Psalm 116:7 NLT*

It is vain for you to rise up early, to sit up late, to eat the bread of sorrows: for so he giveth his beloved sleep.

*Psalm 127:2 KJV*

I've heard this verse in Ecclesiastes summarized as those with *more* can't sleep due to worry of losing what they have. Perhaps. But the ability to rest is a desirable trait for all of us. It increases in value the older I become.

I used to think rest was for the lazy. I spent tireless days and restless nights spinning my wheels to get ahead of the next thing I had to do and attempting to be all things to all people. I had an abundance of obligations and a scarcity of rest. I worked multiple jobs because that the example my father set. There was no time for rest. Rest felt foreign to me, like I was forgetting to do something. I had to slowly change my mindset to realize a candle burning at both ends burns out quicker.

Resting does not equate to laziness. Babies grow from rest. So do we. Work and rest are a partnership. They need each other. If you work, you need rest and when you rest, your work will improve because everything is balanced. If you love, your soul needs rest from fear or worry. In nature, the ground rests in winter to be able to bloom in the spring. Rest may feel like boredom for children, but boredom gives birth to creativity.

Rest sometimes can be mental as much as physical rest. If you lie awake at night, unable to move into sleep mode, your body is resting but your mind is not. It takes practice to turn your mind off for true rest. Sometimes it's just a case of giving yourself permission. We all need rest. So if you need permission from someone, anyone, to slow down, rest, and take your time, you have mine.

The Bible points us to who gives us true rest: God. If you have trouble resting—mentally or physically—ask the giver of rest Himself for it. He is where you will find rest. If we plant the seeds, God promises the harvest. We can rest in that fact.

## WorkHearter Wisdom

Do you struggle with rest? Why do you think *not* resting will help you? Do you think you need permission? Try reading Scripture instead. Or pray if you cannot sleep. When you are in the presence of the Lord during prayer, you are in the safest, most peaceful place to rest and sleep will come quickly. Don't feel guilty for sleeping in during winter, even the plants are sleeping with the pollinators within their leaves.

# Angels Among Us

Do not forget to show hospitality to strangers, for by so doing some people have shown hospitality to angels without knowing it.

Hebrews 13:2 NIV

When my oldest daughter was in preschool, we were driving early one chilly morning when she pointed and told me to look at the people on the roof of a building. My curiosity was piqued, since it was so cold outside. I looked to see if they were replacing the roof on the old building. When I looked up, there was not a single person up there. She was surprised I could not see anyone. Yes, she was little, but I do believe there are angels among us. The Bible tells me so.

Winter brings many beggars on the side of the road and in parking lots asking for help. Whether they have been stranded by a flat tire, broken down car on the side of the road, or ran out of money to get to their destination, they need hospitality and grace from strangers. I may never see what my contribution, however small it might be, helps them but it doesn't mean it isn't needed.

These days it gets harder to know who is truly in need of hospitality. All we can do is let the Holy Spirit lead us. Scripture states we will not know if we are helping angels or not, so why risk it? The safest way to teach our children how to help strangers is to use the resources of nonprofit organizations and familiarize ourselves with those organizational needs. It can be something as simple as a lemonade stand to raise funds for foster children ministry to give them a safe place to wait on their placements.

## WorkHearter Wisdom

What organizations exist in your community to help others? How can we participate as a family to demonstrate hospitality to strangers for our children who haven't seen what that looks like? If you don't know where to start, a good place for children to recognize other children needing hospitality is locating nearby foster child organizations, toy drives, and angel tree donation spots. If we foster in them a willingness to show hospitality, they will foster a love for others and learn to recognize the need.

## Mary and Martha

But Martha was distracted by all the preparations that had to be made. She came to him and asked, "Lord, don't you care that my sister has left me to do the work by myself? Tell her to help me!"

"Martha, Martha," the Lord answered, "you are worried and upset about many things, but few things are needed—or indeed only one. Mary has chosen what is better, and it will not be taken away from her."

Luke 10:40–42 NIV

I tend to think staying busy helps the tears from pouring out. If I'm grieving a change in seasons for my child, a change of seasons for myself or a loss that hurts me down to the quick, I look for tasks. When our beloved dog, Bud, was diagnosed with cancer and the outlook looked grim, I came home from the vet and got busy. I cleaned out the pool, I checked on my vegetable garden, and I boiled an egg. My husband, on the other hand, sat quietly under the shade of our only tree and rubbed Bud's back crying his eyes out. He was preparing for what spot might be his burial plot while I was busy avoiding it. We all grieve differently. Some allow the grief to wash over them and fully release the tears and pain. Others, like myself, avoid the pain and try to do anything to keep it an arm's length away.

Well, you may have guessed from another story about eggs that my boiled egg didn't end well. No, not because I forgot about it and the water boiled out with a terrible smoky smell filling my kitchen. No, I rushed the process and got quite frustrated when I couldn't peel the egg appropriately. I tried peeling it while it was still scorching hot and most of the egg came off with the shell. It was not therapeutic or healing, it was frustrating. I envied how my husband could accept it and just be without having to do tasks to avoid it. He was choosing the better option. I chose doing things for, but he was doing with.

When we are grieving a loss or in a season of lonely parenting, one thing is needed. Sit with it. Sit with it and allow it to be the only thing you do. Other tasks will prolong the inevitable breakdown. You eventually have to allow yourself and agree to grieve.

## WorkHearter Wisdom

God gave us many stories of men who were stubborn and didn't listen to His instructions. I find this story of two women, Mary and Martha, touching because it is two women who acted differently in the presence of Jesus—one who was focused on being fully present and the other distracted/busy. I focus on living for Jesus more than living with Jesus. Our children will be quite different from us and from each other. It is important not to compare them to each other, but be fully present with them. Distraction can draw us away from choosing what or who is better. Sometimes, being with them is needed more than doing for them.

# Losing Sight

> No one will be able to stand against you all the days of your life. As I was with Moses, so I will be with you; I will never leave you nor forsake you.
>
> Joshua 1:5 NIV

I witnessed a young daughter not more than fifteen months old lose sight of her father briefly in a crowded airport. She did the only instinctive thing she could—she cried out. He heard her and although he wasn't far from her, he quickly went to her, speaking only words of reassurance. He was the only individual in that airport who could reassure her in that scared moment. He didn't punish her or yell at her for leaving his side. She was naturally walking in the confidence that he would be near.

Driving at night takes extra concentration; add weather issues, and it can be scary. As someone who needs assistance with vision anyway by wearing glasses, I often try to squint when I can't see driving at night. By squinting, I am trying harder to focus and gain clearer sight. I also turn down the radio and tell my kids to be quiet, but when all else fails I have to call out to God in prayer. Praying while driving and wrecking has a been a saving grace for me. In my last vehicle wreck, I remember calling out "Help me Jesus" as the airbag deployed. My instinct knew He was the only one who could help me in that moment.

We often lose sight of Christ and like a child we do the only thing we instinctively know to do—call out for help. We can confidently walk in the knowledge He will always be near even when we don't see him in the circumstance.

**WorkHearter Wisdom**

Our job as parents is to reassure our children we will not leave them. As they grow into adults, that same assurance is theirs in Christ when they leave the nest. Are we reassuring them that Christ will never leave them so they won't be afraid? Are we displaying this in our own lives so they can witness it as truth?

# Flamingo Flamboyance

She opens her mouth with wisdom and loving instruction is on her tongue.

Proverbs 31:26 HCSB

"Come to me, all you who are weary and burdened, and I will give you rest."

Matthew 11:28 NIV

Flamingos are well known for their pink color, but they are not born pink. They become pink by their diet and what they are fed from their parents. Their parents meet during a dance. A flock of flamingos dancing is called a flamboyance. The term *flamboyant* is defined as an elaborate or colorful display. My late grandmother gave me a large topaz ring years ago. When asked why she chose to give it to me, she said because I was flamboyant. That word has stuck with me for years, without my really knowing its definition.

Flamingos can lose their pink pigments during parenting chicks, because it is so intense they use much of their food feeding their young. When their color fades to white, it signals to other flamingos to allow them to rest and not join in the dancing. They lose what makes them flamboyant. They do eventually return to their pink color with time. Interestingly, flamingos also use more energy standing on two legs than standing on only one. They have a locked resting position making it physiologically easier to stand and balance on one leg.

Learning about the process of flamingos losing their pink color reminded me of how much of myself I lost while learning to how to parent my babies. The process during newborn, toddler, and teen years is so intense, I lost all expectation of sleep, hygiene, sanity, and the ability to reason properly. On the physical appearance, my hair was falling out daily and I was sweating profusely. Praise God it was short-lived. My babies were not born cynical, negative, or critical. They only learn that from their parents. What I feed and pour into them is what they will grow into as teens and adults. Words I use to describe them while they are young will stick with them, even if they don't understand the meaning. I don't have to be colorful in my language when I can simply be comforting.

Also, moms were made to balance. Like flamingos, we can juggle multiple things at once when it comes to parenting using one arm or standing on one leg. However, I still need to make time for self-care a priority. Taking a lesson from the flamingo, my signal as loss of my flamboyance to my family is my nightly bath routine. When the day has drained me of all my flamboyant energy, I take to the tub. I know the more hectic life gets, the more I need God to give me rest.

### WorkHearter Wisdom

Can we all agree to let our mouths be careful and our tongues be tamed and just give other moms—and even our kids—a break? How can we better give loving instruction to our children? What self-care priorities can we take when we are drained? Thank you, Lord, for being a place of rest when I am weary.

# Snow Days in the South

My dear brothers and sisters, take note of this: Everyone should be quick to listen, slow to speak and slow to become angry.

James 1:19 NIV

If you have ever lived in or visited the South in the winter, you already know that if we get any kind of accumulation of ice or snow it is usually slow to melt. Even the tiniest bit of ice/snow or wintry mix accumulation is slow to melt since it took so long for the ground to allow it to stick. Our Southern ground has a tough time letting go. We are a little hard-headed in that way. We cancel schools and businesses, and we empty grocery store shelves if we even hear the 4 letter word *snow* in the forecast.

When the ice/snow melts, we have lots of water pooling around making a sloppy mess. Water is a powerful force, whether it is a trickle or a flood, a stream or snowflakes. Ice can form quickly from a small pool of water if the conditions are frigid cold.

The ice and snow shimmers and shines but once it's gone, the leftover melted is not beautiful. The remnants of what was once a beautiful scene is unrecognizable once it quickly changes its appearance with rising temperatures. A more damaging aspect of ice and snow melting quickly in our area is ice damming. It can leak into our homes.

Our beautiful relationships with our loved ones can quickly change to ugly disagreements and leave a messy pile if we don't adjust when conflict heats up. If we ice out our loved ones when arguing and tensions rise, we can create leaks that damage our families for a long time. Instead, we heed the words of *slow to speak* and *slow to be angry* and *quick to listen*.

## WorkHearter Wisdom

How many times at bridal showers or weddings do you hear this verse about taking note of being quick to listen but slow to speak and slow to anger? Advice we need to keep our cool in our homes and family is found in this verse. God is more than capable to defend us in a situation that incites anger. If we trust He is able, we can remain comfortably quiet when the enemy attacks our families. This is not our battle to fight.

# Breathe Easy

When times are good, be happy;
but when times are bad, consider this:
God has made the one
as well as the other.

Ecclesiastes 7:14 NIV

Because you know that the testing of your faith
produces perseverance.

James 1:3 NIV

Acclimating to high elevations takes time. I spend more time being out of breath than being able to breathe easy. Eventually, the small walks at a slight incline become easier. Parenting teens can feel like climbing a mountain at a steep incline where nothing is ever said, done, or dressed right in teen angst eyes. It is a tough season to acclimate to. It takes our breath away and only gives us labored breaths regularly.

Every winter I decide to start a new workout routine at the gym. This past year I decided to start a cold plunge in our pool in winter. Getting out of a warm bed to go workout in the gym is a cakewalk compared to getting out of bed for a cold plunge. At first, I could only dip for a second. I worked up over time to staying in until I could catch my breath. Then I realized it got easier—as it often does after it's hard. When I go inside, I have learned to appreciate how I made it through a tough time.

We appreciate the sun after the clouds. We appreciate the ocean more after witnessing the power of a storm. We love the snowy cold breezes after being stuck inside with cabin fever. We appreciate the falling leaves after they have shown us their brightest colors.

## WorkHearter Wisdom

Difficult life seasons have the same effect. We need time to acclimate to these seasons of life. Once acclimated to the tough times, life seems to get easier. Even hard times can be appreciated in hindsight—after they are over and survival is imminent. As we overcome, we learn not to fear the challenging times and easily tell life to "bring it" once we are able to catch our breath. We and our children will be challenged or have our faith tested by this world. We may never acclimate to being tested, but we have the hope that it will produce perseverance. In good or bad times, God is Lord of all.

# Growing Cold

Let the message about the Messiah dwell richly among you, teaching and admonishing one another in all wisdom, and singing psalms, hymns, and spiritual songs, with gratitude in your hearts to God.

Colossians 3:16 HCSB

As dry ground and heat snatch away the melted snow, so Sheol steals those who have sinned.

Job 24:19 HCSB

Cold can spread as quickly as heat can spread, but it's harder to get cold if you are already warm.

Cancer also spreads and grows faster in a cold environment, according to research studies. Hold that thought.

On two different travels out west, we were stopped in our tracks by snow. How each began (warm, happy) made all the difference in how it ended. In the first, we were driving up to Pikes Peak to a doughnut shop, but the park rangers stopped us from reaching the peak due to worsening conditions. The goal of warm doughnuts in our hungry bellies was so measurably close but grew cold in that instant. We took the winding path safely back down the mountain and ate a consolation meal instead, grateful that we weren't stuck on a mountaintop.

On a different trip, my family flew to Denver for a Breckenridge ski trip during spring break. We ran into delay after delay with flights, shuttles, and rental cars. When we finally left the airport, a snowstorm began to quickly cover the only roadway into Breckenridge. We were once again greeted with officials in uniforms stopping us to tell us to turn around. But we had a hotel on the other side of the mountain, and a prepaid ski lesson first thing in the morning. We were cold and weary in body and mind. Frustrated. Our attitudes were cold and the annoyance grew. We were not thankful. Sometimes a goal we have gets rejected, stopped cold, or criticized. When life is out of our control (all the time), we can choose gratitude in our hearts. Our hearts don't have enough room for gratitude and annoyance together. No one has ever been gratefully annoyed.

Thankfulness needs to start as soon as we wake up whether we are morning people or not. It sets the tone of our entire day. Communication and nearness to God affects our day and kids and parenting. Our days have the power to grow solely on how strong of a start they begin.

## WorkHearter Wisdom

The scripture speaks about the Christian life and having peace control our hearts. It also commands that we be thankful. Our thankfulness keeps our hearts warm. A warm heart is not easily caught off guard or made cold. Extra layers of protection for our hearts come from a deep relationship with God and His Word. If we start our days and seasons with warm hearts, the cold has a much tougher time getting in. Let's keep our hearts from being snatched away by dwelling in gratitude.

## Fireplace Freedom

You, my brothers and sisters, were called to free. But do not use your freedom to indulge the flesh; rather serve one another humbly in love.

Galatians 5:13 NIV

Your heart must not be troubled. Believe in God; believe also in Me.

John 14:1 HCSB

When it is frigid cold and layers are worn to protect from the freezing wind and temperatures outside, there is a freedom of having a fireplace to thaw out next to inside. My kids will strip down to their first layer of clothing after being outside in the snow/ice. They quickly fling off their thick and heavy coats, pants, boots and hats wet from the snow with the freedom of a bird flying from a cage.

Happily tired, with rosy cheeks and frozen hair, they will go straight to sit in front of the fireplace, like a weight has been lifted. They sit with their eyes gazing upon the dancing warmth to thaw out waiting on their hot cocoa in a mug.

Hot cocoa is a winter staple in our home. It warms them on the inside while the fireplace is warming them on the outside. It's a joyful song in their day to be able to warm up this way. Maybe that's why singing around a campfire or fireplace started in the first place? It is noted that campfire singing originated at camp gospel revival meetings to unite people in action and infusing certain values.

Often our troubles can weigh us down and trouble our hearts, but we are called to be free. I want my kids to know the Father waits for them when they need freedom from a heavy heart. As parents, we know all we need to do to prevent our hearts from being troubled is to believe in God and Jesus accepting the release of burden He offers to us. When our heart starts to grow cold, the warmth of His love is like a fireplace on winter days. It's simple but it's what we all need. His Word gives simple instructions for a freedom in our hearts.

## WorkHearter Wisdom

Our trouble wears down our heavy hearts. Sometimes we don't even know what we are carrying around and all we need is to sit in front of the fire of Christ's love to melt away those troubles and lose the heavy weight. What weight needs lifting? What burden you've placed on yourself needs to die off in the winter season to set you free? What song is He singing to your troubled heart today?

# Snowflakes

Now you are the body of Christ and individually members of it. And God has appointed in the church first apostles, second prophets, third teachers, then miracles, then gifts of healing, helping, administrating, and various kinds of tongues.

1 Corinthians 12:27–28 ESV

Snowflakes are mesmerizing to me. Every year I get older but when I see them, I turn into a child. When I was younger, I would try to catch them on my tongue—knowing they would melt away and be gone. As an adult, I want to catch them on my camera so I can study them even after they have melted. It will always amaze me how much intricate detail our heavenly Father puts into a small frozen piece of precipitation that only lasts long enough to barely be appreciated—often only seconds in the South. I will not ever get over the fleeting beauties' impact on my life.

All of the snowflakes together combine to make a blanket of snow that covers the ground and stills the noise. Yet I imagine a snowflake symphony in my mind when they are falling. All the quiet here on earth but musical harmonies from each flake as they fall to the ground. Snow doesn't melt as fast when it's a blanket. A blanket of snow will cover every patch of dirt, blade of grass, and icy puddle on the ground—just as God's love for us will cover a multitude of transgressions. We are covered no matter the season.

Snow doesn't keep—and neither do babies. The beauty of a newborn is fleeting. I miss my babies being babies, but oh so love my grandbaby era. I will appreciate them even more. The beauty of youth is fleeting. I miss how fat I thought I was when I was a teen/young adult. The beauty of old age is also as fleeting as a sunset here to shine for a short amount of time allowing us to bask in the color of its light. Oh, how I miss my grandparents' wrinkles, toothless grins, and the way their arthritic hands grabbed mine, hugs holding on tight every time they saw me.

As Christians, we are the body of Christ joined together to create a community. We use our unique talents and gifts to contribute to and support the body of Christ. The uniqueness of a snowflake may not stand out individually, but as they join together to make inches of snow, they are vital to the blanketing. As a cord of three strands is not easily broken, linking arms with other moms takes longer to break us down. As mothers we can feel unique and alone at the same time. We might think we lose our uniqueness by joining in community but the overall impact is longer lasting.

## WorkHearter Wisdom

If we are in a group alongside other moms and share our unique snowflake stories, we can quiet the noise of our daily lives and all that bombards us on a regular basis. It can ground us together and give us a reprieve from the hustle we feel compelled to strive for. God tells us that we all have unique gifts. Gifts that He has appointed or designed for us. Gifts that could be fleeting if used alone, but joined with the body of Christ we can rejoice together. Mothering by yourself is much harder. Don't do it alone. God made us to need each other. Embrace the gift of others today.

# Missing Pieces

Above all, love each other deeply, because love covers a multitude of sins.

1 Peter 4:8 NIV

The stillness of being under a thick cozy blanket while it's snowing is incomparable. Snow falling outside will quiet our pace and slow down our hurriedness. There's a lot to be said about the power of still. In the South, snow causes delays, closures and setbacks. I'm still learning that temporary setbacks can be used as lessons and blessings. If our power goes out, I need to rely on the linemen to help get power restored. If my son or daughter's car slides off the road, they need to rely on a tow truck to pull them out of a ditch.

We all need each other and all the parts are honorable. My children have broken homes in terms of divorced parents. They have missing pieces of family at Christmas and other holidays from one side of their family when they are with the other side. This is a broken part of their life. They still have as much love from their parents but it is spread into two homes/places.

At times, we may try to love each other more deeply to compensate for that brokenness. The brokenness runs deep, and we can't fix the broken parts of their story. However, broken parts can be still be used. What we think are our "unpresentable parts" were given honor by God to be used. My kids have a selfless love for other kids whose parents are divorced. They understand each other on a level that no one else can. God gave us the power to heal our broken pieces and restore what's missing. His love covers us and all of our brokenness.

## WorkHearter Wisdom

Do you have what you might call a missing piece in your life? Are you at peace with your missing piece? How do you handle it?

# WorkHearter Wisdom: Twenty Things I Wish I'd Known as a First-Time Mom

1. Baby sounds are short-lived. Savor the sounds and noises they make even in the middle of the night. The quietness of the 2:00 a.m. wake-ups will be missed. Keep everything quiet—no TV, no phone, no music. Embrace the stillness. Listen for the God whispers.

2. Keep TV and screens away from baby as long as possible. Instead, read to them every night. These days and nights pass quickly and you can't get them back once they are gone.

3. Sleep when the baby sleeps the first couple of months. Cleaning, laundry, cooking, and organizing can wait. Sleep will keep you sane.

4. Take a shower when you feel overweight. Wash your hair. Even though it doesn't shed any pounds, you will feel refreshed.

5. Do not diet after childbirth. Eat real food. Your body just went through the valley of the shadow of death and it needs to be nourished, not deprived.

6. Take care of yourself by prioritizing your health. Walk every day once you are able with baby in a stroller or with a wearable sling/pouch. Drink lots of water. Hydration is the savior of sensible thinking with postpartum brain.

7. You don't have to let every single person touch your belly while you're pregnant—or hold your baby. However, don't wait until the baby is older to let elder relatives enjoy them. Older people do get great mental benefits from holding newborn babies, so if there has to be a choice, let the elderly hold them.
8. Do not volunteer for anything the first year. Not church, not school, not sports, not family events. You don't need to give now to feel worthy, you are giving the most to your baby. It takes a whole year for your body to heal after birth, so you need the whole year to heal.
9. You have nothing to prove to anyone. You don't have to go anywhere or do anything for anyone who expects your presence during this season. You also don't have to know how to do anything perfectly. You are not and will not under any condition be a failure.
10. Take your mom or mother-in-law's advice, even if it's not asked for. Believe or not, there are golden nuggets in their experience that are helpful, even if you think it's outdated.
11. If you feel bad, don't feel bad about it. You are recovering and deserve to be taken care of, even while you are caring for a newborn. Even though no one has ever died from lack of sleep, you will feel exhaustion like you never have before.
12. Ask for help. Be specific. If you need a meal, a moment to yourself, or just a conversation with an adult, ask. Everyone is different and some people (me) feel like intruders after someone has had a baby; they do not want to disturb you, especially not knowing the sleep schedule.
13. Don't move or start a new task or hobby or travel overnight until after the baby is sleeping through the night. Do not cut your hair, either. No drastic changes until regular sleep

is back in your routine. Babies can sense any type of stress, even the good kind. Relax in the mundane and monotonous. There will be plenty of time for new adventures. This season is short and passes quickly.

14. Take photos of your baby every day or every week. They change daily and you often don't see it until you look back on baby photos and the time has passed. Let people take your photo with the baby. Who cares if you don't have makeup on! These days are fleeting and you can't redo them or recreate them.

15. Don't take everything so seriously. Be silly and laugh with your baby/toddler. Dance, dance, dance. They can sense when you are stressed and it stresses them without even knowing why.

16. Ask questions. Ask all the questions. You will not look dumb. No one knows what they are doing with their first child and even subsequent children can be different experiences. It's not a big deal to not know what you are doing.

17. Be patient with your husband. He doesn't know what he's doing either. You had nine months to get used to the idea physically and mentally daily. His new reality may have just started when the baby was born.

18. Animal instincts are real. If you have a pet that is protective of the baby, lean into that instinct. Your mama bear instincts will also be keenly aware as a new mom. Trust them. You don't need to explain them to anyone. Jesus stood up for us, it's OK to do the same for those we love.

19. You will worry about your children no matter their age. Worry doesn't help any situation. It robs you of sleep, joy,

time, and being fully in the moment. It only gives you anxiety, stress, moodiness, and strife. Instead, pray. Prayer provides healing, peace, patience, and protection.

20. Be thankful for every scar, extra pound of weight, and increased size on your body. Our scars are reminders of what we overcame and lived to tell about—so be proud.

For I am the LORD your God
    who takes hold of your right hand
and says to you, Do not fear;
    I will help you.

Isaiah 41:13 NIV

The Lord himself goes before you and will be
    with you; he will never leave you nor
forsake you. Do not be afraid; do not be
    discouraged.

Deuteronomy 31:8 NIV

# Pile It On

For the mouth speaks from the overflow of the heart.

Matthew 12:34 NASB

In winter, I pile on the layers. I love the feel of furry fleece. I love warm boots. I have multiple beanie hats. I also enjoy baking and eating what I have baked. Even if I snack and graze on the dish I'm making, I feel it's my duty to taste test it once finished. Therefore, I pile on extra pounds as well.

As a teen, my mom would often put me out of the car to walk home when I had an attitude. When I got in an argument with her, I would pile on insults. I slung curse words and dagger glares in her direction. I would take it too far and damage the relationship. It's amazing God let me survive that time in my life. (Even funnier in His humor, He allowed me to live on the other side. I'm slightly kidding, my teenage kids were not nearly as bad as I was as a teen.)

Somehow I didn't learn from these defense tactics. I would push and test to distract anyone from seeing my weak spots or my scars. No matter how much I piled on the layers of damage or built up walls with hurtful words, my heart was not focused on Jesus. I was not mad at my mom or anyone else when I behaved this way. I was mad at myself. My heart was speaking to me, and I was out of control.

All through Jesus's teaching, the chief priests, elders,

scribes, and Pharisees mocked Him with insults and spoke evil against Him when their hearts were not in line with God. They mocked Him on the cross while He was dying. They were angry they didn't have control and used words to attempt to destroy any power in the truth about Him. They were focused on turning attention away from Jesus and when they couldn't turn it away, they changed the focus to hurtful words and actions. When my heart is focused on Jesus and balanced with God's Word on a daily basis, I can pile on love and truth to myself and others freely.

## WorkHearter Wisdom

I need to pile on Jesus in layers of love for my daily battle with my need to control: I wear my pants with the prayer of peace and patience that I have the exact portion today will need. I wear my shirt with the self-control I need to resist insulting others. I wear shoes on my feet with the focus of faith that God is in control. I wear gloves of goodness and gentleness. I wear a jacket of joy. I wear a keepsake to remind me that kindness can outlive yesterday. If I pile on these layers, it helps me be a mouthpiece of gratefulness and grace given to me so I can give to others.

## Buried In an Avalanche

We were buried therefore with him by baptism into death, in order that, just as Christ was raised from the dead by the glory of the Father, we too might walk in newness of life.

Romans 6:4 ESV

I've not in any way experienced an avalanche but like quicksand videos, I've seen enough of it simulated on TV that I am perfectly fine lacking personal experience on the matter in the literal sense. That is not a life experience I need, hear me, Lord? Let me be clear, no way I would want to be in an avalanche or quicksand.

Parenting a teenager feels like an avalanche with all the places to drive them, items to buy for them, appointments to make for them, and things to pick up after them. I have often felt like a chauffeur more than a family member. Not to mention the avalanche that is the mess of their bedroom.

Avalanches are not just falling rocks and shaky ground—parenting feels like that as well. As soon as one task is done, another comes on top of your head so fast you can't catch your breath. We feel like we are being buried by the overwhelming all that comes with parenting a teenager. One more wrong move will bury us.

Sin can feel like it's burying us. One lie leads to another lie to cover up a lie and then we are so deep in the lie that we can't see daylight anymore. Paul speaks about being buried with Christ in baptism and raised to walk in newness of life.

I have been buried figuratively in many avalanches of life. Stress, grief, work, laundry cause me to be overwhelmed; and I lose the ability to breathe when I have too much to do. I feel paralyzed like I'm in quicksand and don't know what to do next.

One day since I couldn't do anything right as the parent of a teenager anyway, I decided to try to get them to reluctantly talk about their life during the car ride. Surprisingly, they told me they felt buried also by the pressure of school, grades, sports, friends, and life in general with changing hormones that didn't help. As moms and kids we are allowed to say it out loud. We are holding on together.

Knowing more about what they are going through at the same time was freeing as a parent. I was alone as the parent in the car, but not alone in the feeling of being buried by life. We share the same lost breaths with overwhelming tasks.

As Christians, we die to sin and are buried with Christ in the act of baptism so that we can be new and walk in life. Our church says it this way during a baptism service: "Buried with Christ in death, raised to walk in new life." We close our eyes in baptism and rise out of the water with our eyes opened. We only must be buried once and walk in the newness the rest of our life. The avalanche doesn't keep appearing or trying to bury us. Buried with Christ is a freedom not a burden.

## WorkHearter Wisdom

How do you cope with that feeling of being overwhelmed, of being buried in responsibilities or worries? Father, I pray that you will lift us out of the mud and the pit when we feel buried. Give our feet a firm place to stand in the avalanche circumstances of life. Free us from the paralyzing quicksand of never-ending to-do lists. Thank you for raising us and giving us the ability to walk in the newness of life.

# Worry or Wonder

> After He said these things He spit on the ground, made some mud from the saliva, and spread the mud on his eyes.
>
> John 9:6 HCSB

We don't get many ice storms in Tennessee, but when we get them it shuts everything down. In 1994 there was one so bad, my parents didn't have electricity for two weeks. They had to drive thirty minutes from home to my place to take a hot shower.

Fortunately, we didn't lose electricity and found the ice on the trees breathtakingly beautiful. It was captivating, I would drive to the neighboring town where they had no electricity just to see the icy trees. My perspective only saw beauty because I had no pain involved. My kids only see rainy puddles as fun because they don't worry about muddy shoes getting into cars or clothes to wash. When we try to see through our kids' eyes, it is a new perspective. They see wonder and we see consequences or worry. They don't need to know the next step, the next day or the next thing they have to do. They don't care if they get dirty.

Jesus also used mud to clear up a blind man's vision. He used spit and dirt to spread on the man's eyes to heal his vision. The blind man was able to see again, which was a miracle. The

Pharisees only saw it as a sin to heal on the Sabbath. They worried He was not from God. They only saw the mud and not the wonder of wholeness he was giving.

## WorkHearter Wisdom

We all need a new perspective or new eyes sometimes. We need our eyes to open to the glory and blessings of parenting. It is a gift and a chore at the same time, but if we focus on the chore we miss the gift. We only see the worry in the mud and not the wonder of the miracle.

## Divorce and Death

My eyes are swollen from grief; they grow old because of all my enemies.

Psalm 6:7 HCSB

There are five stages of grief/loss, we're told. Loss can be loss of life or loss of relationship. The stages are characterized as: anger, denial, bargaining, depression, and acceptance. If you are in the midst of any stage of grief or loss, it feels like a winter season. You feel alone. You feel isolated. You feel cold or that you are getting the cold treatment. Something in life has died during this season, similar to trees and plants and grass dying in winter. The color of life feels far away and distant.

Even when the sun comes out in winter, you don't feel warm. We need more clothes, more food, and more sleep in winter. We can't predict the end of winter once it starts, but it overstays its welcome in our lives quickly.

Our parent/child days can feel like winter when it is a season we don't prepare for or can't predict the end of the trying time. Preparing for the winter seasons of parenting involves savoring the sunny summer days of warmth with our child's smile and laughter. It includes stocking up on the joys of being with our children. Time will come when we experience an empty nest that is cold and quiet, when we will need to retrieve our stored memories of warmer times.

Winter is a season of rest. Rest comes when our children leave our homes, but parenting doesn't end. It becomes a long-distance relationship.

Loss can lead to distancing ourselves from others out of fear of failure or loss again. In death, much like winter, we remember the good and choose not to focus on the bad. Divorce is different, in that we remember the bad more than the good. We experience the death of this relationship in a way to justify the end of it. When loss of life is experienced, we glorify the life that is gone. When death of a relationship is experienced, we justify that it is over. Our children feel the loss of life in divorce and lose their comfort of family life. They don't justify the end of it, but will glorify the life that is gone, even if they accept it. They will hibernate in a winter season for life about their parents' divorce. My parents divorced when I was twenty-three. I was living on my own at the time, married and expecting my second child, but I was still mourning that loss years later. My parents kindled a kinder relationship as co-parents by celebrating holidays and milestones with us together. For over twenty years, we have the gift of both our parents together even though they aren't married anymore.

## WorkHearter Wisdom

We will stay in the cold season of loss until we have rested in the peace that God gives us to survive the winter. He is our redemption. All sorts of things are happening in winter when it looks dead. But confession and kindness can warm our hearts in winter seasons and our kids' hearts. So we need to be kind to ourselves after a loss. Kindness will warm our cold hearts. Hearts change like seasons. We don't have to fear the changes if we bring the kindness as kindling.

# Nearsighted

How can you say to your brother, 'Brother let me take out the speck that is in your eye,' when you yourself do not see the log that is in your own eye?

Luke 6:42 ESV

I have better vision up close than far away. I often need to remove my glasses to see or read up close but cannot see anything without my glasses far away. Bugs also seem to fly close to my face, so I can have a knee-jerk reaction when I see them. Yet when I go to swat them, they fly away and I cannot see them anymore.

Inadequate eyesight reminds me of the parable Jesus told about our ability to see a speck in other's eyes but not a log in our own. He said that we should first remove our logs and then we can see more clearly to remove a speck in someone else's. I have friends who are farsighted but can't read a restaurant menu unless they hold it with their outstretched arm at a distance or put on reader glasses. I catch myself thinking I'm glad I don't have to do that, then I realize we are both visually impaired in varying degrees.

I am nearsighted in vision but also in my way of doing daily tasks. I turn down the radio so I am not distracted in a parking garage or trying to parallel park my car. (I am also guilty of having my turn signal on for far too long before I need to turn.)

We all have gaps in our "vision." So if we all have logs in our eyes and all our brothers and sisters have specks, we all need to seek better vision into ourselves in order to help each other.

## WorkHearter Wisdom

This holds true in my faith life as well: I only see the part of my story that I can grasp quickly and not the faraway vision that God has for me. When I look back on my life, I see the faraway pieces that fit together, but in the present time I confess I am nearsighted. God can see the whole picture. He has a bird's-eye view of our life and every decision in it. His vision is clear. We need to lean on His sense.

# Finding Worth in the Waiting

> For I consider that the sufferings of this present time are not worth comparing with the glory that is to be revealed to us.
>
> Romans 8:18 ESV

When you grow up and still live in the South, you know the four seasons are typically two long seasons of summer and winter and tantalizingly short seasons of spring and fall. As an adult Southerner, I can say we are constantly wishing for one of the long seasons to end. When we are in the long days of heat or bitter cold, we are wishing and hoping for the next season. We are seeking what is worth waiting for.

As a child, though, I was hoping for longer winters, which meant more snow days, and longer summers, which postponed school starting. I failed to enjoy the season of childhood I had while I was in it.

The seasons of our life—especially parenting—are long while we are in their midst, but looking back on them, it seems they pass so quickly. We tend to appreciate them more once they are over. While we are waiting for the toddler or teen years to pass quickly, they seem to drag on. Yet when we look back at old photographs, videos, or even our own memory snapshots, we see the beauty of those fleeting years. Or as a character on *The Office* famously said, "I wish there was a way to know when you're in the good old days before you've actually left them."

As a mom, there is a way to do this. If you have more than one child you can see that the good old days passed quickly with your first child—so you can choose to be intentionally mindful with your other children. As a daughter or granddaughter, the seasons of being a child or grandchild are also fleeting. This is experienced firsthand when you watch your parents and grandparents grow older and eventually pass away. We experience these seasons in both suffering and joy, but once they are gone we only remember the joyful pieces. The suffering part seems to be less significant to us once the season is over.

## WorkHearter Wisdom

The Hebrew word for wait means to look eagerly for or to bind together. When we wait with the Lord, we tie up/bind our lives with Him as our partner. When we bind our lives with Him, we recognize when to pause and wait. We eagerly await His next move while staying contently still. The worth in the waiting is watching the good old days play out in front of our eyes. Better days may feel like they are behind us, especially when we are suffering, but God says glory days are indeed ahead of us. He should know. He wrote the book about the worthiest of waiting —the Messiah.

## Heated Seats and Harsh Words

Therefore, no condemnation now exists for those in Christ Jesus.

Romans 8:1 HCSB

It took me more than thirty years of driving experience to own a car with heated seats. They are comforting on cold winter days when I need to drive. I often don't want to leave the seat of my car when I get to my destination due to being so comfortable sitting in the heated seat.

Being in the hot seat in life, though, is not as comforting. The dictionary has a variety of words for *hot seat*—under pressure to perform, in a position of uneasiness or anxiety, under scrutiny, or even just having a lot of responsibility. When I got a speeding ticket and sat in the "hot seat" in front of traffic court to await the fate of my ticket, I was under the scrutiny of a judge, in this instance. I would be sweating no matter the temperature or type of clothing I wore, because I was very anxious for the outcome. I wasn't sure I could speak when called upon by the judge, and I did experience a stutter and flubbed my words. It felt like all eyes were on me in the courtroom and I was the center of attention—but not a in a positive way.

As mothers, we need to remind ourselves that our children feel this way about us when they misbehave or get into trouble.

We reassure them that we love them and we give out the consequences for their actions. We must be mindful to do this in love and not condemn them. The worst way to display this is repeatedly reminding them of what they did wrong. We can discipline and *let it go*. We can make their hot seats more comfortable by watching our words and giving them the same freedom in love that Christ gave to us. We see this example in Romans.

## WorkHearter Wisdom

Paul reminds us that there is no condemnation for those in Christ Jesus. We are free from criticism and scrutiny. We are also free from punishment. Jesus took our place in the hot seat and gave us the comfort of knowing that we are set free. He spoke for us and His word is the final fate. Modeling this type of love for our children gives them a concrete example of Christ's grace for us. Let's also not judge young mamas. We all make mistakes when starting something new. Give the reassurance needed as they fumble through this new season of motherhood.

## Rainy Days and Funerals

> Blessed are those who mourn, for they will be comforted.
>
> Matthew 5:4 NIV

No one feels at home at a funeral home, I think. It's not a place anyone lives or visits regularly enough to feel like a "home." So why do they call them funeral homes? Who feels at home there? Strange as it sounds, people do feel at home at funeral homes, not because of the place but the familiar people who come to visit. If you haven't seen your great aunt or second cousin from your mother's side in years, they will show up at a funeral home when a family member passes. They will hug you and recognize you before you recognize them. It will feel like home to be surrounded by people who love you and are thinking of you. The uncomfortable reality of losing a loved one is cushioned only by the love of others enveloping you during a dark time.

I didn't want the sun to shine the day of my sister's funeral. It didn't seem fair to be inside a funeral home in a room with windows and see the sun shining outside. I also resented the fact that the sun had the audacity shine on my face when it was such a dark, gloomy day in my heart. I wanted it to mirror the rain happening in my heart. In that way, I think rain and funerals pair comfortably together.

I talked to hundreds of people in the visitation receiving line the day of the funeral. I didn't know all of them but almost all knew my baby sister. The ones who didn't know her well came to see her family to show their support for us. It was heartwarming to be hugged so many times by so many people and that love shined as brightly in my heart as the sunlight outside. The love of others helped me see sunshine in the darkness. As terrible a day as it was, I was comfortable in that funeral home.

## WorkHearter Wisdom

Have you ever resented the weather outside not mirroring what your heart was feeling? Isn't it a blessing God gives us a light to shine in our darkness to bring us comfort? How can we be the comfort a brother or sister needs to feel at home during a time of grief?

# Quiets Moments of Contemplation: Romans 5:1-5

Therefore, since we have been made right in God's sight by faith, we have peace with God because of what Jesus Christ our Lord has done for us. Because of our faith, Christ has brought us into this place of undeserved privilege where we now stand, and we confidently and joyfully look forward to sharing God's glory.

We can rejoice, too, when we run into problems and trials, for we know that they help us develop endurance. And endurance develops strength of character, and character strengthens our confident hope of salvation. And this hope will not lead to disappointment. For we know how dearly God loves us, because he has given us the Holy Spirit to fill our hearts with his love. (NLT)

Parenting requires endurance. Our character will no doubt come into question, but the endurance we develop from problems will strengthen our character and in turn character will strengthen our hope. A hope that will not lead to disappointment. We have such an undeserved privilege to share in God's glory confidently and joyfully. You have often read versions of this verse that begin with the reminder that we have been "justified by faith." No matter the problems you are facing right now, contemplate the Holy Spirit beside you and let your heart be filled with peace.

## Not My Gift

We have different gifts, according to the grace given to each of us.

Romans 12:6 NIV

Organization is not my gift. This is why it took so long to write this book. I have notes written in journals, scrap paper, my phone and computer. I have a method to my madness in where I keep things. It works for me most of the time, until it doesn't. If life gets too stressed or I am in a time crunch, I cannot find anything I need. It's usually my glasses I can't find. I need to wear them every day. This has resulted in multiple pairs of glasses in different areas of my home or car or husband's truck.

I overlook exactly where I thought I put something. My unorganized ways can create anxiety and panic in my life. In those moments, I am humbled and realize once again that organization is not my gift. My gifts are other tasks that come easily and effortlessly to me. My husband is better at organizing. He is meticulous (when he wants to be) and I have to raise a white flag when I get overwhelmed from my complete disorganization. He doesn't shame me or yell at me for my lack of organization. He just helps. He doesn't make me feel less as a person, human, mother, or wife because I'm disorganized or different from him.

Our kids will struggle with certain tasks. What comes easily to us, may be extremely difficult for them. We are put in their life to help them and believe it or not they are put in our life to help us.

## WorkHearter Wisdom

God gave us all gifts and we can use those gifts to help others. Our gifts are not for us. The gifts we don't have, He gives to others. The others may be in our family, in our home, or in our community. None of us are better than the other. As moms, we try our best to do it all, but we can't do it all. When we don't allow others to help, we rob them of the blessing of being a helper. What white flags do we need to wave today and humbly ask for help?

# Fixing To ...

Be dressed ready for service and keep your lamps burning.

Luke 12:35 NIV

Growing up in the South, we say *fixing to* for about everything. It's not just a saying, it's a way of life for me. All my days are wrapped in moments I choose to pass over because I'm fixing to be. Either, I'm fixing to go somewhere, fixing to get ready to go somewhere, or fixing to leave to go somewhere—instead of just being in the moment that won't ever come again.

It's hard to just be when we live in such a hectic busy way of life today. We miss out on the wonder and blessings of today and what is right in front of us at this very moment.

Time is not our friend. As I age, I find this to be more and more true. I pray for my children. I pray for their salvation. I pray they will be ready when Jesus returns. I don't want them fixing to be ready or fixing to get ready. I want them to *be* ready. I want to be ready. I want everyone I know to be ready.

We need to be ready to meet Jesus because His Word tells us He will come when we don't expect Him. Help us ready our children and ready ourselves as your servants, Lord. Help us to not miss out on the beauty in the waiting.

## WorkHearter Wisdom

I want to care for my children until they are ready to leave the nest, but I know timing is important for them to be ready when Jesus comes. When He returns, there will be no time to get ready.

If I need to live in a fixing to state of mind, it should be I'm fixing to meet Jesus and how do I want to prepare for that meeting. How do I want to prepare my children for that meeting? Do I want all my loved ones to be able to meet Him too one day and do I want to be proud of how I got ready for that day?

## Deep Breaths

We are hard pressed on every side, but not crushed; perplexed, but not in despair; persecuted, but not abandoned; struck down, but not destroyed.

2 Corinthians 4:8–9 NIV

Downward spirals all start somewhere. With me, it starts with disappointment. A friend tells an untruth or cancels long-term plans. I feel abandoned, confused and disappointed all at once. Disappointment leads to discouragement almost immediately with me. I dwell on why it happened and what I did to contribute to the outcome. Disappointed and discouraged, and if I'm not mindful I will get sad enough to be driven to despair. This despair is not a place that allows long-term visits. The spiral down into despair is quick and relentless. Despair is defined as the absence of hope. If I give in to despair, it will inevitably keep me from doing God's will.

When I recognize these spirals in my children, I remember what helps me when my life starts to spiral down. Looking up is my positive position. When I look up, I am thankful. I don't have to be in a constant state of confusion. When I look up, I see the big, open blue sky on sunny days. I see snowflakes falling like tiny masterpieces on winter days. I breathe in deep breaths when I look up. Breathing deep helps my heart calm down. A calm heart is seldom troubled. Remaining calm can be a saving grace when we are hard-pressed.

Breathing is taken for granted, but is incredibly important for survival. We breathe in and breathe out without much thought until we need to take deep breaths. During childbirth, breathing is the focus during labor pains. You breathe through the pain. Controlled breathing is helpful when surviving extreme heat or cold. You breathe through the discomfort. God breathed life into Adam. God-breathed scripture is a living hope for survival to help us breathe deep through the trials.

## WorkHearter Wisdom

A spiral goes up or down. We usually only hear of downward spirals, but have you ever seen a spiral staircase? It does go both ways—up and down. And usually before the first step you take a deep breath and maybe utter, "OK, here we go." The good news is we can go up from a downward spiral. We can spiral up if we turn our eyes up instead of down. Our hearts can be struck down but not destroyed. With God's breath into our lives, they can also heal. God gave us this hope. If God is faith and hope and love, how I can abide in Him without hope? Breathe His Word in deeply today and release those troubles from your broken heart. OK? Here we go, let's breathe deep.

# Getting Out of Debt

Owe no one anything, except to love each other, for the one who loves another has fulfilled the law.

Romans 13:8 ESV

When my son was in preschool daycare, I went through a divorce. The child support was set by the court, but the weekly payment was sometimes delayed or weeks behind.

As a young single mother, this took a toll financially. Paying for groceries and utility bills along with gas to get to work took priority over paying for childcare. The owner of the preschool was once a single mother herself. I wrote her a letter pleading for grace in the last two weeks before my son started kindergarten. She was gracious and canceled my debt. She didn't have to do this, as she had a business that had indeed provided a service.

In her simple act of grace, she lifted a weight that helped me tremendously. The monetary factor may have been $150, but the peace factor was priceless. Having one area of my life out of debt was a relief. I was indebted to her. I could not pay her back with money, but I made sure to give back the only way I could by spreading a positive word about her business and service she and her employees provided.

Debt is a heavy weight no matter the amount we owe. We can never get out of that debt we owe to Christ. We are indebted but not a borrower. God is not the lender. He is the giver. We are the receiver. He gave us more than we could ever repay so He asks us to owe each other love and nothing else. He knew debt was heavy, and He knew love was owed. Love was given and love is all that is to be repaid. Pass it on.

## WorkHearter Wisdom

Has anyone ever forgiven a debt you owed? How did this free you? How did you pass on this blessing of grace? How can you pay it forward to someone who needs grace?

## Funeral Surprises

But by the grace of God I am what I am, and his grace to me was not without effect. No, I worked harder than all of them—yet not I, but the grace of God that was with me.

> 1 Corinthians 15:10 NIV

When my sister died just shy of thirty-one years old, I learned so many new stories from friends. It was like rediscovering a person and her secrets of helping others. Those positive stories were welcome new information after we learned the darker secrets of her drug addiction.

I don't remember when people started to wear a little color attire at funerals, but it's during my lifetime. I only remember having one black dress to wear at short notice until my sister passed and we decided to wear her favorite color, blue. My memory of that day is a blur, but I remember vividly one beautiful soft pink outfit worn by my husband's grandmother. She, too, had lost a sister, and yet she was a bright light shining through the dark clouds hanging over us that day.

I decided then that I wanted my friends and family to wear their brightest colors to my memorial service when it's my time to go. My loved ones brought bright colors into my life, and I hope they brighten up a gloomy day of anyone who may be grieving my passing. I hope they tell the stories of how God's immeasurable grace made me who I was, and nothing I accomplished could have been done without it.

## WorkHearter Wisdom

Give this some thought. Your family thinks they know everything about you. Leave them with a few surprises that will help soften their grief and turn tears to smiles. You could leave each of your children a letter, for example. Or a video of yourself telling them your wishes for their lives.

# Love Languages of God

Every good and perfect gift is from above, coming down from the Father of the heavenly lights, who does not change like shifting shadows.

James 1:17 NIV

Gary Chapman wrote a book—*The Five Love Languages: How to Express Heartfelt Commitment to Your Mate*—and defined them as gifts, words of affirmation, acts of service, quality time, and physical touch.

And God sends us all the love language in every season:

His love language of gifts are sunrises and sunsets in all seasons. He sends us cool breezes on hot days of summer; He provides shade trees in those dry dog days of summer. God gives us sunshine on cold days of winter, and creates snowflakes to remind us of how much detail He puts into the tiniest creations. God created flowers to bloom in the spring. He paints a tapestry of color in the fall when the leaves change color. God gave us bird songs in all seasons.

His love language of words of affirmation are throughout the Bible and in the whispers from our loved ones. His wise words are repeated in hymns of praise.

His love language of acts of service are from the hands, arms, and feet of His followers.

His love language of quality time is in the quiet moments

spent with Him in prayer. He is always available to spend time with us. We don't even have to ask for an appointment on His calendar—we have His direct line to sit with Him during trial or joy.

His love language of physical touch is from loved ones' hugs. His gave us hands to hold and arms to wrap around us when we need it most.

God's gifts can be temporary and only for a season—like the ages of our children. Babies, adolescents, and teens are only that age for a season and the gifts of watching them grow during those seasons are temporary. The trials of those seasons are temporary as well.

### WorkHearter Wisdom

Although the seasons will continue to change, His love and grace does not change and His gifts are perfect. Look for them everywhere. He loves you in every love language.

## Church Is not Supposed to Hurt

So in Christ we, though many, form one body, and each member belongs to all the others.

Romans 12:5 NIV

Now about your love for one another we do not need to write to you, for you yourselves have been taught by God to love each other.

1 Thessalonians 4:9 NIV

In my past, I spent more hours at church than I did at home. I volunteered, taught, and spent hours working and attending services all year long. I didn't know how to say no to an opportunity to volunteer. I took photos and taught during vacation Bible school at the same time. I volunteered with youth lock-ins, youth trips, and youth creative movement. When I didn't have money to tithe, I volunteered my time. I drove people to and from church. I couldn't carry it all no matter how much I tried, but I didn't want to let anyone down. It was too much for a single person let alone a married one. It wasn't sustainable. I tried to be more than one member of the body of Christ. I thought if I could do more I could more than make up for my past mistake of breaking up my family unit. I saw church as family and wanted to spend time with that family also, but my family at home was starving for my attention. I only hurt both family relationships by trying to take on more than I could carry while no one noticed I needed to serve

God by serving my family first.

Christ spoke of our role in the church body to work together and to belong to a family of believers. If one is hurt, it hurts us all. Eventually, I was so worn out I had to leave. No one had seen me. But, we can't give up on church even when it hurts or we feel unseen, misunderstood, or unheard. Instead of giving up altogether, after some time I knew I needed community, tried another church organization and heard the three words I most needed to hear after my hurt: "You're safe here." Those words, like spoken from the pulpit ones often do, spoke directly to me. And, just like that, I felt seen again. Don't give up on community just yet. Church isn't just a building to attend, it's the living body of Christ and God wants you to be a part of it.

## WorkHearter Wisdom

Our children are easily hurt by perceptions and change. If their pastor changes, they take it personally. If their teacher changes or friends move, they feel abandoned. Our job as believers in Christ and parents is to nurture them and grow them into the knowledge that Christ loves them, understands them and hears them no matter who is feeding them. God will provide the food for his family. And, above all the hurt, He sees them.

## When You Can't Do Anything but Cry

In the same way, the Spirit helps us in our weakness. We do not know what we ought to pray for, but the Spirit himself intercedes for us through wordless groans.
Romans 8:26 NIV

Jesus wept. John 11:35 NIV

And even the very hairs of your head are all numbered.
Matthew 10:30 NIV

The death of my sister was different than any other family member's death I've experienced. It is still different. I understand why the shortest verse only says "Jesus wept." No other explanation was needed. It was all He could do, cry. He was fully man and fully God and He empathized with Mary's emotion. I know that feeling of how no words would come out, only tears. Everything I tried to do for days after Brooke's death led to tears. I'd take a shower and cry. I'd look at family photos and cry. I cried for my parents who lost their baby. I'd wear my favorite lotion, which was also hers, and it'd make me cry again. I'd put on clothes and cry because she loved to shop. I'd see her everywhere. I tried to be alone to let the tears out. She was my baby sister for thirty years. I barely remember life before she came when I was nine years old. I felt like her second mom. I was full of sorrow and it spilled out everywhere I went, and with everything I did. Crying will deplete your energy. I was a nursing mom during that time and my milk stopped. My body was spending so much energy crying it stopped producing milk for my baby. On top of everything else, I did not feel like a good mom.

It's quite amazing to me now to look back and realize I got out of bed and got dressed or even left the house during those times. All I remember is crying. During that time, my days were a blur. That blur was from the tears that filled my eyes most of my waking hours. It is comforting to know that Jesus in all His majesty also stopped what He was doing and wept when He was sorrowful. He knows how I felt, He cried with me and He carried me through that difficult time. All my tears matter to Him as all the hairs on my head are numbered. He empathizes with me and lets me weep. He knows my hurt as well as He knows the hairs on my head.

## WorkHearter Wisdom

Maybe you have had a time when all could do is cry from similar sorrow not knowing how to get through or understand how others were doing their daily routine with ease. Take comfort in knowing even Jesus wept when the sorrow consumed Him and we have the Spirit to intercede for us in our weakness. Allow Him to carry you until you can stand on your own. After time helps you heal, you can help someone else stuck in the heavy pit of sorrow by understanding in that moment all they can do is cry.

Have you experienced days blurred from weeping over a loss or from sorrow? Have you ever just wanted someone to know how much hurt you have in your heart? How can you help carry the burden of others after you've experienced what they are experiencing?

# Troubled Heart

Do not let your hearts be troubled. You believe in God; believe also in me.

John 14:1 NIV

When my sister died, I felt a grief that was crippling to me personally. Even more than my own battle with grief, it was also debilitating to watch my parents grieve. I could not imagine their pain. The only peace I had was knowing that she knew the Lord. No matter how much we hurt, we will see her again. On another positive thought, we knew she was no longer struggling with addiction.

My sister battled alcoholism before she turned twenty-one. She had three DUIs before she was legally able to purchase alcohol. I worried all the time about her causing a car wreck while she was drinking and driving that could kill someone else. She was sentenced to jail, halfway houses, rehabs, and post rehab centers. When alcohol became too obvious to hide, she turned to opioid drugs. From what we know now, she was an addict most of her adult life, if not all of it. The first tear-filled words out of my father's mouth moments after she passed were, "She's not addicted anymore."

His heart was troubled but he was right. Her place had been prepared, and she was not battling addiction any longer. Our hearts were heavy with grief in the days and months after her death. But our hearts had been troubled for so long with worry for her when she was on earth—while we were mentally preparing for an untimely death—that at least that part of our hearts healed and were not troubled anymore.

## WorkHearter Wisdom

What troubles have hurt your heart? How has God renewed your belief in Him during or after those troubling times?

## Forgive That Regret

Pay attention to yourselves! If your brother sins, rebuke him, and if he repents, forgive him.

*Luke 17:3 ESV*

It would be better for them to be thrown into the sea with a millstone tied around their neck than to cause one of these little ones to stumble.

*Luke 17:2 NIV*

And where these have been forgiven, sacrifice for sin is no longer necessary.

*Hebrews 10:18 NIV*

Elisabeth Kübler-Ross has written a well-known book on the stages of grief: denial, anger, bargaining, depression, acceptance. You can't get to acceptance by skipping a stage, and you can go through each stage more than once. As a sister of an addict, I would add two more stages: regret and forgiveness. In that order. Instead of forgive and forget—because forgetting is a rare possibility in grief—you have the weight of regret.

Forgiveness is difficult in grief if the person you need to forgive is gone, but you also have to forgive yourself, which is where the regret comes into play. Regret is a nasty mean-minded stage that talks to you as if you could have known what would happen. It takes all the hindsight in a situation and gives it a front row seat in your mind so you can't look past it.

Being an older sister traditionally comes with responsibility. I was nine years older than my late sister. I took care of her, babysitting her when she was young. She spent the night at my house several times after I moved out and got married. She lived with me when she was fifteen for about six months during our parents' divorce. As a young, struggling wife and mother, I made so many mistakes during that time, overlooking her needs as a teenager. Years later, I learned of her addiction and felt responsible, even though I never bought her alcohol. My sister Tracy and I tried to proactively protect our sister Brooke, taking her on a sober senior beach trip, since all her other friends were partying with alcohol on the beach. It was just the three of us and we had a blast.

What else could I have done? How could I have stopped it? I felt the heavy weight around my neck when she passed. I didn't do enough to help her. I didn't save her. During those times of deep grief regret, I recounted details weeks, months, or years prior. Things I had missed or didn't notice that are now so clear in hindsight. After a lot of time, sleepless nights, and prayer, I forgave myself and my sister. I forgave her when she didn't get a chance to forgive herself. I also forgave myself. I had to or it would have been impossible to face another day.

Forgiveness is a wonderful thing for everyone who has regrets. We can't atone our sins or regrets. Jesus already did that.

## WorkHearter Wisdom

Who do you need to forgive today? Have you forgiven yourself for regret in your life? Forgive yourself for that regret today in the same way Christ has already forgiven you.

## Place Is Important

And he said, "Where have you laid him?" They said to him. "Lord, come and see."

John 11:34 ESV

Sometimes I drive by the house I grew up in and wonder what it looks like inside now. I would go up and ask to look inside if I was brave. I had some formative years in that house. Home is an important place. My children still talk about our first or second house. They don't miss the house, but the memories make the place special to them. They miss the love they shared in that place.

Church can be an important place too. Even if church is a community to you and not a building. Pews are a safe place for me, especially pews in the back row. I like the buffer between me and the piercing words of a sermon. After my grandmother passed away, I wanted to go sit on her couch and at her kitchen table and remember her. Even though I know it is not the house I miss, it's her and how she made it a home. It was her place, and being in it I had a piece of her back with me. My parents visit the cemetery where my younger sister is buried. I thought it was silly until I realized they needed a place to go talk, visit, and spend dedicated moments remembering her.

People move. Addresses change. It happens more often these days, but place is important to us sentimental folks. Place is important for a number of reasons, but many times it's because we experienced something great or something tragic. Jesus wanted to know where His friend was laid after death. The place his body was put mattered to Him. After they told Him, he processed his grief by weeping. He had empathy for the grief they were feeling. As mothers, we feel empathy for our children as soon as they are born. My parents go to my sister's burial place because they miss my sister tremendously, but they also go to process the great burden of grief they carry every day.

### WorkHearter Wisdom

What places are important to you? Why? How can you relate to others or have empathy for those who have a place that is meaningful to them?

# Quiets Moments of Contemplation: Hebrews 11:1

Faith is being sure of what we hope for. It is being sure of what we do not see. (NIV)

The fundamental fact of existence is that this trust in God, this faith, is the firm foundation under everything that makes life worth living. It's our handle on what we can't see. The act of faith is what distinguished our ancestors, set them above the crowd. (MSG)

Living by faith requires leaning on faith every single moment we are awake. From the time we hear the alarm to the time we get into a vehicle to drive to our first destination point of the day, we know we have no control over how much traffic is involved or how grouchy our kids or spouse are that morning. We hope for smooth mornings and safe travel mercies, and we have to be certain of God's goodness every step of the way. But when life throws us a not-so-fair scenario, such as child illness, our faith is tested. If our faith is strong, we will do what is required of us to take care of our child and know with all certainty *this too shall pass*. Even though we can't see past the missed deadline, missed work day, missed school day, or seeing our child in pain, only an assurance in what we hope for that can't yet be seen will sustain us in those moments. Faith takes our shaky hands when we have those "scared to death" days and holds them in an unwavering calm those without faith cannot fathom.

# Extravagant Gestures

Then Mary took about a pint of pure nard, an expensive perfume; she poured it on Jesus' feet and wiped his feet with her hair.

John 12:3 NIV

I think grandparents are the pros of extravagant gestures. My mom bought my son his first car. It was an extravagant gesture, but to her it was a simple gift for her grandson.

Extravagant gestures can also just be showing up. Showing up to a funeral when someone has lost their daughter or sister or dear friend. Funeral home visits and deathbed hospital visits are the pouring oil on Jesus's feet kind of extravagant. It was costly and couldn't be regained. Those visits take our time and effort which is expensive—since once it's spent you can't get it back. When you have nothing to give but yourself and your time, it is an extravagant gesture. You can give without any money in the bank. The sacrificial gift of your presence is more precious than gold.

When my sister died, I was shocked by how many of my old friends I hadn't seen in a long time came to the visitation. Both of my ex-husbands came to the funeral home. They both brought food. A lot of people showed up because they knew what grief felt like and how hard this day was going to be for us. After the funeral was over and we were talking about the visitation list, I realized how extravagant their gesture was—not just to me, but my parents. My mom wrote every person a thank-you note, giving her something of comfort to do with her time of grief. My dad constantly repeated the number of people who came, bringing him comfort knowing his baby girl was remembered. We were all surprised by the turnout. I still remember the face of every visitor. They were kind and loving just a like a grandparent is to a child. They had lived through this and knew their presence was needed.

In confession, before this time I didn't regularly attend funerals of friends who'd lost loved ones. I didn't want to say the wrong thing and be awkward, which is how I usually am. Now I know how many times I missed being able to give someone the gift of my presence as an extravagant gesture.

## WorkHearter Wisdom

Have you ever thought about how much of a gift it is to simply *be present* with someone? All Jesus wants to receive as a gift from us is to be present with Him.

# Three Words

Whoever does not love does not know God, because God is love.

1 John 4:8 NIV

I was once a photographer by trade, which led to my teaching career. I heard and repeated this quote often: "A picture is worth a thousand words." Yet the root meaning of the word *photograph* does not contain the word *picture* at all. The definition can be narrowed down to three words: *drawing with light*. You cannot take a photo without light.

In the same way, you can't show love without bringing your personal light to the situation. Showing love to someone you know well is drawing light into their life worthy of a thousand words.

When I was consumed by grief, I took solace in photos of my sister. I was thankful others had taken them, especially if we were in the photo together. A thousand words aren't needed during difficult times. *I love you* is the most common three-word phrase for those in relationship. Other powerful three-word phrases that speak a magnitude of love: How are you? I know you, I appreciate you, and I am sorry.

When I tell my kids "I know you," what I'm really saying is *I know what you are thinking* or *I know how you feel*. I'm telling them I know them so well because I pay attention to them and how they are affected. I truly see them and know.

"I appreciate you" is a small phrase that could brighten anyone's day. Especially if their love language is words of affirmation.

Asking someone "How are you?" when you know they are grieving is a sign that you care. Most of the time, you know they are not doing well but you ask the hard question anyway. Most often, the response is "Thank you so much for asking." There's a reason for that. You acknowledge their feelings are real, and they don't feel alone at that moment because you cared enough to ask. When you lose someone you love, you get angry because the world is not stopping for everyone like it has for you.

"I am sorry" is tough for parents to say to their kids. Saying "I am sorry" is saying "I love you enough to admit I'm wrong."

And the last three words of our Savior on the cross: "It is finished." Nothing else needed to be worthy of salvation. These are the greatest words of love ever spoken. He didn't need a thousand words to paint the most beautiful picture of grace. Jesus gave us the freedom to receive great love with only three words. He is our model, showing love and light can be spoken with a few words in a variety of ways. God is love so we need to know God to love well. One day our life will be finished and how well we loved others will be the words spoken about us when we are gone.

**WorkHearter Wisdom**

When have you avoided someone for fear of saying the wrong thing, during grief or a time of disappointment? How can you show you care by taking a moment to send a text or email ... or asking them in person how they are? What three words need to be said to someone you love today? Jesus showed us the power of words on the cross. And, we don't need many to show love.

## Hard Candy Skinny Christmas

Keep your lives free from the love of money and be content with what you have, because God has said,
"Never will I leave you;
never will I forsake you."

Hebrews 13:5 NIV

My dad worked multiple jobs when we were growing up. He would often say, "It's going to be a hard candy skinny Christmas this year." I had no idea what he meant or knowledge of the Dolly Parton song at the time. We were fed and clothed and always had a gift under the tree, so I didn't notice how hard it was for my parents to make ends meet until I was older.

When I had children of my own. I learned quickly what that term meant. Christmas is a difficult time for parents when children are old enough to realize there are not many gifts under the tree. When I was a single parent, I was barely making those ends meet to keep food on the table. My kids didn't really know the extent. They just remember not having a lot of snacks in the house and not going out to eat at restaurants. They were cared for and loved. They remember that, I hope.

You may not have much, but learning to be content with what you have is an important lesson for parents and children alike. As a mom, even when you just don't have much left to give, life can still be sweet with God by our side.

## WorkHearter Wisdom

How great a gift it is to know God will never leave and will never abandon us. How can we show our children we won't leave them no matter how tough it gets? How can we teach them to trust that God will never leave them either?

# Lessons Learned

He lifted me out of the slimy pit,
 out of the mud and mire;
he set my feet on a rock
 and gave me a firm place to stand.

Psalm 40:2 NIV

Even to your old age and gray hairs I am he, I am he who will sustain you. I have made you and I will carry you; I will sustain you and I will rescue you.

Isaiah 46:4 NIV

When I was five years old, I had a baby sister, Tracy, and toddler brother. We came home from church with my mom to an icy driveway. Mom had attempted to climb up our steep driveway with her car in low gear in the ice and snow before, but she gave up that losing battle and parked on the road to allow us to walk up the driveway. The only problem was my faux patent leather shiny black shoes. I couldn't walk up that driveway any easier than she could drive it. I was crawling on my hands and knees crying for help. I was sliding even on my knees. My mom was carrying a baby in one arm and a toddler in the other. She couldn't possibly carry me too. The neighbors heard me I was so loud. All I knew to do was cry out for help. I feared if I slid too far down the drive, my mom wouldn't be able to get to me in time before I reached the road at the rocky bottom of the driveway.

When my cry wasn't answered, I learned to help myself from this early experience. As the oldest child in the home, I had to do a lot for myself so my mom could help my younger siblings. Even as a young mom myself, I had to rely on figuring it all out because my mother still had other children to raise herself at home. But, even as an adult I often wanted to cry out like my 5-year-old self for help.

There are times we cannot possibly carry alone all that we are responsible for. We only need to remember to cry out for help. He can carry it and come alongside us to help every step of the way. He will always answer when we call out to Him.

## WorkHearter Wisdom

I used to wonder if Jesus was going to be there for me. I don't wonder that anymore. I was scared more than I wasn't. When we live in fear, we let evil win. Fear is not from Him. We are free from fear. His hands are never too full for me and I can cry out to Him on my hands and knees when I'm sliding down a slippery slope. Even if I make it all the way to rock bottom, He will be there to pick me up. Lord, remind me sometimes I need more than a little help. I know you never tire of hearing my cries. Thank you for always coming to my rescue.

# This Little Light of Mine

Do not conform to the pattern of this world, but be transformed by the renewing of your mind. Then you will be able to test and approve what God's will is—his good, pleasing and perfect will.

Romans 12:2 NIV

You are the light of the world. A city situated on a hill cannot be hidden. No one lights a lamp and puts it under a basket, but rather on a lampstand, and it gives light for all who are in the house.

Matthew 5:14-15 HCSB

Your word is a lamp for my feet,
   a light on my path.

Psalm 119:105 NIV

I love candles burning in my home every fall and winter. I learned an easy hack to put them out without inhaling the smoke caused by blowing them out. Now I cover them with a metal top. They burn out quicker than blowing them because the oxygen they need to burn is eliminated. Fire can't light or burn without oxygen.

When you reduce your gift—your light—to fit the size of others' expectations by conforming to the pattern of the world or what they can handle, it is dimmed and a dim light is closer to burn-out than a flame. We should be growing our light—and instead of trying to conform to the world, our light should be a lamp for others to find hope. If we don't think there is room for our light to shine, we give in to the darkness by dimming it or making it smaller. We can't help lead others to Christ with our lights dim. Darkness needs a bright light. If you are in a period of darkness and don't know which way to go, the Word is the lamp you need to guide your next steps. It is the oxygen we need for the flames to grow and shine bright. A small spark can start a fire with little oxygen and it takes more water to put it out. What we kindle in our thoughts, actions, and lives will grow. We need our light strong so we can show our children how to shine. How do we grow our light? We spend time in the Word. We spend time listening to God in prayer. We show kindness to others. We practice patience. "This little light of mine, I'm going to let it shine. Let it shine. Let it shine. Let it shine."

## WorkHearter Wisdom

When the frost or snow is on the ground in winter, you can see a clear difference between the shade and sunny areas. The shaded area is still dark so it's colder and takes longer for frost/snow to melt. Others need our light/gift to warm their hearts when they are in a dark season. If you need a sign how to use or recognize your gift to help others, come to Him in prayer but listen first before you speak. Spend a few moments being quiet and listening for direction/answers. He already knows your needs. He already knows what you're going to say but is happy to sit with you to spend time with you. He knows that the more time you spend with Him the more at peace you will be. If you are not at peace about a decision, or the decision feels rushed, it is likely not from God. His will is good for us, His will is perfect for us. His will is pleasing to us. When we are in His good, pleasing, and perfect will, He gives us the oxygen we need to shine so bright no one can dim our light.

# When a Piece of Your Heart Is in the Ground

He heals the brokenhearted
and binds up their wounds.

Psalm 147:3 ESV

I'm one of those people who didn't fathom or understand why someone would lie down by a gravesite or take a picnic lunch to a cemetery. I *was* one of those people until it happened to me. I'll admit I went to my Granny's grave not long after she died. I knew she wasn't there. I knew about dust to dust. I knew she didn't hear me, but I went and cried while I talked to her. It was healing. It was therapeutic. I didn't visit frequently, but I needed to that day.

When my sister died, I would often hear friends reference what they took to her gravesite. And suddenly I totally got it. They knew she wasn't there, they knew about heaven. But when a piece of your heart is put in the ground, you gravitate toward it to heal. The scar on the piece of your heart needs time and action to heal. If a gravesite was the last place you had a moment with that piece of broken heart, the action you take to visit a gravesite and get feelings off your chest or to put pretty flowers that remind you of that person, it puts a salve on the broken part of your heart.

Our children need a space to find healing for their wounds.

Practically, from us it can look like a kiss on a scrape of a child, a hug or space for a nap for a teen, an ear for an adult child, or the relief of a prepared meal for our children when they become newborn parents struggling to find a routine.

## WorkHearter Wisdom

We can't give out peace if we don't have it first. Moms need to let our own scars heal in order to help our children's broken hearts. We are peace for our children-their sanctuary—so we need to have our own peace to be able to give it to them. Think about this.

PART 4: THE WEARY DAYS OF WINTER

# Church In a Gay Bar

The darkness is passing away and the true light is already shining. Whoever says he is in the light and hates his brother is still in darkness. Whoever loves his brother abides in the light, and in him there is no cause for stumbling.

1 John 2:8–10 ESV

When my sister died, all of us were in a state of shock. Part of that shock was we didn't even know she was using drugs again. There had been no signs of it. I had blamed and resented her friends for influencing her. After news of her death spread around to her friends and the gay community she loved, they jumped into action to minister to our family.

The following Sunday after her funeral would have been her birthday, so they hosted a fundraiser in her honor. None of us had ever entered a gay bar before, but we were not only invited, our family were guests of honor. We sat at a reserved table with front-row seats to the auction held by her friends. They raised over $10,000 for her funeral expenses. There were no strings attached. They opened their hearts and their wallets for us. They loved my sister so they showed it, even through their own grief, by caring for her devastated family.

That night was everything a church does in ministry. We were welcomed. They saw a need and filled the need. They ministered to a grieving family. They gave to us and we received. They loved us even if we hadn't loved them well in the past.

My sister's death changed me forever. That night changed me forever. I decided to be more like those who loved me unexpectedly and, therefore, be more like Jesus. You may have a story of someone who loved you with no expectation in return. You may be the one who gives that love to others.

## WorkHearter Wisdom

Have you ever been on the receiving end of a gift that you could never pay back? Did you realize it at the time? Have you been able to pay it forward?

# Hardest Part of Grief

> Brothers and sisters, we do not want you to be uninformed about those who sleep in death, so that you do not grieve like the rest of mankind, who have no hope.
>
> 1 Thessalonians 4:13 NIV

The hardest part of grief is moving on, or seeing others move on when you want to stand still. Feeling guilty is real when moving on in the midst of grief.

Yet even Jesus paused to weep (John 11:35). The universal sign of respect during a funeral procession is to pull over on the side of the road with your flashers on until the processional has passed by, showing the family and friends that you have the respect for their loss to pause for a moment and remember the life they are grieving.

We don't stop traffic forever. Even if you want to sit in your grief and linger, moving on eventually has to happen. You still have to shower, eat meals, drink water. No matter how difficult it is to take those first steps of moving on with daily life without your loved one, it is vital to survival. Moving on hurts.

And when you least expect it, days, weeks, months, and years later, grief can come back to you in waves. It can be small, big, or unpredictable in nature. The grief wave can knock you down or carry you out further into the deep blue sea of grief. You can't fight it. Grief is real even if it doesn't feel real yet.

Lean into it and let it be. There's something indescribable about being so close to the edge of overwhelming grief; but knowing it's too deep to go far alone without assistance brings us closer to God. It is a humble way of acknowledging how small we are next to a great big God.

Inevitably, no matter what you do or don't do, babies will be born and other deaths will occur. The earth will continue to spin. The best way to move on is to help others who have experienced loss. Attending funeral visitation or memorial services is important to those grieving, to show they are not alone in their moments of despair. It also shows them it gets easier to live with the grief than try to fight against it.

We all want to be remembered. The memories help us to recover and heal in the grieving process. They help us laugh and smile again. We have hope that this life is not the end.

## WorkHearter Wisdom

Loved ones are missed when they leave because the fond memories of them embodied love done for us on earth. Part of those memories return through the people who visit when you lose a loved one. They remind you of the gift of love God has given to all of us.

Elephants in a herd grieve loss for weeks/months. If the largest land mammal in the world mourns loss through community, I think we can pause and empathize too.

The ability to love one another is the easiest part of grief. You don't have to say a word. You just show up. Your presence is encouragement. It shows the hope that our Lord gave to all of us and that the loss they feel is real. Like Jesus did, it's OK to pause and weep if you want. Sometimes, we need a good cry.

# Walking Track to Nowhere

Therefore, my dear friends, as you have always obeyed- not only in my presence, but now much more in my absence-continue to work out your salvation with fear and trembling.     Philippians 2:12 NIV

In winter, a walking track is my saving grace for staying active. I do not want to get out of my warm bed when it's freezing cold outside. Even when I took my kids to school, I had a habit of getting back into bed instead of walking outside. The local gym has an indoor walking track that I took advantage of on rainy and cold days.

Unfortunately, unlike my outdoor trail with plenty of space and routes to walk, the gym walking track is narrow and only goes in one direction, around and around. It seems counterintuitive at times, with no incline or variation in path. I've noticed on more than one occasion how people get frustrated and impatient if someone in front of them is walking at a slower pace. When they finally have the chance to pass them, they grunt or sigh under their breath. It could be they feel like they are just going in circles, walking to nowhere (and they are doing precisely that). They miss the purpose of walking for exercise. In the end, the elevated heartrate and increased endorphins are the goal, not the passing of the other walkers.

I remember a road rage incident on the highway that happened in front of my vehicle. A truck wanted to pass a car. However, instead of allowing the truck to pass, the car would speed up just enough to prevent it. As it escalated, they both ran off the road and fortunately no one was hurt. They were impatient and wanted resolution immediately. They may not have been walking in circles, but they were frustrated by not getting to pass and it ended in a frightening situation.

When God disciplines our decisions, we get frustrated. We do not want to feel any consequences for our actions. Our children also sigh when we discipline them. We won't see the harvest of our own discipline or our children for years, in some cases. We circle the same issues and mistakes in cycles on a track to nowhere. We want to see the harvest immediately because the discipline we give is unpleasant to us as parents. We yearn for the peace in repeated situations that try our patience. Yet, if we remain obedient, God's will works in us so we can act according to His purpose.

## WorkHearter Wisdom

We don't get to pass over these situations. We have to wait for it and not try to pass it up or run off the road. We have to let go of control for God's will. The peace it brings is a glorious side effect of many missteps and corrections. We are still being sanctified daily as we grow. Later on, when a child leaves the home they grew up in, as parents we can exhale in the peace that they have been trained in obedience and will continue to grow for His purpose.

# Daylight Savings Time

Wait for the Lord; be strong and take heart and wait for the Lord.

Psalm 27:14 NIV

Time is a strange commodity. Daylight savings time has two well-known phrases to remind us to change our clock setting in spring and fall. We "fall back" one hour in fall, but it forces us to have a shorter day of sunlight. It gets dark before we make dinner and we go to sleep earlier.

So what if we looked at it as *fall back* into more rest in preparation of winter? Instead of focusing on why it's dark so early, I can let rest breathe more freely into my day. I have learned to rest when it's winter in my life. Even if it's sunshine and 75 outside, I am tired and weary in a season of life that is cold, dark and dreary, I need rest more than work. Who am I kidding? I stay tired no matter the season.

When our children are growing, they need more sleep. Even though as adults, we are done growing physically, we are always growing spiritually and emotionally. After a season of extreme work and growth in our adult lives, rest is vital to prepare for the next season of growth. As parents, we must rest in our thoughts and worries about our children as well. We can't keep toiling away at the soil of our children's lives without letting the groundwork rest for a season. We wait expectantly during the cold, gloomy season of winter for warmer days of growth. There is beauty in the waiting. It may not be revealed to us ... yet.

## WorkHearter Wisdom

How do you adjust to Daylight Savings Time? Or do you? Do you continue with the same schedule or do you make adjustments? How does it affect your children?

## Last Words

When Jesus had received the sour wine, he said, "It is finished," and he bowed his head and gave up his spirit.

John 19:30 ESV

For it is by grace you have been saved, through faith-and this is not from yourselves, it is the gift of God-not by works, so that no one can boast.

Ephesians 2:8 NIV

Last words are significant like last names—because they follow us. Last words are important because they are the last words. Last words spoken by a loved one on their deathbed, or the last words they said to you before passing can be treasures. Last words of a tearful fight that ends a relationship in the worst possible way can be painful memories. Last words stick with us, whether they were good or bad. They define us and our entire relationship.

The language development of our children is primarily on our shoulder their first years of life. Children learn the language parents speak. They are listening, hanging on our every word. And the last words they heard from us are very important.

Thus, our children need to hear comforting, encouraging last words from us on a daily basis. When we wake them up, tuck them into bed at night, when we leave for work or drop them off at school, they need to hear loving and life-giving words from us. They will not know this positive language nor be able to give it if they don't hear it first from us.

## WorkHearter Wisdom

I want my last words on earth and in any relationship to be life-giving. The last words of Jesus on the cross are significant to His followers: "It is finished." He gave us freedom with His last words. Since He finished it, we don't have to do anything. His last words were life-giving. The daunting task has been completed for us. An incredibly heavy burden has been lifted for us without any assistance from us. We feel love and grace when others help lift our burdens. Jesus embodied love and grace with His last words.

## Last Names

But now thus says the LORD, he who created you, O Jacob, he who formed you, O Israel: "Fear not, for I have redeemed you; I have called you by name, you are mine."

Isaiah 43:1 ESV

Having a different last name than my older children is confusing to most people. I know they are mine, and they look like me. The fact that everyone doesn't know we are family is not important to me.

God feels this way about us even when we change our names—He knows us and calls us by our name because we are His. I can change my name multiple times, but that fact will remain: I am known by Him. If your last name changes due to adoption, divorce, marriage, or remarriage, does who you *are* change? No. If you couldn't find a keychain with your name spelled correctly when you were younger, did that mean you were any less loved? No.

When our children marry and change names, they are no less our children. They will always be our children. Even when we are eighty and our children have *grand*children—they will still be our babies in our hearts. Our children will change more than their names in their lifetime. But they will not change the fact of being ours.

## WorkHearter Wisdom

God feels the same about us as we change throughout life. He knows we are His. Even if others don't know us, He does. We don't have to explain whose daughter or sister we are to Him. We look like Him and He delights in us.

## Quiet Moments of Contemplation: 1 Chronicles 4:10

Jabez cried out to the God of Israel, "Oh that you would bless me and enlarge my territory! Let your hand be with me, and keep me from harm so that I will be free from pain." And God granted his request. (NIV)

This prayer of Jabez is simple but powerful. Prayer is an action that humbles us before our creator. Prayer is an action that seeks help from our heavenly Father. Prayer is an action that protects us from becoming hard-hearted. Prayer is an action to practice patience while we wait. Prayer is an exercise to improve our listening skills. Prayer is a petition to trust that Jesus knows what to do with our words.

We have the same power to pray over our homes, over our lives, and over our fears and doubts. We can have a stronger relationship with God by simply praying. When it feels like nothing is happening, everything is happening during prayer. There is not a time to avoid prayer. Even if we feel unworthy. Prayer is not based on our worth, but His worth is what makes prayer so powerful.

## Choose to Be Numb or Choose Who to Become

> Do everything without grumbling or arguing, so that you may become blameless and pure, "children of God without fault in a warped and crooked generation."
> Then you will shine among them like stars in the sky as you hold firmly to the word of life.
>
> Philippians 2:14-16 NIV

> He must become greater, I must become less.
>
> John 3:30 NIV

For a long time, I thought God and I had an unspoken, unwritten understanding—that my loved ones would be around until old age and only die of natural causes. I thought this way because when I lost my grandmother when I was twenty-three, I was devastated. I missed her terribly. I didn't think I would ever recover. She was my biggest fan. She made me feel so special. I thought she was the only family member who understood me and that loss left a hole in my heart. I wasn't mad at God when she died, but I reasoned that she was at an age for it to be acceptable.

Almost twenty years went by before I lost another close loved one. So, understandably I felt numb after my sister died. Grief is shocking, devastatingly painful, and full of blame. I blamed myself, my family, and, of course, her for dying too young. I complained about the timing and everything else.

In those moments, I had to decide what to do moving forward. I had to choose to remain numb from all the loss, revelation of deceit, and grief ... or I could become a better person. I could become a better friend by the example she set. I could become a better sister. I could become a better daughter by checking in on my parents and spending time with them doing fun things—like she did often. There's always a choice, even when something is taken from you or chooses to leave you. I chose to become better. I choose to become less so He can become greater.

### WorkHearter Wisdom

Have you ever been confronted with a choice like this—be numb? Or feel and grow? What precipitated the choice? Did you make the right choice, or did you bury yourself until another event forced you to reconsider? How are you handling it these days? Let's work today without complaint and shine bright like the stars together.

## Head and the Heart

And he said, "Truly I tell you, unless you change and become like little children, you will never enter the kingdom of heaven."

Matthew 18:3 NIV

When my sister died, the last song she heard before she took her last breath was by the band named The Head and the Heart. I had not heard it until it was chosen for the memorial playlist. She was way cooler about music than I ever will be.

Some of what my heart heard in that song were the words I sang along with the song even though they were wrong. I didn't know the lyrics, all I knew in that moment was my sister and the ache of losing her.

The head and the heart can be connected or disconnected. We can be led by one or the other. My daughter would try to read a book by the pictures on the page before she could read the words. She would create a story from the artwork and read it out loud proudly and confidently. Her heart was in it, even if her head knowledge was not. Kids cannot understand sarcasm and translate scenarios in a literal sense. Their head knowledge about connections and language is still forming. Their hearts are leading them 100 percent into any task they attempt without having 100 percent knowledge.

I can sing with my whole heart in worship yet not sing the right words in church. My heart is in it 100 percent but my head knowledge is only about 80 percent. God lovingly sees that child in me who is 100 percent in it. He doesn't worry about the adult who's just trying. All that matters is that Jesus can tune our hearts.

## WorkHearter Wisdom

Our babies know in their hearts a full love for their moms before they have any head knowledge of who we are. They learn about us as parents and our rules and expectations after. Their heart leads our relationship. Our knowledge of Jesus starts in our heart and follows with head knowledge of who He was and still is today. How can we let our heart open with faith like a child lead us when our adult mind tells us all odds are stacked against us?

# Doxology

Praise God, from whom all blessings flow;
Praise Him, all creatures here below;
Praise Him above, ye heavenly host;
Praise Father, Son, and Holy Ghost. Amen.

—Thomas Ken, 1674

## Acknowledgments

I would like to thank my mom, my late grandmothers, my mother-in-laws, my sisters, my cousins, my aunts, my friends, and my daughters who have shaped my life. I only know some of what they sacrificed for me, as my children will only know parts of what I sacrificed for them. They were my protection, so I fiercely protect my own children.

Secondly, thank you to all the mothers, moms, mamas, stepmoms, grandmothers, aunts, cousins, and sisters out there that fill in the gaps of our children's lives and step up to help to raise them as only a village can. Thank you to every woman outside my own family I've met in my life whether you have been a friend, foe, boss, colleague, mentor, teacher to me. I am grateful for all the lessons learned. Thank you to all the moms who inspire me by your strength. Thank you for sharing your stories, wins, failures. Thank you to the moms of multiples, moms of special needs, adoptive moms, birth moms, single moms, widow moms, moms of terminally ill children, and all the moms who have lost a child. Your endurance and perseverance has helped me as a mom more than you could ever know.

Thanks to my late sister Brooke for being my sister despite how tough I made it for you. Thank you for giving me an example of a better person I can strive to be. Thank you Lord for all my sisters. What a gift.

Thank you to the girls who will one day be moms with hopes and dreams that get lost inside our mama hearts to be the best parent we can for our children. Work hard but WorkHearter with all our hearts to live out the best calling as moms to our sons and daughters.

Thank you to my husband, Michael, for allowing me to dream. The freedom you give freely for me to pursue the ideas I have is a special gift I've never known before you. I know my expectations are higher than anyone could ever meet, but you work so hard trying and I love you more for that.

Thank you, Bob Goff, for dreaming big and helping me to do the same. Thank you, Kimberly Stuart, for your kind words, mentorship, and much-needed laughter. Thank you, Jon Acuff, for not only helping me start but also inspiring me to finish and stop overthinking.

I would like to acknowledge the late Jarrid Wilson for the words you gave the world and helping me start this journey.

Thank you to my editor, Jamie Chavez, for your patience and expertise.

Thank you to all the pastors and teachers who introduced and taught me more about Jesus. Namely Pastor Michael Duff, who taught me about the meditations of my heart; Pastor Mike Glenn, who gave me Kairos moments and taught me I don't have to afraid anymore after going through the fires of life; and Dr. Chris Brooks, who taught me how to empty my hands to have peace, letting go of fear and anxiety along with the act of dancing every day.

Thank you, Jesus, for all you have given me-the ultimate sacrifice. I pray I've done my best at raising some of the next generation.

Thank you to all the ones who have saved my life whether by doing the Heimlich to keep me from choking, or pulling me out of the ocean to keep me from drowning, providing for me, taking me to the doctor/hospital, giving me life-giving shots weekly or pulling me out of despair and giving me hope: my mom, my dad, my grandmothers, my sisters, my friends, my daughters, my son, my husband and my Jesus.

Last but not least, thank you to all my wonderful children. God gave me more than I could ask or imagine with all four of my unique gifts from above. Each one of you has richly blessed my life with much love, laughter, lessons, and life-giving hope giving me my greatest work/purpose. Thank you for sticking it out with me and growing up alongside me.

# Scripture Reference

| | | | |
|---|---|---|---|
| Proverbs 19:21 | ix | Ephesians 4:26 | 66 |
| Colossians 3:23-24 | xv | John 16:33 | 68 |
| Psalm 19:14 | 3 | 1 Corinthians 16:13 | 71 |
| Psalm 62:5-6 | 5 | 2 Timothy 4:2 | 73 |
| Matthew 10:30-31, Colossians 4:6 | 9 | Mark 4:22 | 75 |
| Jeremiah 17:8 | 11 | John 13:14 | 77 |
| Revelation 21:5, John 15:2, | | John 21:21, Matthew 6:34 | 79 |
| James 5:7 | 13 | Matthew 6:25-34 | 81 |
| Matthew 18:12-14, Luke 11:9 | 15 | 2 Corinthians 14:18 | 84 |
| John 7:37-38 | 17 | Luke 6:38 | 86 |
| Romans 8:28 | 19 | Proverbs 12:20 | 88 |
| Matthew 13:24-25, 28-30 | 20 | John 12:15 | 90 |
| Lamentations 3:22-23, | | Micah 6:8 | 92 |
| 2 Timothy 2:25-26 | 23 | Psalm 73:26 | 94 |
| Luke 12:25, Luke 8:14 | 25 | Matthew 13:44 | 96 |
| 2 Corinthians 5:17 | 27 | Matthew 7:24-25 | 98 |
| Matthew 14:30, Matthew 6:21-22 | 29 | Exodus 35:31, James 4:2 | 100 |
| 1 Peter 5:6-7 | 32 | Philippians 4:6-7 | 102 |
| Acts 1:8 | 34 | John15:2, Psalm 118:24 | 107 |
| Philippians 4:6-7 | 36 | 1 John 4:18 | 109 |
| Proverbs 3:5-6 | 38 | Proverbs 3:6 | 111 |
| 2 Samuel 22:31 | 39 | Isaiah 64:8 | 113 |
| Mark 9:40 | 41 | Isaiah 43:2 | 115 |
| Ecclesiastes 3:1-8 | 43 | Psalm 89:9 | 117 |
| Mark 3:25 | 46 | John 4:10 | 119 |
| James 5:13 | 48 | Psalm 119:103, Proverbs 16:24 | 121 |
| Hebrews 12:14 | 50 | Mark 9:50, Matthew 5:13 | 123 |
| Matthew 22:37-39, John 15:12 | 55 | Psalm 139:14 | 127 |
| Philippians 2:3-5 | 56 | Galatians 5:22-23 | 128 |
| Acts 20:35 | 58 | Colossians 3:15 | 131 |
| 2 Thessalonians 3:16, Isaiah 61:3 | 60 | Matthew 18:6, Mark 10:15 | 133 |
| Psalm 23:1-6 | 62 | John 14:26 | 135 |
| John 4:14 | 64 | Mark 1:22, 1 Corinthians 2:2 | 137 |

| Reference | Page | Reference | Page |
|---|---|---|---|
| 1 Corinthians 13 | 141 | Psalm 34:8 | 236 |
| Philippians 1:6 | 143 | Colossians 3:16, Ephesians 5:19, | |
| Matthew 12:33 | 145 | 1 Corinthians 14-15 | 238 |
| Ephesians 6:10-18 | 147 | Psalm 32:8 | 240 |
| Matthew 13:32 | 150 | 2 Corinthians 4:16-19, | |
| Luke 16:10, Matthew 17:20 | 152 | Matthew 9:37-38 | 242 |
| Proverbs 10:11, Proverbs 27:17 | 155 | Ephesians 4:26-27, | |
| Hebrews 11:1 | 158 | Colossians 2:8 | 245 |
| Philippians 1:6, 2 Peter 3:8-9 | 160 | Proverbs 15:4 | 247 |
| Matthew 5:16 | 162 | 1 Corinthians 3:23 | 249 |
| Matthew 7:3, Luke 6:41 | 164 | Matthew 4:4 | 253 |
| 2 Cor 12:10, Ephesians 4:29 | 166 | Proverbs 22:6, | |
| Proverbs 22:1 | 168 | 2 Corinthians 8:12 | 254 |
| Galatians 6:9 | 172 | Mark 13:10, | |
| 1 Peter 5:8, 2 Corinthians 11:14 | 173 | 2 Corinthians 4:16-18 | 256 |
| Mark 4:14-20 | 176 | Psalm 138:8 | 259 |
| Isaiah 55:8 | 179 | Matthew 6:19-21 | 261 |
| 2 Corinthians 10:5 | 181 | 1 Peter 5:7, Proverbs 21:26, | |
| Job 14:7-9 | 183 | Psalm 37:4 | 263 |
| James 4:7 | 185 | John 14:6 | 265 |
| Isaiah 43:18-19 | 187 | Matthew 7:7 | 267 |
| Galatians 5:13 | 189 | John 10:27 | 269 |
| Proverbs 18:12 | 191 | Luke 23:43 | 271 |
| Psalm 118:5 | 193 | John 8:12 | 273 |
| Psalm 39:4 | 195 | 1 Timothy 6:17 | 275 |
| Ephesians 3:20-21 Ecclesiastes 4:9-10 | 197 | Acts 17:24, Romans 10:15 | 277 |
| | 200 | Colossians 3:12 | 280 |
| Luke 7:38 | 202 | Matthew 6:11, 1 Peter 2:2 | 282 |
| 1 John 2:11 | 205 | 1 John 1:7, Revelation 4:11 | 284 |
| John 3:8, 2 Timothy 3:16 | 207 | Romans 10:14-15 | 286 |
| 1 Peter 4:10 | 213 | Matthew 5:38-40 | 288 |
| Psalm 23:5 | 215 | Ecclesiastes 4:10, Hebrews 13:1 | 290 |
| Hebrews 12:11 | 217 | Ephesians 4:32 | 292 |
| 1 Timothy 5:3, James 1:27 | 219 | Galatians 6:2 | 295 |
| James 1:26 | 221 | John 4:48 | 297 |
| John 6:12 | 223 | 1 Peter 2:21 | 299 |
| 1 Thessalonians 5:18 | 225 | Isaiah 30:21 | 301 |
| Isaiah 40:31 | 227 | 1 John 3:18 | 302 |
| Ecclesiastes 3:1 | 228 | Ecclesiastes 5:12, Psalm 116:7, | |
| Psalm 121:1-2 | 231 | Psalm 127:2 | 307 |
| Galatians 3:26 | 232 | Hebrews 13:2 | 309 |
| Philippians 4:8 | 234 | Luke 10:40-42 | 311 |

| | | | |
|---|---|---|---|
| Joshua 1:5 | 313 | Romans 12:5, 1 Thes 4:9 | 366 |
| Proverbs 31:26, Matthew 11:28 | 317 | John 11:35, Matthew 10:30 | 368 |
| James 1:19 | 319 | John 14:1 | 370 |
| Ecclesiastes 7:14, James 1:3 | 321 | Luke 17:3, Luke 17:2, | |
| Colossians 3:16, Job 24:19 | 323 | Hebrews 10:18 | 372 |
| Galatians 5:13, John 14:1 | 325 | John 11:34 | 374 |
| 1 Corinthians 12:27-28 | 327 | Hebrews 11:1 | 376 |
| 1 Peter 4:8 | 330 | John 12:3 | 378 |
| Isaiah 41:13 | 335 | 1 John 4:8 | 380 |
| Matthew 12:34 | 336 | Hebrews 13:5 | 382 |
| Romans 6:4 | 338 | Psalm 40:2, Isaiah 46:4 | 384 |
| John 9:6 | 341 | Romans 12:2, Matthew 4:14-15, | |
| Psalm 6:7 | 343 | Psalm 119:105 | 386 |
| Luke 6:42 | 345 | Psalm 147:3 | 389 |
| Romans 8:18 | 347 | 1 John 2:8-10 | 391 |
| Romans 8:1 | 349 | 1 Thessalonians 4:13 | 393 |
| Matthew 5:4 | 351 | Philippians 2:12 | 395 |
| Romans 5:1-5 | 353 | Psalm 27:14 | 397 |
| Romans 12:6 | 354 | John 19:30, Ephesians 2:8 | 399 |
| Luke 12:35 | 356 | Isaiah 43:1 | 401 |
| 2 Corinthians 4:8-9 | 358 | 1 Chronicles 4:10 | 403 |
| Romans 13:8 | 360 | John 3:30, Philippians 2:14-16 | 404 |
| 1 Corinthians 15:10 | 362 | Matthew 18:3 | 406 |
| James 1:17 | 364 | | |

## About the Author

Michelle Hollingsworth is a mom to four with more than twenty-nine years of experience; wife to her contractor husband Michael; a military spouse; and former public school educator. Her vocational background is photography, psychology, and education, but she has always heard the call to write. She has been working on this devotional since her sister passed away, tying her Bible studies to real life experience.

She is a Tennessee-raised daughter of divorced parents who celebrate every holiday and birthday together as one family. As a divorced parent herself, she appreciates those who work diligently to co-parent in love for the sake of their children. Michelle loves to travel but home to her is in the hills of Tennessee or the white sandy beaches of the Florida Panhandle.

Read more at workhearter.com and follow her at @workhearter.

www.ingramcontent.com/pod-product-compliance
Lightning Source LLC
Chambersburg PA
CBHW020334010526
44119CB00002B/62